DEMOGRAPHIC AND PROGRAMMATIC CONSEQUENCES OF CONTRACEPTIVE INNOVATIONS

REPRODUCTIVE BIOLOGY

Series Editor: Sheldon J. Segal
The Rockefeller Foundation
New York, New York

THE ANTIPROGESTIN STEROID RU 486 AND HUMAN FERTILITY CONTROL

Edited by Etienne-Emile Baulieu and Sheldon J. Segal

CONTRACEPTIVE STEROIDS: Pharmacology and Safety

Edited by A. T. Gregoire and Richard P. Blye

DEMOGRAPHIC AND PROGRAMMATIC CONSEQUENCES OF CONTRACEPTIVE INNOVATIONS

Edited by Sheldon J. Segal, Amy O. Tsui, and Susan M. Rogers

GENETIC MARKERS OF SEX DIFFERENTIATION

Edited by Florence P. Haseltine, Michael E. McClure, and Ellen H. Goldberg

GOSSYPOL: A Potential Contraceptive for Men

Edited by Sheldon J. Segal

IMMUNOLOGICAL APPROACHES TO CONTRACEPTION AND PROMOTION OF FERTILITY

Edited by G. P. Talwar

A Continuation Order Plan is available for this series. A continuation order will bring delivery of each new volume immediately upon publication. Volumes are billed only upon actual shipment. For further information please contact the publisher.

DEMOGRAPHIC AND PROGRAMMATIC CONSEQUENCES OF CONTRACEPTIVE INNOVATIONS

Edited by

Sheldon J. Segal

The Rockefeller Foundation
New York, New York

Amy O. Tsui

University of North Carolina at Chapel Hill
Chapel Hill, North Carolina

and

Susan M. Rogers

National Research Council
Washington, D.C.

PLENUM PRESS • NEW YORK AND LONDON

Library of Congress Cataloging-in-Publication Data

Demographic and programmatic consequences of contraceptive innovations
/ edited by Sheldon J. Segal, Amy O. Tsui, and Susan M. Rogers.
        p.   cm. -- (Reproductive biology)
    Papers presented at the Conference on the Demographic and
Programmatic Consequences of Contraceptive Innovations, sponsored by
the National Research Council's Committee on Population and held at
the National Academy of Sciences, Oct. 6-7, 1988.
    Includes bibliographical references.
    ISBN-13: 978-1-4684-5723-0   e-ISBN-13: 978-1-4684-5721-6
    DOI: 10.1007/978-1-4684-5721-6
    1. Birth control--Developing countries--Congresses.
2. Contraceptives--Developing countries--Congresses.
3. Technological innovations--Social aspects--Developing countries-
-Congresses.   I. Segal, Sheldon J. (Sheldon Jerome) II. Tsui, Amy
Ong. III. Rogers, Susan M. IV. Conference on the Demographic and
Programmatic Consequences of Contraceptive Innovations (1988 :
National Academy of Sciences) V. National Research Council (U.S.).
Committee on Population. VI. Series.
    [DNLM: 1. Contraception Behavior--congresses. 2. Contraceptive
Agents--congresses. 3. Contraceptive Devices--congresses.
4. Developing Countries--congresses. 5. Family Planning-
-congresses.   HQ 766 D383 1988]
HQ766.5.D44D46   1989
363.9'6'091724--dc20
DNLM/DLC
for Library of Congress   89-23083
                                                              CIP

Proceedings of a conference on Demographic and Programmatic Consequences
of Contraceptive Innovations, sponsored by the Committee on Population,
held October 6–7, 1988, at the National Academy of Sciences, Washington, D.C.

© 1989 Plenum Press, New York
Softcover reprint of the hardcover 1st edition 1989
A Division of Plenum Publishing Corporation
233 Spring Street, New York, N.Y. 10013

Note

The project that is the subject of this report was approved by the Governing Board of the National Research Council, whose members are drawn from the councils of the National Academy of Sciences, the National Academy of Engineering, and the Institute of Medicine. The members of the committee responsible for the report were chosen for their special competences and with regard for appropriate balance.

This report has been reviewed by a group other than the authors according to procedures approved by a Report Review Committee consisting of members of the National Academy of Sciences, the National Academy of Engineering, and the Institute of Medicine.

The National Academy of Sciences is a private, nonprofit, self-perpetuating society of distinguished scholars engaged in scientific and engineering research, dedicated to the furtherance of science and technology and to their use for the general welfare. Upon the authority of the charter granted to it by the Congress in 1863, the Academy has a mandate that requires it to advise the federal government on scientific and technical matters. Dr. Frank Press is president of the National Academy of Sciences.

The National Academy of Engineering was established in 1964, under the charter of the National Academy of Sciences, as a parallel organization of outstanding engineers. It is autonomous in its administration and in the selection of its members, sharing with the National Academy of Sciences the responsibility for advising the federal government. The National Academy of Engineering also sponsors engineering programs aimed at meeting national needs, encourages education and research, and recognizes the superior achievements of engineers. Dr. Robert M. White is president of the National Academy of Engineering.

The Institute of Medicine was established in 1970 by the National Academy of Sciences to secure the services of eminent members of appropriate professions in the examination of policy matters pertaining to the health of the public. The Institute acts under the responsibility given to the National Academy of Sciences by its congressional charter to be an adviser to the federal government and, upon its own initiative, to identify issues of medical care, research, and education. Dr. Samuel O. Thier is president of the Institute of Medicine.

The National Research Council was organized by the National Academy of Sciences in 1916 to associate the broad community of science and technology with the Academy's purposes of furthering knowledge and advising the federal government. Functioning in accordance with general policies determined by the Academy, the Council has become the principal operating agency of both the National Academy of Sciences and the National Academy of Engineering in providing services to the government, the public, and the scientific and engineering communities. The Council is administered jointly by both Academies and the Institute of Medicine. Dr. Frank Press and Dr. Robert M. White are chairman and vice chairman, respectively, of the National Research Council.

Committee on Population

ALBERT I. HERMALIN (Chair), Population Studies Center,
University of Michigan
FRANCISCO ALBA, El Colegio de Mexico
DAVID BELL, Center for Population Research, Harvard University
JULIE DAVANZO, Economics Department, The Rand Corporation
MAHMOUD F. FATHALLA, World Health Organization
RONALD FREEDMAN, Population Studies Center, University of
Michigan
WILLIAM N. HUBBARD, Hickory Corners, Michigan
CHARLES B. KEELY, Department of Demography, Georgetown
University
RON J. LESTHAEGHE, Interuniversity Programme in
Demography, Vrije Universiteit Brussel
DIANA B. PETITTI, Division of Family and Community Health,
University of California, San Francisco
JAMES E. PHILLIPS, The Population Council
T. PAUL SCHULTZ, Department of Economics, Yale University
SUSAN SCRIMSHAW, School of Public Health, University of
California, Los Angeles
JAMES TRUSSELL, Office of Population Research, Princeton
University

Conference Contributors

Jalaluddin Akbar, International Centre for Diarrhoeal Disease Research, Bangladesh

Jose Barzelatto, World Health Organization, Geneva

John O.G. Billy, Battelle Human Affairs Research Centers, Seattle, Washington

Esther Boohene, Zimbabwe National Family Planning Council

Arthur Campbell, National Institutes for Child Health and Human Development, Bethesda, Maryland

Robert C. Caplan, National Academy of Sciences, Washington, D.C.

Harry E. Cross, U.S. Agency for International Development, Washington, D.C.

John G. Crowley, U.S. Agency for International Development, Washington, D.C.

Jose Donayre, United Nations Fund for Population Activities, New York City, New York

Barbara Entwisle, Carolina Population Center, University of North Carolina, Chapel Hill

Mahmoud F. Fathalla, World Health Organization, Geneva

Jacqueline Darroch Forrest, The Alan Guttmacher Institute, New York City, New York

Judith Fortney, Family Health International, Research Triangle Park, North Carolina

Walter Fox, Ortho Pharmaceutical Corporation, Raritan, New Jersey

Duff G. Gillespie, U.S. Agency for International Development, Washington, D.C.

Noreen Goldman, Office of Population Research, Princeton University

William R. Grady, Battelle Human Affairs Research Centers, Seattle, Washington

Stanley K. Henshaw, The Alan Guttmacher Institute, New York City, New York

Mian Bazle Hossain, International Centre for Diarrhoeal Disease Research, Bangladesh

A.A. Zahidul Huque, International Centre for Diarrhoeal Disease Research, Bangladesh

Anrudh Jain, The Population Council, New York City, New York

Barbara Kelley, British Overseas Development Administration, London

Cynthia Lloyd, United Nations, New York City, New York

Luigi Mastroianni, University of Pennsylvania Hospital, Philadelphia

W. Parker Mauldin, The Population Council, New York City, New York

Hedi Mhenni, Office National de la Famille et de la Population, Tunisia

Donald H. Minkler, University of California, San Francisco

Lorenzo Moreno, Westinghouse, Columbia, Maryland

Axel Mundigo, World Health Organization, Geneva

Gordon W. Perkin, Program for Applied Technology in Health, Seattle, Washington

Susan Philliber, State University of New York, New Paltz

James F. Phillips, The Population Center, New York City, New York

Malcolm Potts, Family Health International, Research Triangle Park, North Carolina

Scott R. Radloff, U.S. Agency for International Development, Washington, D.C.

John A. Ross, Columbia University, New York City

Sheldon J. Segal, The Rockefeller Foundation, New York City, New York

Jacqueline Sherris, Program for Applied Technology in Health, Seattle, Washington

George Simmons, University of Michigan, Ann Arbor

Joanne Spicehandler, The Population Council, New York City, New York

J. Joseph Spiedel, Population Crisis Committee, Washington, D.C.

Bruce Stadel, Food and Drug Administration, Rockville, Maryland

Felicia Stewart, Valley Center for Women's Health, Sacramento, California

Haryono Suyono, National Family Planning Coordinating Board, Indonesia

John W. Townsend, The Population Council, New York City, New York

Amy O. Tsui, Carolina Population Center, University of North Carolina, Chapel Hill

Manuel Urbina-Fuentes, Direccion General de Planificacion Familiar, Mexico City

Mechai Viravaidya, Population and Community Development Association, Bangkok

Charles F. Westoff, Office of Population Research, Princeton University

Bradman Weerakoon, International Planned Parenthood Federation, London

Jae Mo Yang, Planned Parenthood Federation of Korea, Seoul

Preface

This volume contains papers presented at the Conference on the Demographic and Programmatic Consequences of Contraceptive Innovations, which was sponsored by the Committee on Population and held at the National Academy of Sciences, October 6–7, 1988. The papers consider how new contraceptive methods currently being developed and changes in the use of already available contraceptives could affect contraceptive practice, levels and patterns of abortion use, and the health of women. In addition, several of the papers review the probable consequences of introducing new technology into family planning programs in developing countries. The Committee on Population sponsored this conference in order to stimulate thinking and to provide a forum for scientists, family planning program managers, and donor agency personnel to exchange information and ideas about these important issues. The committee is publishing these papers to expand the discussion of consequences of contraceptive innovations and to give scientists, policy makers, and members of the public who could not attend the conference an opportunity to learn about new developments in fertility control and their likely consequences for individuals and the societies in which they live.

NEED FOR NEW METHODS

While a strong case can be made that the pill and the intrauterine device (IUD) have contributed to declines in the level of unintended pregnancies around the world, it is also clear that for many couples existing methods present problems. High discontinuation rates for many contraceptive methods imply either user dissatisfaction with available choices or lack of knowledge of proper practice of those methods. Abortion rates remain high in both developed and developing countries, reflecting both the lack of availability of existing methods and their often high failure rates in everyday use.

At the same time, since the 1960s the number of contraceptive users has increased tenfold and the demand for services continues to expand. Modern contraceptive use is a primary determinant of declining fertility in the Third World. Even so, approximately two out of three women of reproductive age in developing countries (excluding China) are not currently using any method of contraception. Part of the difference in contraceptive prevalence from country to country is due to a country's development status and to coverage of the health care system. Many specialists believe that more and different contraceptive methods would improve the access to family planning services of couples in many Third World countries. In both developed and developing countries, users and providers of contraceptive services worry about side effects and the consequences of prolonged use of many of the available methods; there is a need for methods that are associated with fewer side effects.

There is also a need to examine the potential demographic impact of new contraceptive technologies. What would be the effect of new methods in developed countries, many of which already have low—indeed sometimes below replacement—fertility, and in developing countries, where fertility is generally much higher? On the basis of available data, is it likely that new methods would have a substantial impact on fertility rates, or would they merely substitute for current methods? Would new technologies have the potential for reducing abortion rates, and would they do so by encouraging nonusers to practice fertility control, or would their presumed greater effectiveness make the difference? A particularly important aspect of the problem concerns the ways in which new technologies may have an impact on family planning programs in developing countries through their effect on personnel, program budgets, and distribution systems. Little previous attention has been given to the cost of the proposed new methods or how they would be provided given the limited medical infrastructure available in many developing countries.

CONFERENCE PROGRAM

With the help of a conference steering committee, the Committee on Population invited 24 experts to prepare papers on topics related to the effects of new contraceptive technologies and changes in contraceptive practice. In addition, 15 other scholars were asked to comment on the papers or to serve as moderators for discussions. Presentations on the first day of the conference examined the potential consequences of the introduction of new contraceptive methods or changes in contraceptive practice for fertility and health. Papers on the second day addressed problems associated with the management of family planning programs and the introduction and dissemination of new and already existing contraceptive technology.

At the time of the conference, there were a number of new contraceptive methods in the research pipeline. These included improvements to old methods—medicated condoms and disposable diaphragms, for example—and fundamentally new technology—for example implant systems for delivering contraceptive steroids, antipregnancy vaccines, and the so-called menses-inducing pill, RU-486. All these methods are for women. The prospects for a new male contraceptive are not nearly as bright. A great deal of work remains to be done before any of these methods will reach the public. Moreover, declining investments in contraceptive research have slowed innovation and dissemination. It will be years before most of the new technology has been adequately tested and made available for mass distribution. In the meantime, therefore, improvements in contraceptive practice will provide the most important mechanism for couples around the world to increase their ability to control their fertility.

The participants agreed that well-designed family planning services and well-informed providers and users are critical elements for the successful adoption of new methods and for the effective use of the available technology. Increased attention is needed to strengthen the family planning infrastructure through education and training, as well as development of the specific service delivery components. More effective contraceptive practice represents the most likely way that unintended pregnancies will be reduced for the foreseeable future.

This volume is organized into five sections. Part I examines new leads in contraceptive development and provides a review of historical perspectives on the introduction of new contraceptives. Part II discusses the fertility impact of changes in contraceptive practice and reviews the demographic, programmatic, and psychosocial factors affecting contraceptive effectiveness. The potential effects of new methods for reproductive health and the use of abortion are reviewed in Part III. Issues associated with introducing new technologies, including a case study of the introduction of Depo-Provera in Matlab,

Bangladesh, are detailed in Part IV. Part V focuses on the administrative and operational processes associated with introducing new methods in developed and developing countries. The financial resources required to support adequately the demand for and delivery of family planning services are reviewed and projections for the next 20 years are estimated.

ACKNOWLEDGMENTS

The Committee on Population is particularly grateful to the steering committee that organized the conference. The chair of that committee, Amy Ong Tsui, carried out the largest share of the work associated with the conference. Other members of the steering committee included Jose Donayre, Jacqueline Forrest, Anrudh Jain, Sheldon Segal, and Charles F. Westoff. Members of the steering committee designed the conference program, outlined the topics to be addressed, and reviewed each presentation.

We are also grateful to the discussants, panel members, and moderators whose papers and remarks have not been included in this volume. Particularly important in this regard are a series of panel discussions and presentations by program managers from the developing world. The conference participants heard presentations from Esther Boohene of Zimbabwe, Hedi Mhenni of Tunisia, Haryono Suyono of Indonesia, and Manuel Urbina-Fuentes of Mexico. A second panel discussion reviewed the problems and opportunities faced by international donor agencies as they work to increase the effectiveness of contraceptive practice. Participants in this panel included Arthur Campbell with the National Institute of Child Health and Human Development, Jose Donayre of the United Nations Fund for Population Activities, Barbara Kelley of the British Overseas Development Administration, Mechai Viravaidya of the Population and Community Development Association in Thailand, and Bradman Weerakoon of the International Planned Parenthood Federation.

The Committee on Population appreciates the financial assistance it receives from the Agency for International Development, the William and Flora Hewlett Foundation, and the Andrew W. Mellon Foundation, which made the conference and the publication of these papers possible. The committee would also like to thank Chalmers Claris of the Carolina Population Center for production of the conference brochure and Maura Fitzpatrick of the Alan Guttmacher

Institute for assistance in hosting the meetings of the conference steering committee.

The committee also appreciates the work of its study director, Peter J. Donaldson, and of Susan M. Rogers, the staff officer with principal responsibility for implementing the suggestions of the steering committee and managing the conference as well as the publication of this volume of papers. The committee particularly appreciates the work that the editors of this volume, Sheldon Segal, Amy Tsui, and Susan Rogers, have put forward to ensure that the conference presentation would be available to the widest possible audience.

The Committee on Population is also grateful to the National Research Council staff who assisted in the publication of these papers. Special thanks are due to Eugenia Grohman, associate director for reports of the Commission on Behavioral and Social Sciences and Education, who encouraged the publication of these papers and worked closely with the committee staff to see them into print. We would also like to thank Carol Foote for preparation of this manuscript, Estelle Miller for composition services, and Michael Hayes for editorial assistance, and Barbara Rice for production help.

The committee is grateful for the work done by those preparing the papers, commenting on them, organizing the conference and individual sessions, and completing all the administrative and editorial work required for publication of this volume. The papers reflect the views of the authors themselves and not the Committee on Population, the National Research Council, or the organizations with which the authors are affiliated.

Albert I. Hermalin, *Chair*
Committee on Population

Contents

Part I
Review of New
Contraceptive Methods

Contraceptive Innovations:
Needs and Opportunities

SHELDON J. SEGAL

INTRODUCTION

People who wish to limit their fertility do so primarily in pursuit of family or individual aspirations to enhance their chances for personal fulfillment and to provide a good home and opportunities for their children. These aspirations are often frustrated, as high rates of unwanted pregnancy exist side by side with the desire to limit fertility. Contributing to this paradox is the fact that contraceptive measures, under conditions of actual use, often do not provide the desired protection against pregnancy (Trussell and Kost, 1987).

Several objectives can be identified in efforts to develop better contraceptives. First, there is the need to give greater assurance of effectiveness for those who wish to prevent or postpone childbearing. A simple calculation based on the estimated worldwide total of users of each contraceptive method and the reported method failure rates (Segal and Mauldin, 1987) reveals that each year 10 million to 30 million pregnancies occur as a result of contraceptive failure. Throughout the world many of these accidental pregnancies are voluntarily terminated, whether or not abortion is legal. Consequently, a significant portion of the global total of over 30 million annual abortions (Tietze and Henshaw, 1986) are done because the contraceptive methods that were used failed to work properly. Research to improve the effectiveness of contraception is, in fact, research toward the prevention of abortions.

Second, there is a need to provide methods that reduce the side effects associated with the most effective methods now available.

3

Couples are faced with the choice between using the more effective methods with varying degrees of uncomfortable side effects or health hazards and methods that are safer but less effective in preventing pregnancy.

Third, there is the need to provide methods that are better suited to the distribution systems of developing countries and that are more acceptable to people who do not now use contraceptives.

National priorities may differ with respect to contraceptive technology. In many countries only a small percentage of eligible couples use some form of fertility regulation (Mauldin and Segal, 1986). They must concentrate on extending access to currently available methods. Increasing contraceptive prevalence, however, is not unrelated to the type of technology the family planning services are attempting to deliver. Methods that are simpler to use and better in other respects make acceptance and distribution easier.

Countries such as the United States, China, or Japan have other priorities for contraception research. In these countries, at any one time about 75 percent of married couples of childbearing age use some form of contraception (United Nations, 1984). Improved contraception is important for providing current contraceptors (and future users) with greater effectiveness and convenience along with fewer health risks. In the United States and China, countries in which three out of four eligible couples use some form of fertility regulation, each year about 25 percent of pregnancies terminate as voluntary, legal abortion—a revealing insight into the failure rates of current methods in actual use. In Japan, where the highly effective oral contraceptives are not widely available and abortion is used by some as a primary means of fertility limitation, the figure is closer to 50 percent (Segal, 1984).

In the years ahead totally new methods of contraception as well as improvements in existing methods can be expected. To be available for use in the remaining years of this century, however, any new contraceptive method requiring regulatory agency approval by now must have reached the clinical investigation stage. A basic research lead or clever invention that is not yet in clinical trial is unlikely to be translated into a contraceptive method for general use before the calendar closes on the twentieth century.

It is possible, therefore, to look ahead to the contraceptive scene over the next 10 to 15 years and identify the new methods or major modifications that can be expected. Admittedly, prognosticating on the outcome of research in progress is fraught with uncertainty. A similar undertaking 3 years ago (Atkinson, Lincoln, and Forrest, 1986) forecast the registration of 10 new contraceptive products by the end of 1988. Two have kept to the anticipated time schedule. All others have been subjected to delays for reasons that could not have been predicted. Uncertainties notwithstanding, a perspective on the state of contraception research is presented in this paper. Not intended to be an inventory of all research leads that are being pursued, this review represents the author's judgment of prospective methods or major modifications of existing methods that have a realistic chance of success in the next 10 to 15 years.

POSSIBLE METHODOLOGICAL BREAKTHROUGHS

Subdermal Implants for Women

This long-promised contraceptive method is now a reality for women of the 12 countries where it has been approved for marketing. It is in the final stages of testing or registration in many others. By late 1988, the number of users was over a quarter of a million.

Eighteen years ago an author wrote, "A capsule small enough to be inserted under the skin . . . can be filled with an adequate supply of progestin to last for more than three years. . . . This form of low-dose progestin contraception, reversible and simple, may be one of the next developments in contraceptive methodology" (Segal, 1971). The method is indeed simple, but the process of developing it proved not to be. More than two decades after the first research report (Segal and Croxatto, 1967), the first version of the new technology, named NORPLANT® implant, is just beginning to become available for general use in some countries, and in others the registration process will not be completed until the 1990s. The file for new drug approval submitted to the U.S. Food and Drug Administration (FDA) consists of 56 volumes containing about 19,000 pages of data and information. The average review time for an application of this scope is about 2 years.

The NORPLANT® method entails the introduction of a progestin in small silastic tubes beneath the skin. The progestin diffuses out slowly to provide contraceptive protection for several years. The diffusion rate is controlled by the chemical structure of the progestin and the surface area of the silastic implants. The method provides long-term contraceptive action without requiring attention except for initial placement and eventual removal. The use of a progestin only in the implant is a safety advantage compared with conventional oral contraceptives, which contain a combination of a progestin and estrogen.

NORPLANT® has been used in clinical trials in 37 countries and has involved over 45,000 acceptors (Population Council, 1988). Data from an aggregate of hundreds of thousands of women-months of use have been analyzed. Consequently, the method's performance characteristics are well defined under various circumstances of use around the world. Effectiveness is high. A pregnancy rate well below 1 per 100 women per year is characteristic of most studies. In an Indonesian study, for example, the cumulative 5-year net pregnancy rate per 100 women was 1.8. Continuation rates were 96 and 92 percent for the first and second years, respectively. By the end of the fifth year, four out of five women were continuing to use the original set of implants (Affandi et al., 1987). The main reason for discontinuation was for problems of irregular menstrual bleeding. Another example is Egypt, where the 5-year experience is similar; the net cumulative pregnancy rate was 1.6 (Salah et al., 1987). Chinese investigators are undertaking a study in which 10,000 women are using NORPLANT® implants. Over 1,000 have been observed for 2 years of continuous use of the method. Few women have discontinued using NORPLANT® for either medical or personal reasons. Three pregnancies have occurred, giving a 2-year cumulative pregnancy rate of 0.1 (Gu et al., 1988).

NORPLANT® implants can be removed at any time. Several studies involving hundreds of women established that fertility occurs at a normal rate after removal. Growth and development patterns of babies born to mothers who stopped using the method to have planned pregnancies have been monitored. There is no evidence of any deleterious effects (Diaz et al., 1987).

NORPLANT® is an effective, safe, reversible method of long-term contraception. For women, one visit to a clinic can replace 3 to 5 years of daily pill-taking and provide a higher level of contraceptive protection. The one-time administration feature is a considerable advantage both to the user and to service delivery systems. It simplifies the logistical problems associated with replenishment of renewable contraceptives and reduces the number of clinic visits required by most reversible contraceptive methods. Based on the pricing established so far in countries where NORPLANT® has been introduced commercially, the cost is about equivalent to the local cost of 1 year of oral contraceptive pills when purchased by the consumer in a pharmacy or drugstore.

At least three second-generation silastic implant contraceptives are in the initial stages of clinical study. While the original NORPLANT® product requires the placement and eventual removal of six small tubes, the newer versions seek to simplify the procedure by reducing the number. The convenience of fewer implants is particularly important at the time of removal, when an occasional subdermal capsule may be hard to reach. One modification involves a change in the configuration of the silastic implant itself. Designated as NORPLANT®-2, this version has been studied extensively and has proved to have performance characteristics over 3 years of use comparable to those of the original NORPLANT® (Sivin, 1988). It requires a set of only two soft-rod implants, each of which is slightly longer than those in the six-implant system. When manufacturing problems, recently encountered, are overcome, NORPLANT®-2 will be proposed for registration as a 3-year implant method in many countries, including the United States and India.

A second modification is to use a progestin with higher potency than the standard levonorgestrel used in the NORPLANT® systems. With a high enough progestin potency, a single implant might provide a sufficient surface area to achieve a contraceptive level in blood. Exploratory studies have started with at least three single-implant systems (Odlind, 1988; Wiedhaup, 1988:11; Coutinho et al., 1984a). This may be a long process, because introduction of a new progestin requires new information on release rates, blood levels, optimal dosages for bleeding control, duration of action, metabolic effects, and restoration of fertility. It is expected that any of the single-implant methods now being explored would have a shorter life span than either NORPLANT® system. The development program with the progestin desogestrel adds the objective of reducing the diameter of the implant in order to further simplify the insertion process.

In another approach to implant contraception, researchers seek to avoid the need for removal of empty silastic tubes or rods by using a biodegradable implant as the carrier for the contraceptive progestin. One system which is undergoing initial clinical trials is named Capronor. The outer tube is made of biodegradable polycaprolactone, an innocuous rubberlike substance that is readily absorbed by the body. The progestin levonórgestrel is dissolved in a vehicle that is also bioabsorbable. Clinical work reported so far, involving 40 volunteers, is directed toward finding the proper size and number of implants needed to achieve contraceptive levels of the progestin in blood. In these preliminary tests, implants were left in place for 45 days, but it is expected that the system will last 18 to 24 months before a new implant would be required (Hall and d'Arcangues, 1988).

There are no data on the performance of Capronor as a contraceptive method. Its advantages would be simplicity because it is a one-implant system that does not require the removal of an empty tube. Bioabsorbability, however, introduces a new issue. Once dissolution begins, probably a few months following insertion, the implant would not be removable (Hall and d'Arcangues, 1988). This could prove to be a limitation when removal is required for personal or medical reasons.

Another biodegradable implant system uses the progestin norethindrone (NET) as the contraceptive agent. The steroid is heat-fused with a cholesterol base, molded into a pellet the shape and size of a grain of rice (Gupta, 1977), and is inserted under the skin. Efforts to find the right size and number of NET pellets have been proceeding sporadically for many years (Gupta et al., 1984). Using a new production method, pellets have been prepared recently that are expected to last approximately 1 year before a new set of four pellets would be required. A first-phase trial in 35 women is in progress (Archer, 1988). Until there is sufficient information available, it is not possible to evaluate the prospects and advantages of this most recent version of NET pellets.

As with other biodegradable implants, removal of NET pellets may prove to be a problem. Removal is of particular concern if a woman experiences prolonged or heavy bleeding. Under such circumstances the progestin should be discontinued. If this cannot be done because removal of the pellets is not successful, it would be necessary to make some attempt to prevent further blood loss, particularly in women who may already be anemic. Estrogen therapy has been used for this purpose, although the efficacy of this cannot be assured.

These concerns indicate the breadth of experience that will have to be acquired before the usefulness of biodegradable implants can be assessed.

A Pill to Terminate Pregnancy

Advances in the biology of cell receptors have progressed at a rapid pace in recent years, bringing a cascade of new discoveries and insights. Identification of specific receptors for steroid hormones has been of seminal importance. This knowledge has already been applied for the diagnosis and treatment of gynecologic cancers and other diseases. A new application, the prevention or termination of early pregnancy, looms ahead as chemists synthesize molecules that can compete with progesterone for its receptor sites on target cells of the uterus.

Progesterone stimulation of endometrial target cells is essential for the prevention of menstrual sloughing of the uterine lining. Without progesterone the uterus cannot nidate a fertilized egg and pregnancy cannot become established. Compounds that occupy progesterone receptor sites without transforming the target cells from the nonstimulated to the stimulated state prevent the natural hormone from carrying out its progestational role and are, therefore, contragestational.

The first of this new class of progesterone antagonists to be tested for its effect on pregnancy is mifepristone (RU-486), a compound similar in its structure to progestins that behave like the natural hormone. A clever change in one portion of the molecule causes RU-486 to lose progestational activity and converts it into an efficient antagonist (Teutsch, 1985). The first clinical study using RU-486 to interrupt early pregnancy was published in 1982 (Hermann et al., 1982). In the short time since then, adequate information has been gathered by the sponsoring company to successfully seek approval for registration in France, where the compound was first synthesized. Approval for use has been obtained also in the People's Republic of China. This was based on a filing that incorporates data from government-sponsored trials in China completed in 1988. Studies with RU-486 as a contragestational agent have also been carried out in other countries, including Sweden, the United States, and India. The Swedish investigations have been particularly important because they disclosed that the efficiency of RU-486 in preventing pregnancy is enhanced when prostaglandin is administered concurrently (Bygdeman and Swahn, 1985).

When women take oral tablets of RU-486 for 1 to 3 days, progestational support to the endometrium is interrupted and a menstrual bleeding usually ensues. This simulates what happens during the menstrual cycle, when progesterone levels drop and menstruation begins. If this occurs in a cycle when fertilization has occurred, the fertilized egg or early embryo is discharged with the menstrual flow. The efficiency of RU-486 treatment has proved to depend more on the length of time postfertilization than on the dose of drug used. When treatment is begun within 10 days after a missed period, the drug terminates pregnancy in 85 percent of the cases. For women who have had 8 weeks of amenorrhea before beginning RU-486 treatment, the success rate is about 63 percent. Waiting longer drops the success rate even further (Van Look, 1988).

Using RU-486 together with prostaglandin increases the effectiveness of both drugs as abortifacients. A single dose of RU-486 combined with a vaginal suppository containing a prostaglandin analogue increases effectiveness to nearly 100 percent for women who are not beyond 2 weeks past the missed period (Psychoyos and Husson, 1987). The prostaglandin dose required for this synergistic effect is about one-tenth the dose employed when prostaglandin alone is used to induce abortion. Consequently, the treatment avoids the unpleasant and frequently intolerable side effects associated with prostaglandin use.

Product registration filings and most investigations are now proceeding on the basis of treatment with the two drugs combined. RU-486 is given orally and prostaglandin is given by vaginal suppository, intramuscular injection, or oral tablet.

This new menses-inducing therapy is an important alternative to surgical termination of early pregnancy and the vacuum aspiration procedure sometimes referred to as menstrual regulation. It is not, however, a method of abortion that can simply be sold over the counter for use without clinical backup. RU-486 plus prostaglandin must be used under supervision. In some cases, prolonged heavy bleeding occurs, which could be life-threatening if it is not controlled. This is usually caused by incomplete emptying of the uterine contents. The exact percentage of cases in which this occurs is uncertain but like the overall success rate itself, it depends on the length of gestation when the treatment is initiated. Postabortion infection is another eventuality that must be recognized early and treated promptly.

The receptor-blocking activity of RU-486 suggests several other uses of the compound in gynecology, in clinical endocrinology, and for other methods of fertility regulation. Tests in monkeys show that RU-486 may be effective as a once-a-month menstrual regulator (Collins and Hodgen, 1986). When tried in women, there was sufficient disruption of menstrual regularity or variability in response to make the procedure, in its present form, unfeasible (Nieman et al., 1987). Work is proceeding to overcome these difficulties with RU-486 and related compounds. The compound has also been used early in the menstrual cycle and has been found to delay ovulation (Swahn and Bygdeman, 1988). Whether this observation can be used as an approach to contraception requires further investigation.

In the years ahead, products consisting of RU-486 and some form of prostaglandin will be available in many countries. They will be important for fertility regulation and they will help reduce maternal mortalities resulting from illicit, unclean abortions throughout the world.

Hormones as Vaginal Contraceptives

Synthetic estrogens, rather than naturally produced estradiol, are used in combination oral contraceptives because the natural hormone is not active when taken orally. It is too rapidly metabolized when the blood carries it directly to the liver from the gut. In an effort to take advantage of the safety advantages of using the natural estrogen, scientists have developed hormonal contraceptives that utilize the ability of the vaginal epithelium to absorb steroids. Vaginally absorbed hormones enter the general circulation and therefore avoid the first pass to the liver. This and avoidance of daily pill-taking were the rationales behind early studies undertaken with contraceptive vaginal rings (CVRs) (Mishell et al., 1970). Molded of silastic into a ring about the size of a diaphragm rim, the first CVRs were designed to release progestin alone, but soon afterward the focus switched to progestin-estrogen combinations. The steroids used were the progestin levonorgestrel and natural estradiol at doses high enough to suppress ovulation (Mishell et al., 1978).

An acceptability survey carried out early in the development of this new method indicated a favorable user reaction. A woman can be instructed to insert the ring in the vagina. It is left in place for 3 weeks and is then removed for a week, simulating the schedule of daily pill-taking when oral contraceptives are used. In most cases, withdrawal bleeding occurs during the week the ring is left out. This system was carefully evaluated in an international study involving over 1,000 volunteers, and its acceptability and effectiveness were established. Pregnancy rates were similar to those from the use of low levels of oral contraceptives (1.0 per 100 women-years), and most users were satisfied with the method (Sivin et al., 1981a,b).

As clinical chemistry data were accumulated, however, unfavorable changes in the ratio of HDL-cholesterol to LDL-cholesterol were observed (Ahren et al., 1983). Even though the total cholesterol levels were not elevated, this potentially adverse finding discouraged further work with that particular version of the CVR. Nevertheless, the method had proved itself in terms of effectiveness and bleeding control (menstrual blood loss), the two essential elements of a successful hormonal contraceptive. This has encouraged trials of CVRs with different progestin-estrogen combinations (Wiedhaup, 1988:11). One of the few contraceptive research undertakings in the pharmaceutical industry, the 3-ketodesogestrel flexible vaginal ring now in preliminary trials, may make an appearance on the contraceptive market sooner than methods for which commercial sponsors have to be found.

Substantial information has been accumulated on the performance of a CVR that derives its contraceptive action by the release of a low level of a progestin only. In a key study, women have used this ring for an aggregate of over 8,000 women-months. The pregnancy rate is 3.6, and a 1-year continuation rate of 49 percent was observed (Landgren, 1987). Sufficient data on performance and toxicity were accumulated to project introductory studies in several countries by the end of 1987. At the eleventh hour, the manufacturer of the plastic (Medical Grade Elastomer 382) used to manufacture the ring discontinued its production. The minuscule market for medical uses of the product, including vaginal rings and silastic rod implants, would not enable the company to recover the costs of new tests required by the U.S. Environmental Protection Agency (EPA). Several expert toxicology panels gave the material a clean bill of health after reviewing the EPA's questions and concerns. Nevertheless, it became necessary to seek a replacement for the plastic material used to make the CVR. The time schedule for the introductory studies of this device, therefore, has been set back until a new manufacturing arrangement can be worked out and tests can be performed to ensure that the new device's performance matches that of the original. The same misfortune has delayed a contraceptive vaginal ring that was designed to use the natural hormone progesterone so that it could be used by lactating women to extend the period of lactational amenorrhea.

There is, however, an approach to the use of hormones as vaginal contraceptives that remains in clinical trials, the combination pill administered per vaginum. The idea to test this approach emerged from the experience in testing contraceptive vaginal rings. One investigator noticed that the method's problems were associated with the silastic ring itself and not the hormones that were being released (Coutinho et al., 1982). Since steroids are readily absorbed across the vaginal mucosa, why not use the vaginal route instead of the oral route for administration of the conventional pill? Like the vaginal ring, this approach would retain the advantage of bypassing the gut and avoiding the first pass to the liver. The initial volunteers were women who wished to discontinue oral contraceptive use because of nausea and other gastrointestinal symptoms. The studies to date have shown that the pill is equally effective by the vaginal route of administration, that some side effects are reduced compared with those from oral contraceptive use, and that the method is acceptable to most women who participated in the trials (Coutinho et al., 1984b). Blood levels of levonorgestrel, the progestin used in the combination pill tested, are about the same as those achieved when the pill is taken orally (Alvarez et al., 1983).

An international study involving 700 women in eight cities is in progress in which two progestin-estrogen combination pills used vaginally are being compared. By mid-1989 enough data will be available to evaluate not only the overall performance of this method but consumer interest as well.

An Antipregnancy Vaccine

The 1980s have been called the age of vaccines as scientists, armed with the powerful tools of molecular biology and dramatic advances in understanding of the immune system, attempt to develop an array of new vaccines to combat diseases such as malaria, hepatitis, acquired immune deficiency syndrome (AIDS), and leprosy. Among the most advanced experimental programs is a vaccine to prevent pregnancy. The process is long and sometimes frustrating. Foremost, it is necessary to identify the appropriate antigen—the molecule that stimulates the body's immune system to produce neutralizing antibodies. Using this antigen, the next step is to prepare a vaccine that will elicit a strong enough response to be biologically meaningful. Low levels of antibody formation are not protective. Sometimes, the titers can be increased by using adjuvants. These are substances such as bacterial cell wall lipids or synthetic molecules that stimulate the immune system to produce a stronger reaction.

There are several fertility-regulating vaccines in clinical trial. The most comprehensive program is in India, where government-sponsored research places high priority on finding an effective and safe vaccine. In many centers around the country, volunteers are participating in a study to select the best antigen among several candidates (Talwar and Singh, 1988). The basic approach is to interfere with the action of the human pregnancy hormone, human chorionic gonadotropin (hCG). This protein hormone is essential for the establishment and maintenance of pregnancy. The gene for its production is one of the first to be turned on once the fertilized egg begins to divide. Without the action of hCG, which stimulates the ovary to produce progesterone, the lining of the uterus would slough off and a menstrual flow would occur, carrying with it the fertilized egg. hCG is the message that alerts the woman's reproductive system that a fertilized egg is present. The system is not infallible, however; scientists estimate that wastage of fertilized eggs occurs spontaneously in about one-third of cycles in which fertilization occurs.

The origins of the program in India trace back to the mid 1970s, when investigators made a breakthrough in enhancing antigenicity by linking a portion of the hCG molecule to a carrier protein. The scientists in India used tetanus toxoid as the carrier and the beta-subunit of hCG as the primary antigen (Talwar et al., 1976). The first trials proved the feasibility of the approach; 60 out of 63 volunteers developed antibodies which neutralized hCG when tested in the laboratory. None of the women had manifestations of toxicity. This finding was confirmed quickly by a study involving 15 women in Scandinavia and Latin America. Fourteen women developed neutralizing antibodies. Each of these volunteers was observed carefully for 4 years after their antibody titers were allowed to drop to undetectable levels, and no evidence of health impairment emerged (Nash et al., 1980).

Specific issues were identified in the pioneering studies with the Indian vaccine, designated as beta-hCG-TT. The antibody response was not uniform. Some women produced neutralizing titers of antibody; others produced only low levels. A manufacturing problem emerged when batch differences appeared in the tetanus toxoid used as the carrier protein. This surprising nonuniformity had to be overcome to meet regulatory agency requirements. It was necessary, also, to improve the linkage process between the beta-subunit and the tetanus toxoid molecule.

Probably, the most important cause for delaying further work on the beta-hCG-TT after the initial trials was the fact that antibodies cross-reacted to some degree with the pituitary hormone luteinizing hormone (LH). Although a cross-reaction was anticipated because of structural similarities, there was no way of assessing the significance or safety implications of this finding. This uncertainty prompted a comprehensive 9-year study in monkeys that failed to disclose any toxicity or pathology resulting from the cross-reaction (Thau et al., 1987). Consequently, new trials with beta-hCG-TT could resume in India and have been in progress since May 1986. Three different antigens are being tested and two carrier proteins are being used (tetanus toxoid and a portion of the cholera toxin). Each has the advantage of creating a vaccine that can provide some degree of immunity against a life-threatening disease.

Once a single vaccine is selected on the basis of antibody titers that are developed and the absence of side effects, the government of India will authorize a study of its effectiveness in actual use. Until such data are available, it is not possible to predict the degree of efficacy, acceptability, or other implementation issues that will arise when this antifertility vaccine becomes available.

Another trial was done in Australia, under World Health Organization sponsorship, using a vaccine prepared with a different antigen but based on the same principle of intercepting hCG. In order to avoid a cross-reaction with LH, only a small portion of the beta-subunit molecule is used for linkage with the carrier protein. A consequence of this modification is that antibody-stimulating potency is reduced compared with that in vaccines using the entire beta-subunit. This Australian trial involved 30 volunteers who were observed for 6 months (Griffin, 1988). The study has demonstrated that all the immunized women respond to the vaccine by producing antibodies. While data to determine whether these antibodies are capable of neutralizing hCG have not been reported, the Australian investigators believe that the titers produced by most of the women would be sufficient to prevent pregnancy. Inactivation of the hormonal message of hCG, they propose, may not be necessary. The antibodies could act locally on the surface of the dividing egg and thus prevent implantation, a postulate derived from observations in an experiment done with baboons (Griffin, 1986).

Authorized by the U.S. Food and Drug Administration, an international team of investigators is reinvestigating the beta-hCG-TT vaccine, using a preparation that does not have the manufacturing variability problems inherent in the original vaccine. Data on the uniformity of response will be available in 1989.

The hCG-based antifertility vaccine is far along in the development process, if viewed in the context of vaccine development in general. It will be several years, however, before information is available on basic facts like effectiveness, schedule of boosters required, reversibility, or side effects. A version of this vaccine could be ready for general use in some countries in the next decade. Considering India's leadership role in this research, it is likely to be among the first countries to provide this new method of fertility regulation to its people.

Pills, Implants, or Injections for Men

Some years ago, writing in the *Village Voice*, author Jennifer MacLeod called attention to the negative features of available contraceptive technology for women by speculating on the reaction of men if they were required to endure comparable health hazards and indignities (Segal, 1972). Her description of mythical male methods, portrayed with Swiftian irony, may prove to have been prophetic.

Among current research approaches, the most extensive clinical experience has been accumulated with an oral contraceptive method that men take every day for 60 days before switching to a less frequent maintenance dose. This is the pill for men developed in the People's Republic of China. It is based on the use of gossypol, the yellow pigment found in cottonseed. First tested as a male contraceptive in 1974, the idea of using gossypol sprang from medical detective work that revealed that uncooked cottonseed oil was responsible for an epidemic of infertility in a rural area.

More than 10,000 Chinese men have taken large doses of gossypol. Most of these were volunteers in the initial countrywide study. When the results were published in 1978, a success rate of 99.4 percent was reported (National Coordination Group on Male Antifertility Agents, 1978). Actually, this so-called success rate referred to the percentage of men whose sperm count dropped to levels believed to be incompatible with fertility. It was reported that some men in the study experienced a decline in blood levels of potassium, which the body needs for normal muscle function. The report did not attempt to quantify the hypokalemic (low potassium) effect because it varied widely from center to center, ranging from 0 to 6 percent.

Two subsequent studies in Beijing, smaller in size and more carefully controlled, confirmed the antifertility action of gossypol at a dose of 20 mg/day (Liu and Lyle, 1987; Liu, Lyle, and Jian, 1987). In these studies, too, lower blood potassium levels were observed after several months of use. Unfortunately, the Beijing studies, like the initial all-China trial, had methodological problems that confound the interpretation of potassium changes. Without an appropriate animal model, it has not been possible to clarify the validity and magnitude of the gossypol/potassium relationship, but this is too important an issue to be left unresolved.

Efforts to find analogues of gossypol that retain antifertility activity have not succeeded, but it has been possible with advanced laboratory procedures to separate two chemical variants, positive and negative gossypol, and study them individually (Matlin et al., 1987). Early results indicate that the antifertility action in men can be achieved with the negative form alone, thus allowing a 50 percent reduction in dose (Matlin et al., 1985). Tests in progress will establish whether this reduces the chances of hypokalemia without sacrificing effectiveness. Meanwhile, Chinese chemists are working on bulk production methods that would lower the cost of manufacturing negative gossypol.

Elsewhere, work is in progress to identify, by a simple urine test, individuals who are considered likely to be susceptible to the hypokalemic effect of gossypol (Jennings and Reidenberg, 1988). This would make it possible to selectively exclude some men from using the method, just as some women are excluded from using oral contraceptives or intrauterine devices (IUDs).

The acceptability and usefulness of gossypol as a male contraceptive will be influenced by its reversibility. When a large group of men take the standard dose of gossypol for 12 months and then stop, 1 year later about 80 percent have resumed normal sperm production. It takes even longer for sperm to appear in the ejaculates of some portion of the remainder, and some remain azospermic after several years of observation. Exact percentages in each category are not defined, but it appears that the chances for irreversibility increase with the dose and length of use (Meng et al., 1988). With the lower doses of gossypol now being tested, the objective is to achieve an antifertility effect by stopping sperm motility without fully inhibiting sperm production. This approach may reduce the chances of prolonged azospermia.

Couples could opt to take oral contraceptives in alternate years, with the woman using the conventional pill and the man using gossypol. With this couple method, each partner would share the responsibilities of contraception and the risks for each would be reduced. This regimen would also accommodate the need for an overlapping contraceptive measure during the time required for an adequate fall in sperm count or motility after the man starts to use gossypol.

There is ample evidence that gossypol treatment does not reduce the production of male sex hormone by the human testes, so that this method does not require replacement hormone treatment. Even after a year of gossypol use, men retain normal plasma testosterone levels (Coutinho et al., 1984c).

If gossypol is the product of traditional medicine and medical sleuthing, the other main line of work toward a reversible male method is the result of sophisticated fundamental research. In 1971 two American biochemists, destined to win the Nobel Prize for this discovery, announced independently the structure of LHRH (LH and releasing hormone [RH]). This is the small polypeptide produced by the hypothalamic region of the brain which stimulates the production of the pituitary hormones LH and folicle-stimulating hormone (FSH) (Monahan et al., 1971; Schally et al., 1971). By controlling the release of these gonad-stimulating hormones, LHRH indirectly controls the production of both sperm and testicular androgens. When chemists synthesized analogues that were either highly potent agonists (mimics) or antagonists of LHRH, it was quickly learned through animal experiments that either type could interfere with the action of endogenous LHRH. The result was a suppression of sperm production by the testes and hormone production as well.

This means that any method based on LHRH suppression would have to include testosterone or another androgen to maintain physiologically normal male sex hormone levels. A few agonists were tested with or without testosterone injections, but results were not satisfactory because of the unpredictability of sperm suppression. While some efforts with agonists continue, the current view favors the use of LHRH antagonists (Waites, 1988). This introduces additional obstacles because some antagonists have inherent histamine-releasing activity that would be unacceptable in clinical use (Sundaram et al., 1988).

Whether agonists or antagonists, LHRH analogues are polypeptides that lose their activity when taken by mouth because they are destroyed by digestive enzymes in the gastrointestinal tract. Therefore, a contraceptive method using a compound in this category would have to be administered by some other route. For some years efforts were made to develop a nasal spray delivery form because the nasal mucosa is a good absorptive surface for small molecules. When it appeared that this procedure could not be relied on to deliver a standard dose and that the spray would have to be repeated several times each day, these obvious disadvantages discouraged further efforts to produce a nasal spray contraceptive. The currently proposed modes of administration are by injection or, ultimately, by a long-acting subdermal implant. With the present technology, the longest interval feasible between injections is 1 month. Researchers believe that they can develop a sustained-release implant that will last 1 year. Without some progress on a practical delivery system, the feasibility of an LHRH-based method fades considerably.

Delivery of the required replacement androgen is also not a simple matter because no suitable, orally active androgen is available. Here, too, hope lies in the development of long-acting delivery systems, either injections or implants. In addition, a suitable androgen must be identified and must pass the test of pharmacological safety. Since androgens are involved in such issues as blood lipid levels and prostate stimulation, many toxicity issues will have to be scrutinized carefully under conditions of long-term use.

The road ahead for research on an injectable or implantable male contraceptive seems long. Neither specific compounds nor precise delivery forms are in hand. Until fixed product formulations are set, the required long-term safety, effectiveness, and reversibility studies cannot be started. It is reasonable to conclude that work with LHRH-based contraceptive approaches is still at the stage of determining whether this approach is feasible.

As for the other suggested approach to injectable male contraception, the use of pituitary-suppressing doses of androgens, progestins, or combinations of the two, suffice it to say that it has been over 35 years since this was first attempted (Heller et al., 1958), and some of the basic uncertainties about this approach remain. About 10 years ago a published summary of results of clinical trials with many formulations revealed that with each unacceptably high failure rates occurred. Some men did not respond sufficiently and others experienced breakthrough sperm production after having responded initially (Schearer et al., 1978). Similar work is continuing, but no regimen tested in recent years has yielded results that would be acceptable for contraception. If a clinical trial results in an inadequate success rate, it is not simply a matter of increasing the dose and trying again. The range of doses that can be considered is limited because chronic androgen administration to men at levels that would exceed physiological blood values would be viewed with skepticism by cardiovascular specialists, oncologists, and clinical pharmacologists.

Future prospects for male contraceptive methods will depend on greater understanding of the physiology of male reproduction. Posttesticular maturation of sperm may be susceptible to controlled interference. Specific inhibition of FSH is an intriguing approach because it would avoid the need for supplementary androgen treatment.

When pioneer endocrinologists coined the term *inhibin*, they were suggesting that something other than gonadal steroids signals the pituitary gland to stop producing FSH. Proof that inhibin really exists and, if so, what it is and what it does have been elusive for nearly 50 years. Suddenly, scientists today not only know what it is, atom by atom, but they can produce it by gene technology. An understanding of inhibin's role in normal physiology and how this knowledge might be used for birth control remain for future research.

The concept of using inhibin or anything else to selectively stop the gamete-producing function of the testes suffered a serious setback when research in monkeys revealed that blocking FSH production immunologically does not stop sperm production (Nieschlag, 1985). Since there is another study with opposite results, however, this matter can hardly be considered as settled. This is a serious shortcoming in fertility control research. All too often an important step or principle is influenced by a single research report, without confirmation, because the amount of work in the field is far too limited.

What, then, are the prospects for a new male contraceptive method this century? If China's pill for men does not materialize, and there are some who believe that gossypol's toxicity problems are insurmountable (Waites, 1988), the outlook is bleak. Expectations beyond the next 10 to 15 years depend on basic research and how this information can be converted to applied technology.

IMPROVING PRESENT METHODS OF CONTRACEPTION

Modifications of Oral Contraceptives

Constantly in search of new progestins as limited life spans of existing patents wane, pharmaceutical companies continue to synthesize and study new progestational compounds that can be used in oral contraceptives. Three high-potency compounds that are already on the European market are in the testing or registration process in the United States. When available, they will offer dose reductions below those of existing products, a process that has been going on since the first oral contraceptives were first introduced. For example, a new progestin, gestodene, is used in a pill containing 75 micrograms of the progestin and 30 micrograms of ethinyl estradiol (Wiedhaup, 1988:7). This is one one-hundredth the amount of steroid contained in the first oral contraceptive that reached the market just over 25 years ago. Two other compounds, desogestrel and norgestimate, also serve as the basis for low-dose products. If these high-potency compounds prove to have advantages over existing products, it would be by virtue of reducing the metabolic risks associated with hormonal contraception. This is not assured, however, because the high potency necessary to have reproductive effects may also prevail with respect to other physiological or metabolic functions

Variable-dose products are another modification that is popular with pharmaceutical companies. The changing dosage schedule over the course of a month attempts to follow the pattern of ovarian steroid production. The regimen results in an aggregate steroid dose per month that is below that of the same components taken as a fixed-dose oral contraceptive. The reduction in monthly steroid intake is intended to reduce the risk of progestin-induced changes in metabolic parameters such as glucose tolerance, total cholesterol, and blood-clotting factors.

A pill taken on a non-daily basis is another variant of oral contraception that attracts attention. A weekly pill, for example, has been the subject of investigation for many years. A drug now used successfully for the treatment of uterine fibroids and endometriosis (Coutinho et al., 1986) was first tested as a once-a-week contraceptive pill. The compound, thought to be too androgenic for regular use as a contraceptive in some cultures (Mora, Faundes, and Pastore, 1974), is available as a weekly pill in the People's Republic of China. Its use may spread in the years ahead. The Chinese have also persisted in the use of progestins as a postcoital pill (Lei and Hu,

1981), an approach that investigators elsewhere have found to be too disruptive to the endocrine cycle to be useful.

Modifications of Intrauterine Contraception

Because of their popularity in China, IUDs are used by more women than any other reversible form of fertility regulation. There are an estimated 80 million users worldwide (Mauldin and Segal, 1988), despite the fear, notable in the United States, that IUDs can cause pelvic inflammatory disease. This attitude persists, fueled by litigation associated with the defunct Dalkon Shield, regardless of epidemiological evidence that American women living in stable, monogamous relationships have no increased risk of pelvic inflammatory disease when they use an IUD (Lee, Rubin, and Boruck, 1988).

When modern IUDs were introduced in the 1960s, users were prepared to accept the failure rates of three to four pregnancies per 100 women-years of use for the convenience of a coitus-independent method that offered an alternative to the pill. With the advent of copper-bearing devices in the 1970s, effectiveness jumped upward and the smaller size of the new devices meant that more women could use an IUD without discomfort or pain. The most effective of the copper IUDs, the TCu-380, has a pregnancy rate of less than one per 100 women-years of use. This leaves little room for improvement. There are some spontaneous expulsions, and about 4 percent of users discontinue the method within 1 year because of discomfort or bleeding, but the continuation-of-use rate with the TCu-380 is also improved substantially over that of earlier IUDs (Sivin and Tatum, 1981).

Possibly, these performance features could be improved upon by design changes. One such effort utilizes the contraceptive value of copper without introducing the usual plastic platform, T-shaped or otherwise. This is achieved by stringing a row of small segments of copper tubing on a monofilament polyethylene thread that is inserted into the uterus, in which one end is fixed to prevent expulsion. This flexible device is in the early testing phase with about 40 women.

Comprehensive studies involving thousands of users in many countries have been carried out for several years with a T-shaped IUD that releases levonorgestrel. The failure rate is less than one per 100 women-years. In a large Scandinavian study more than 80 percent of women were still using the method after 1 year (Luukkainen,

Toivonen, and Lahteenmaki, 1987). This is a high continuation-of-use rate for an IUD. An advantageous feature of this device is that users experience a reduction in menstrual bleeding. Like some other long-acting contraceptives, development of this method has been set back by the unavailability of Elastomer 382, the medical-grade silastic used in its manufacture.

The most important advances in intrauterine contraception may not be in new product design but in our knowledge about the method. Understanding the mechanism of action of IUDs and more epidemiological information on long-term use may enhance the acceptance of this method more than the appearance of yet another shape, form, or material would.

Modifications of Injectable Contraceptives

Investigators in Brazil were first to recognize the contraceptive potential of the progestin medroxyprogesterone acetate (MPA), which is prepared in a solution that creates a depot effect when injected intramuscularly (Coutinho et al., 1966). This was the origin of the much-publicized Depo-Provera trimonthly contraceptive which, after 20 years, remains controversial. In spite of the controversy, use of injectable contraceptives has continued, particularly in countries where injections are the preferred method for receiving medications. It is estimated that in 1985, 6 million women were taking injections for contraception (Mauldin and Segal, 1988).

Depo-Provera acts by suppressing ovulation. This accounts for its high contraceptive effectiveness. With long-term ovarian suppression, however, women tend to develop amenorrhea. After 1 year about 40 percent of Depo-Provera users experience an absence of menstrual bleeding. This and other bleeding disturbances are the main reasons that women fail to continue the injections. About 25 percent stop by 1 year and 50 percent stop by 2 years (Hall and d'Arcangues, 1988).

Despite the fact that several national and international medical authorities approve the use of Depo-Provera, it is not likely that any injectable preparation using MPA as the progestin will gain widespread favor. Rejected as a contraceptive by the U.S. Food and Drug Administration, it has been the subject of several hostile hearings by committees of the U.S. Congress. Women's groups in several countries have attacked it as being dangerous.

The development of a trimonthly preparation that retires MPA as the active ingredient may be the best way to increase the use of injectables around the world. Efforts to do this are under way but are at an early stage, so that the performance characteristics of new long-acting injectables cannot yet be judged.

Injectable contraceptives that are given every month have been available for many years (Coutinho and De Souza, 1968) and continue to attract users. It is estimated, for example, that in Mexico over 1 million ampules of progestin-estrogen preparations are sold each year for this purpose. China reports that 1 million women use the method. While there are no particular problems with products now available, they are not distributed in many countries. To promote the adoption of this method in family planning programs, new formulations are being studied (Hall and d'Arcangues, 1988).

Modifications of Barrier Contraceptives

Interest in barrier contraceptives has been increased dramatically because of their importance in preventing the spread of the virus that causes AIDS (human immunodeficiency virus [HIV]) and other sexually transmitted diseases. This has resulted in a sharp increase in the use of condoms in many countries. A study in Nairobi, Kenya, for example, recorded an increase in condom use after prostitutes participated in an AIDS education program (Ngugi et al., 1987).

Research has shown that compounds that can act as spermicides can also inactivate some viruses. The standard spermicidal agent in most vaginal preparations, the detergent nonoxynol-9, can reduce the infectivity of HIV. This has also been shown for gossypol, which has specific antiviral activity for viruses with a protein envelope. It is, therefore, also active against herpes simplex virus type 2, the virus responsible for genital herpes (Wichmann, Vaheri, and Luukkainen, 1982). Studies are now in progress in Africa and Asia to determine the acceptance of condoms that have been pretreated with gossypol or other spermicides. Testing the effectiveness of these medicated condoms will prove to be a difficult epidemiological task.

Inventors have proposed new types of barriers to ensure greater protection against the transfer of bodily fluids during intercourse. One has been named the female condom. It would cover the vaginal vault, including the clitoris and labial portal. Most likely, it would have to be used with an artificial lubricant that could be formulated to include an antisperm/antivirus chemical. As yet, little is known about the acceptability of this vaginal barrier in various cultures.

Other approaches to increasing the variety of choices of barrier methods include disposable diaphragms and plastic condoms. Both are revivals of ideas that have been tried and abandoned in the past, but may be more acceptable now, in the time of the AIDS epidemic.

Modifications in Surgical Sterilization

Choosing surgical sterilization is different from using reversible contraceptives in many ways. None, however, is more important than the certainty that sterilization provides. For couples who are positive that they will not want another pregnancy, short of terminal abstinence, this is their method of choice. As modifications are devised to simplify or make reversible the procedures used for vasectomy or tubal closure, this fact must be kept in mind. To sacrifice any degree of effectiveness is a doubtful strategy.

The most advanced work in this area aims to cause bilateral occlusion of the vas deferens without requiring a scrotal incision. In fact, over 1 million such procedures have been carried out routinely in China, using a sclerosing chemical injected into the vas through a blunted needle. This simple instrument, combined with the use of colored solutions to test the needle's location, simplifies the process of locating the elusive vas lumen (Wu Chieh-ping, honorary president, Chinese Academy of Medical Sciences, personal communication, 1986). Chinese scientists and others are also attempting to inject into the vas polymerizing plastics that could later be removed to restore patency and fertility (Zaneveld, 1988). Failure rates of past attempts to do this have been unacceptable. If sacrificing effectiveness in blocking sperm proves to be a characteristic of the new experimental procedures as well, this would be a poor tradeoff for the prospect of reversibility.

The same principle, the paramount dominance of effectiveness over simplification, reversibility, or both, pertains to efforts to develop transcervical approaches to female sterilization. The openings of the fallopian tubes into the uterus are not always in a predictable location or easy to identify. The task of developing an instrument that can do this reliably without direct visualization has continually frustrated gynecologists and inventors. It is also a daunting challenge to identify the chemical or plastic that is effective and also safe to inject into the highly vascular uterine or tubal lumen.

CONCLUSION

Contraceptive methodology has changed significantly since the introduction of the birth-control pill and the modern IUD over a quarter century ago. Women today use oral contraceptives that are safer than those available in the 1960s. New IUDs are more effective and carry less risk than earlier versions. Surgical contraception for women has been simplified without sacrificing effectiveness. The constituents of spermicidal preparations have been changed to reduce possible toxic effects. New types of vaginal contraceptives are in use. In some countries, contraceptive injections are available. Around the world, nearly a quarter million women are using a long-acting contraceptive implant. Furthermore, research is continuing on all of these methods to improve them even further and to overcome the impediments to their use in developing countries.

Clinical research trials are in progress that, if successful, could add substantially to the array of choices: new contraceptive implants, a contragestational drug that can prevent the establishment or maintenance of early pregnancy, a vaccine to prevent pregnancy that would not interfere with a woman's normal menstrual cycle, and a pill that men could take to prevent sperm formation or motility without impairing libido.

These are *new* contraceptive methods. If all complete the course of research, surveillance, and registration, the number of contraceptive choices would increase sharply over the next decade.

Viewed in the light of overall biomedical research, these achievements by contraceptive researchers are remarkable. A revolution in medical technology is not an everyday event. The vast investment in cancer research, for example, has had important successes, but frustrations remain in achieving major breakthroughs. The burden of AIDS has been upon us for almost a decade, and there is no therapeutic relief in sight. Diseases that afflict hundreds of millions of people are treated essentially the same today as they were 25 years ago.

This is not to say that medical technology has stood still over the past quarter century. Indeed, there have been dramatic changes and advances in some branches of diagnostics, therapeutics and surgery. But a 25-year plateau in treatment modalities for a given disease or condition is not unusual. That contraceptive technology has progressed is a credit to the relatively small band of reproduction research scientists throughout the world and to the policymakers who have established programs and provided funds to support their work.

Beyond the next dozen years, the future depends on the present. Without a continuing investment in today's fundamental research toward a broader and deeper understanding of the reproductive process, society will have to depend on faith, hope, and serendipity for the next wave of innovations.

One hopes that an observer of contraceptive research as we cross over to the new millennium will give little notice to the subjects described in these pages. She or he should be able to describe possible applications of new knowledge about basic issues such as membrane biology, tissue growth factors, cell-to-cell communication, or the fertilization process itself. With scientific advances, methods of fertility regulation could be based on mechanisms that differ from those used today

There is no perfect method of contraception for the world's diverse population. As research continues, however, the array of methods will widen so that each couple may have a better chance to select a contraceptive method that they find appropriate and suitable.

REFERENCES

Affandi, B., S.S.I. Santoso, Djajadilaga, W. Hadisaputra, F.A. Moeloek, J. Prihartono, F. Lubis, and R.S. Samil
    1987   Five-year experience with Norplant®. *Contraception* 34(4):417–428.
Ahren, T., A. Victor, H. Lithell, B. Vessby, T.M. Jackanicz, and E.D.B. Johansson
    1983   Ovarian function, bleeding control and serum lipoproteins in women using contraceptive vaginal rings releasing five different progestins. *Contraception* 28(4):315–327.
Alvarez, F., A. Faundes, E. Johansson, and E. Coutinho
    1983   Blood levels of levonorgestrel in women following vaginal placement of contraceptive pills. *Fertility and Sterility* 41:120–123.
Archer, D.F.
    1988   Phase I biodegradable norethindrone. In *Six Month Technical Report Summary, October 1, 1987–March 31, 1988*. Norfolk: Contraceptive Research and Development, Eastern Virginia Medical School.
Atkinson, L.E., R. Lincoln, and J.D. Forrest
    1986   The next contraceptive revolution. *Family Planning Perspectives* 16(1):19–26.
Bygdeman, M., and M.L. Swahn
    1985   Progesterone receptor blockage: Effect on uterine contractility and early pregnancy. *Contraception* 32:45–61.
Collins, R.L., and G.D. Hodgen
    1986   Blockage of the spontaneous midcycle gonadotrophin surge in monkeys, by RU 486: A progesterone antagonist or agonist? *Journal of Clinical Endocrinology and Metabolism* 63:127.

Coutinho, E.M., and J.C. De Souza
  1968   Conception control by monthly injections of medroxyprogesterone
          suspension and a long-acting oestrogen. *Journal of Reproduction and
          Fertility* 15:209–214.
Coutinho, E.M., G.A. Boulanger, and M.T. Goncalves
  1986   Regression of uterine leiomyomas after treatment with gestrinone, an
          antiestrogen, antiprogesterone. *American Journal of Obstetrics and
          Gynecology* 155(4):761–767.
Coutinho, E.M., J.C. De Souza, and A.I. Csapo
  1966   Reversible sterility induced by medroxyprogesterone injections. *Fer-
          tility and Sterility* 17(2):261–266.
Coutinho, E.M., E.J. Coutinho, M.T.R. Goncaves, and I.C. Barbosa
  1982   Ovulation suppression in women following vaginal administration of
          oral contraceptive tablets. *Fertility and Sterility* 38:380–381.
Coutinho, E.M., A.R. de Silva, C. Carreira, I. Barbosa, V. Dourado-Silva, and
I. Sivin
  1984a   Contraception with single implants and mini-implants of ST-1435.
          Pp. 450–455 in G.I. Zatuchni, A. Goldsmith, J.D. Shelton, and J.J.
          Sciarra, eds., *Long-Acting Contraceptive Delivery Systems*. Philadel-
          phia, Pa.: Harper & Row.
Coutinho, E.M., A.R. de Silva, C. Carreira, V. Rodrigues, and M.T. Goncalves
  1984b   Conception control by vaginal administration of pills containing
          ethinylestradiol and dl-norgestrel. *Fertility and Sterility* 42:478-481.
Coutinho, E.M., J.F.Melo, I. Barbosa, and S.J. Segal
  1984c   Antispermatogenic action of gossypol in men. *Fertility and Sterility*
          42:424–429.
Diaz, S., M. Pavez, H. Cardenas, and H.B. Croxatto
  1987   Recovery of fertility and outcome pregnancies after the removal of
          Norplant® subdermal implants or copper-T IUDs. *Contraception*
          35(6):569–579.
Griffin, P.D.
  1986   A fertility regulation vaccine based on the carboxyl-terminal peptide
          of the beta subunit of human chorionic gonadotrophin. Pp. 43–59
          in G.P. Talwar, ed., *Immunological Approaches to Contraception and
          Promotion of Fertility*. New York: Plenum Press.
  1988   Vaccines for fertility regulation. Pp. 177–197 in *Research in Human
          Reproduction: WHO Special Programme of Research, Development
          and Research Training in Human Reproduction*. Biennial Report,
          1986–1987. Geneva: World Health Organization.
Gu, S., M. Du, Y.D. Yuan, L.D. Zhang, M.F. Xu, Y-L Liu, S.H. Wang, S.L.
Wu, P-Z Wang, Y-L Gao, X. He, L-F Qi, C-R Chen, Y.P. Liu, P. Mo, and I.
Sivin
  1988   A two-year study of acceptability, side effects and effectiveness of
          Norplant® and Norplant®-2 implants in the People's Republic of
          China. *Contraception* 38(6):641–658.
Gupta, G.N.
  1977   Sustained absorption of 3H-norgestrel from s.c. fused pellets in rats:
          A potential totally bioabsorbable implant for human contraception
          (Ab #3833). *Federal Proceedings* 36:977.

Gupta, G.N., B.B. Saxena, R. Landesman, and W.J. Ledger
  1984   Subcutaneous bioabsorbable pellets of norethindrone for contraception
         in women: Phase I: Clinical study, *Fertility and Sterility* 41(5):726–
         731.
Hall, P.E., and C. d'Arcangues
  1988   Long-acting methods of fertility regulation. Pp. 129–150 in *Research
         in Human Reproduction, WHO Special Programme of Research, De-
         velopment and Research Training in Human Reproduction*. Biennial
         Report, 1986–1987. Geneva: World Health Organization.
Heller, C.G., W.M. Laidlaw, H.T. Harvey, and W.O. Nelson
  1958   Effects of progestational compounds on the reproductive process of
         the human male. *Annals of the New York Academy of Sciences*
         71:649–661.
Hermann, W., R. Wyss, A. Ryondel, D. Philibert, G. Teutsch, E. Sakiz, and
E.E. Baulieu
  1982   Effet d'un stercide anti-progesterone chez la femme. *Comptes Rendus
         de l'Academie des Sciences Paris* 294:933–938.
Jennings, M.B., and M.M. Reidenberg
  1988   Adaptation to nephrotoxic chemicals. *Proceedings of the Society for
         Experimental Biology and Medicine* 189:338–343.
Landgren, B.M.
  1987   Vaginal delivery system. Pp. 165–180 in E. Diszfalusy and M. Bygde-
         man, eds., *Fertility Regulation Today and Tomorrow*. New York:
         Raven Press.
Lee, N.C., G.L. Rubin, and R. Boruck
  1988   The intrauterine device and pelvic inflammatory disease revisited:
         New results from the Women's Health Study. *Obstetrics and Gyne-
         cology* 72(1):1–6.
Lei, H.P., and Z.Y. Hu
  1981   The mechanisms of action of vacation pills. Pp. 70–82 in C.C.
         Fen, D. Griffin, and A. Woolman, eds., *Recent Advances in Fertility
         Regulation*. Geneva: Atar S.A.
Liu, G.Z., and K.C. Lyle
  1987   Clinical trial of gossypol as a male contraceptive drug. II. Hy-
         pokalemia study. *Fertility and Sterility* 8:462–465.
Liu, G.Z., K.C. Lyle, and C. Jian
  1987   Clinical trial of gossypol as a male contraceptive drug. I. Efficacy
         study. *Fertility and Sterility* 48:459–461.
Luukkainen, T., J. Toivonen, and P. Lahteenmaki
  1987   Medicated intrauterine devices. Pp. 153–163 in E. Diczfalusy and
         M. Bygdeman, eds., *Fertility Regulation Today and Tomorrow*. New
         York: Raven Press.
Matlin, S.A., A. Belengeur, G.R. Tyson, and A.N. Brookes
  1987   Resolution of gossypol: Analytical and large scale preparative HPLC
         on non-chiral phases. *Journal of High Resolution Chromatography
         Communications* 10:86–91.
Matlin, S.A., R. Zhou, G. Bialy, R.P. Blye, R.H. Naqui, and M.C. Lindberg
  1985   (−)-Gossypol: An active male antifertility agent. *Contraception*
         31:141–149.

Mauldin, W.P., and S.J. Segal
    1986   *Prevalence of Contraceptive Use in Developing Countries: A Chart Book.* New York: Rockefeller Foundation.
    1988   Prevalence of contraceptive use: Trends and issues. *Studies in Family Planning* 19:335–353.
Meng, G.D., J.C. Zhu, Z.W. Chen, and L.T. Wong
    1988   Recovery of sperm production following the cessation of gossypol treatment: A two center study in China. *International Journal of Andrology* 11:1–11.
Mishell, D.R., D.E. Moore, S. Roy, P.F. Brenner, and M.A. Page
    1978   Clinical performance and endocrine profiles with contraceptive vaginal rings containing a combination of estradiol and d-norgestrel. *American Journal of Obstetrics and Gynecology* 130:55–62.
Mishell, D.R., M. Talas, A.F. Parlow, and D.L. Moyer
    1970   Contraception by means of a silastic vaginal ring impregnated with medroxyprogesterone acetate. *American Journal of Obstetrics and Gynecology* 107:100.
Monahan, J., J. Rivier, R. Burgus, S. Amos, W. Blackwell, W. Vale, and R. Guillemin
    1971   Synthese totale par phase solide d'un decapeptide qui stimule la secretion des gonadotropines hypophysaires LH et FSH. *Comptes Rendus de l'Academie des Sciences Paris* 273:508–510.
Mora, G., A. Faundes, and U. Pastore
    1974   Clinical evaluation of an oral progestin contraceptive, R-2323, 5 mg. administered at weekly intervals. *Contraception* 10:145–148.
Nash, H., G.P. Talwar, S.J. Segal, T. Luukkainen, E.D.B. Johansson, J. Vasquez, E. Coutinho, and K. Sundaram
    1980   Observations on the antigenicity and clinical effects of a candidate antipregnancy vaccine: Beta-subunit of human chorionic gonadotropin linked to the tetanus toxoid. *Fertility and Sterility* 34(4):328–335.
National Coordinating Group on Male Antifertility Agents
    1978   Gossypol: A new antifertility agent for males. *Chinese Medical Journal* 4(6):417–428.
Ngugi, E.N., F.A. Plummer, D.W. Cameron, M. Bosire, and J. Ndinya-Achda
    1987   Effect of an AIDS Education Program on Increasing Condom Use in a Cohort of Nairobi Prostitutes. P. 157. Paper presented at the III International Conference on Acquired Immunodeficiency Syndrome (AIDS), June 1–5, Washington, D.C.
Nieman, L.K., T.M. Choate, G.P. Chrousos, and D.L. Healy
    1987   The progesterone antagonist RU 486: A potential new contraceptive agent. *New England Journal of Medicine* 316:187–191.
Nieschlag, E.
    1985   Reasons for abandoning immunization against FSH as an approach to male fertility regulation. Pp. 395–400 in G.I. Zatuchni, A. Goldsmith, J.M. Spieler, and J.J. Sciarra, eds., *Male Contraception.* Philadelphia, Pa.: Harper & Row.
Odlind, V.
    1988   Report to the International Committee on Contraception Research. New York: Population Council.

Population Council
  1988   Contraceptive subdermal implants. *NORPLANT®* *Worldwide* 10:1–4.

Psychoyos, A., and J.M. Husson
  1987   Antiprogestagens: Basic Research and Clinical Aspects. Paper presented at the Second International Symposium of the Japan Family Planning Association, Tokyo, October 24.

Salah, M., A.G.M. Ahmed, M. Abo-Eloyoun, and M.M. Shaaban
  1987   Five-year experience with Norplant® implants in Assiut, Egypt. *Contraception* 35(6):543–550.

Schally, A.V., A. Arimura, Y. Baba, R.M. Nair, H. Matsuo, T.W. Redding, and L. Debeljuk
  1971   Isolation and properties of the FSH and LH-releasing hormone. *Biochemistry and Biophysics Research Communications* 16:392–399.

Schearer, S.B., F. Alvarez-Sanchez, J. Anselmo, P. Brenner, E. Coutinho, A. Latham-Faundes, J. Frick, B. Heinild, and E.D. Johansson
  1978   Hormonal contraception for men. *International Journal of Andrology* 2(Suppl.):680–712.

Segal, S.J.
  1971   Contraceptive technology: Current and prospective methods. *Milbank Memorial Fund Quarterly,* October 49(4)[Part 2]:145–171.
  1972   Contraceptive research: A male chauvinist plot? *Family Planning Perspectives* 4(3):21–25.
  1984   Seeking better contraceptives. *Populi* 11(2):29.

Segal, S.J., and H.B. Croxatto
  1967   Single Administration of Hormones for Long-Term Control of Reproductive Function. Paper presented at the twenty-third meeting of the American Fertility Society, April 14–16, Washington, D.C.

Segal, S.J., and W.P. Mauldin
  1987   Contraceptive choices: Who, what, why? Pp. 305–317 in E. Diczfalusy and M. Bygdeman, eds., *Fertility Regulation Today and Tomorrow.* Serono Symposium, vol. 36. New York: Raven Press.

Sivin, I.
  1988   International experience with Norplant®-2 contraceptives. *Studies in Family Planning* 19(2):81–94.

Sivin, I., and H.J. Tatum
  1981   Four years of experience with the TCu-380A intrauterine contraceptive device. *Fertility and Sterility* 36:159–163.

Sivin, I., D.R. Mishell, A. Victor, V. Brache, T. Jackanicz, and H.A. Nash
  1981a   A multicenter study of levonorgestrel-estradiol contraceptive vaginal rings. I. Use effectiveness: An international comparative trial. *Contraception* 24:341–358.
  1981b   A multicenter study of levonorgestrel-estradiol contraceptive vaginal rings. II. Subjective and objective measures of effects. *Contraception* 24:359–376.

Sundaram, K., A. Didolkar, R. Thau, M. Chaudhuri, and F. Schmidt
  1988   Antagonists of luteinizing hormone releasing hormone bind to rat mast cells and induce histamine release. *Agents and Actions* 25:307–313.

Swahn, M.L., and M. Bygdeman
  1988   The effect of the antiprogestin RU 486 on uterine contractility and sensitivity to prostaglandin and oxytocin. *British Journal of Obstetrics and Gynecology* 95(2):126–134.

Talwar, G.P., and O. Singh
    1988   Birth control vaccines inducing antibodies against chorionic gonado-
            tropin. Pp. 183–197 in G.P. Talwar, ed., *Contraception Research for
            Today and the Ninety's.* New York: Springer-Verlag.
Talwar, G.P., N.C. Sharma, S.K. Dubey, M. Salahuddin, C. Das, S. Rama-
krishnan, S. Kumar, and V. Hingorani
    1976   Isoimmunization against human chorionic gonadotropin with conju-
            gates of processed beta-subunit of the hormone and tetanus toxoid.
            Proceedings of the National Academy of Sciences USA 73(1):218–222.
Teutsch, G.
    1985   Analogues of RU 486 for the mapping of the progestin receptor:
            Synthetic and structural aspects. Pp. 27–47 in E.E. Baulieu and S.J.
            Segal, eds., *The Antiprogestin Steroid Ru 486 and Human Fertility
            Control.* New York: Plenum Press.
Thau, R.B., C.B. Wilson, K. Sundaram, and D. Phillips
    1987   Long-term immunization against the beta-subunit of ovine luteinizing
            hormone (oLH beta) has no adverse effects on pituitary function in
            rhesus monkeys. *American Journal of Reproductive Immunology and
            Microbiology* 15:92–98.
Tietze, C., and S.L. Henshaw
    1986   *Induced Abortion: A World Review,* 6th ed. New York: Alan
            Guttmacher Institute.
Trussell, J., and K. Kost
    1987   Contraceptive failure in the United States: a critical review of the
            literature. *Studies in Family Planning* 18:237–283.
United Nations
    1984   *Recent Levels and Trends and Contraceptive Use as Assessed in 1983.*
            New York: United Nations.
Van Look, P.F.A.
    1988   Post-ovulatory methods of fertility regulation. Pp. 153–173 in *Re-
            search in Human Reproduction, WHO Special Programme of Research,
            Development and Research Training in Human Reproduction.* Biennial
            Report, 1986–1987. Geneva: World Health Organization.
Waites, G.M.H.
    1988   Male fertility regulation. Pp. 199–223 in *Research in Human Re-
            production, WHO Special Programme of Research, Development and
            Research Training in Human Reproduction.* Biennial Report, 1986–
            1987. Geneva: World Health Organization.
Wichmann, K., A. Vaheri, and T. Luukkainen
    1982   Inhibiting herpes simplex virus type 2 infection in human epithe-
            lial cells by gossypol, a potent spermicidal and contraceptive agent.
            American Journal of Obstetrics and Gynecology 142(5):593–594.
Wiedhaup, K.
    1988   View of Contraceptive Development. Background paper for the Com-
            mittee on Population, Subcommittee on Contraceptive Development,
            National Academy of Sciences.
Zaneveld, L.J.D.
    1988   SHUG device study. In *Six Month Technical Report Summary, Oc-
            tober 1, 1987–March 31, 1988.* Norfolk: Contraceptive Research and
            Development Program, Eastern Virginia Medical School.

Historical Perspectives on the Introduction of Contraceptive Technology

W. PARKER MAULDIN AND JOHN A. ROSS

This paper focuses on the role of technology in the adoption of family planning programs. In the process it neglects the crucial importance of a well-organized delivery system; the recruitment and training of workers; a focused information, education, and communications program; ensuring a good medical backup program and organization; and the role of management. At the heart of a strong family planning program, however, is the ready availability to most of the married couples of reproductive age of several modern methods of birth control at reasonable cost, at convenient times, and with adequate information about the advantages and disadvantages of the various methods.

Clearly, the primary instrument of fertility decline during the past several decades has been the use of contraception, including voluntary surgical contraception. We take it as generally agreed that other determinants of fertility decline, including later marriage, have played lesser roles, although later marriage is a very important contributor in the early years of fertility decline in many countries. Therefore, what new or improved technologies have figured in the growth of birth control and the consequent fertility declines? In rough order of importance they fall into five groups: sterilization, intrauterine devices (IUDs), hormonal methods (oral and injectable contraceptives), simpler abortion, and improved condoms.

The other methods—such as diaphragms, foams, and jellies—have been of minor importance. Before 1960, however, those were the principal methods available, along with condoms and, to a lesser

TABLE 1 Estimated Users (millions of persons) of Contraceptive Methods, 1985

Method	Total	Developed Countries	Developing Countries Total	Africa	America	Asia and the Pacific
Sterilization	155	19	135	1	11	123
Female	108	13	95	1	11	84
Male	47	7	40	0	0	40
Hormonal	61	20	40	5	10	26
Pill	55	20	35	4	9	22
Injectable	6	0.3	6	1	1	4
IUD	80	8	72	1	4	67
Condom	38	20	18	0.3	1	16
Vaginal	6	4	2	0	0.4	2
Traditional	58	28	30	3	6	22
Rhythm	16	9	6	1	2	3
Withdrawal	21	15	6	0.4	2	4
Total	398	100	297	10	32	256

NOTE: Numbers may not equal totals because of rounding.

SOURCE: Based on Table A3 in Mauldin and Segal (1988) and U.N. data on number of women aged 15–49 and percent married.

extent, sterilization. We have quite limited information on the trends in the use of these methods over time. Himes (1936) observed that studies in the English-speaking world from 1917 to 1934 showed that large proportions of persons in the reproductive years admitted the use of contraception, and it was found that the most popular methods were withdrawal (one-third), the douche (about one-fourth), and the condom (about one-fourth) in that order. Himes said that the condom is undoubtedly the most important contraceptive *instrument* of the day. National probability samples on this topic had yet to appear, but we accept Himes' generalizations regarding the most used methods of contraception at that time. In the mid-1960s, Levin (1966) estimated that there were 25 million to 30 million users of contraceptives (excluding rhythm and withdrawal) throughout the noncommunist world, or about .5 percent of married women of reproductive age. The majority of those users were in developed countries.

As of the mid-1980s, there were about 300 million users in less developed countries (LDCs) and 100 million users in more developed countries (MDCs) (Table 1); users in developing countries outnumbered those in developed countries by 3 to 1 (Figure 1). Thus, there

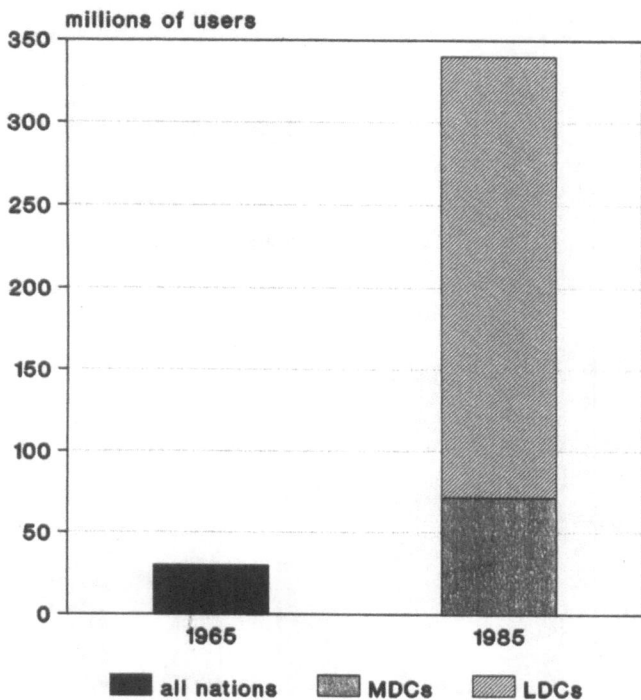

FIGURE 1   Number of users of modern methods of contraception: 1965 and 1985.

has been more than a 10-fold increase in the number of users of supply and clinic-based methods of contraception in the past two decades.

A further, related development has been the change in which a spouse uses a contraceptive method.   Less than three decades ago male methods of contraception were used far more than female methods (Mauldin, 1965), but this has changed dramatically with the introduction of the pill, the IUD, and simpler methods of abortion and female sterilization. Today the ratio of female to male methods of contraception is about 2.7 to 1 (Mauldin and Segal, 1988).

The five technologies mentioned above have been the chief mechanisms by which fertility has fallen, and in that sense they have driven out their predecessors, or at least have cornered a vastly enlarged market of birth-control interest (Figure 2). Historically, they

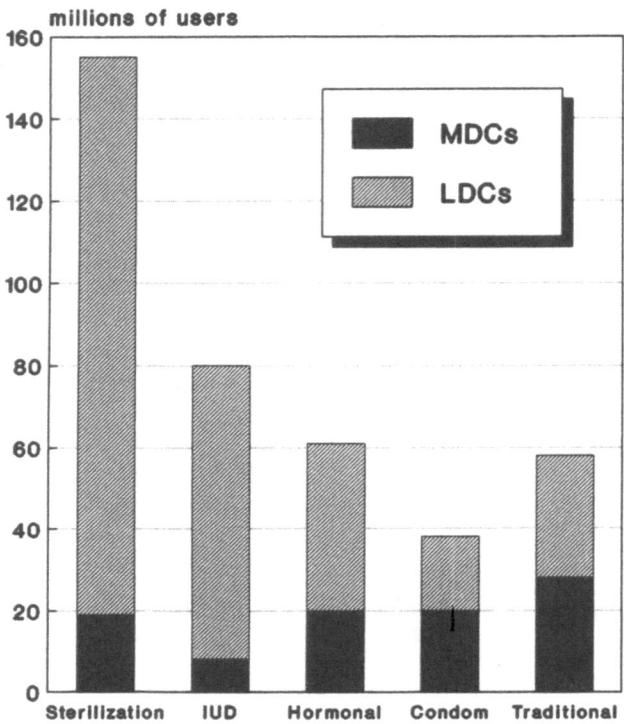

FIGURE 2   Estimated number of users of contraceptive methods in MDCs and LDCs in 1985.

coexisted with the previous methods: the technology-based ones—dilation and curettage for abortion, the thick, nonlubricated condom, the diaphragm, foams, and jellies—and the nontechnological ones—rhythm, withdrawal, and abstinence. Rhythm and withdrawal are important methods of birth control, primarily in developed countries (Table 1). An example of the importance of a new technology is that there were about 3 million users of diaphragms in the United States in 1960 (Levin, 1966), but 5 years later birth-control pills had become very popular and the number of users of diaphragms decreased to 2 million. The estimate for the number of diaphragm users in 1987 was 1.5 million (Forrest and Fordyce, 1988:Tables 3 and 5).

Why this selectivity? Why did the new methods come to dominate? The chief factors are obvious. To a greater or lesser extent, each new method offered one or more of the virtues of the ideal method in ways that the old ones did not: a single action with automatic continuation, actionable by one partner alone, not linked to coitus, less inconvenience, less medical trauma as with suction abortion and simplified sterilization, and low cost. The old ones fail on one or more of these standards. They posed the opposite actions: higher motivational requirements, repeated acts connected to coitus, and so on.

Table 2 gives the details of the new technologies and the improvements that have been made in the older ones. Figure 2 gives the number of contraceptive users by method in the more and less developed countries in 1985, and Figure 3 gives the percent distribution of contraceptives by method used in developing countries, by continent. The following considers the methods in the order shown in Table 2.

1. *Sterilization.* "The introduction of laparoscope should probably be ranked as one of the most important advances in obstetrics and gynecology during the past 10–15 years. It provides specialists with a remarkable diagnostic tool for viewing the reproductive organs, as well as an agile therapeutic and surgical instrument for tubal ligations" (Burkman, Magarick, and Waife, 1980). As a result of the John Hopkins Program for International Education in Gynecology and Obstetrics (JHPIEGO program), hundreds of laparoscopes and laparocators have been shipped to a large number of institutions throughout the developing world. "There have been almost 40,000 trainees from over 4,000 institutions in 122 countries. Over 400 medical schools and almost 200 nursing schools have faculty members who have been trained and are themselves involved in training others. This is an accomplishment of which JHPIEGO can justly be proud" (Brady, 1988:12). The Association for Voluntary Surgical Contraception (AVSC) also shipped more than 700 laparoscopes and laparocators during the 1970s and 1980s. Many other organizations also supplied these instruments to physicians in developing countries; thus, the numbers of laparoscopes and laparocators sent to developing countries run into the thousands. Figure 4 presents data on the countries that rank highest in the proportion of couples who use sterilization.

2. *IUD.* The invention of modern IUDs is credited to Dr. Jack Lippes, who developed the original "loop." It and other IUDs were studied by many academic investigators around the world, so that before IUDs were available commercially on a large scale, a vast amount of data on their performance and safety had been gathered by the public sector (Segal, 1987). The IUD is relatively inexpensive,

TABLE 2 New or Improved Birth-Control Technologies

Method	Improvements
Sterilization	
Female	Minilap, laparoscope,[a] laparotomy: outpatient basis, local anesthesia, simple equipment with minilap, and low-cost, extended availability.
Male	No major change that is widely used (no scalpel method used by the Chinese).
IUD	Breakthrough new method.[a] Numerous types, all giving extended protection in one step. Insertion by paramedics in some countries. Permitted distribution by mobile teams and private physicians. Stimulated the creation of national programs that was abetted later by sufficiently low pill prices to permit mass distribution.
Oral contraception	Breakthrough method. Evolved to low dosage and to minipill. Attractive packaging. Distribution through shops and lay workers extended availability.
Injectable	Breakthrough new method, offering 3 months of protection in one injection. Appealed to the popularity of injections in developing countries; amenable to application by paramedics and pharmacies (and at home, as in Matlab) (restricted availability in many countries that follow U.S. Food and Drug Administration cautions; hence, limited effect on fertility).
Condom	Lubricated and made thinner. This in part stimulated increased advertising and distribution by the private sector and increased use in programs.
Other birth control method	
Abortion	Vacuum aspiration method reduced risk, trauma, and side effects. Also led to the menstrual regulation subtype, which obscured whether an abortion had occurred or not and so expanded availability.

[a]An additional reason for rapid diffusion was fascination by the medical establishment with the method. The laparoscope could be used for numerous abdominal procedures; this added to its utility, and this also gave an acceptable reason to acquire it when the climate toward sterilization was conservative.

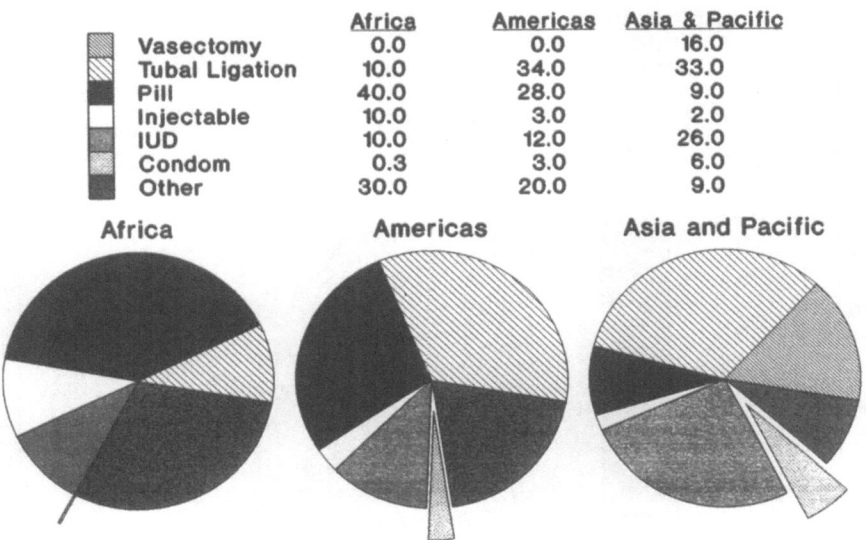

	Africa	Americas	Asia & Pacific
Vasectomy	0.0	0.0	16.0
Tubal Ligation	10.0	34.0	33.0
Pill	40.0	28.0	9.0
Injectable	10.0	3.0	2.0
IUD	10.0	12.0	26.0
Condom	0.3	3.0	6.0
Other	30.0	20.0	9.0

FIGURE 3   Percent distribution of contraceptive users by method used in LDCs in 1985.

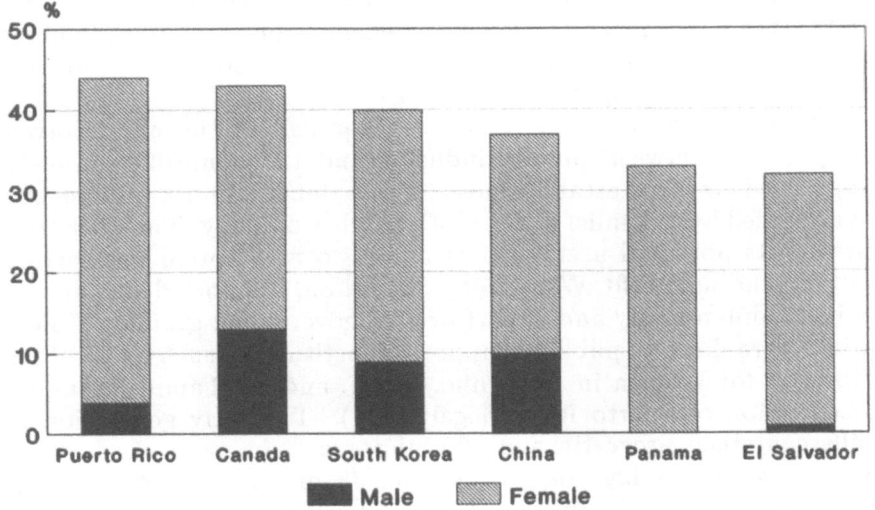

FIGURE 4   Percentage of couples using sterilization in selected MDCs and LDCs in 1985.

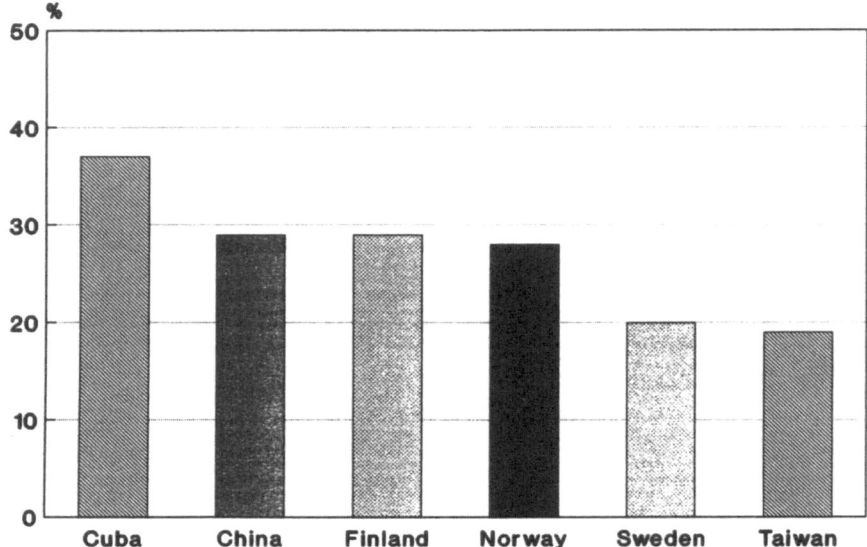

FIGURE 5   Percentage of couples using IUDs in selected MDCs and LDCs in 1985.

provides protection for years, and is highly effective. Insertion typically is done by medical personnel, but in some countries paramedical personnel have been trained and are permitted to do insertions. The IUD served as a focal point for implementation of family planning programs in a number of countries. Figure 5 shows the countries with the highest proportion of IUD users.

3. *Oral contraceptives.*   The development of the pill involved cooperation between private industry and the nonprofit, publicly supported research establishment. The patented 19-nor steroid was synthesized by a chemist at the G. D. Searle Company. The work that proved its potential usefulness as an oral contraceptive was carried out by the nonprofit Worcester Foundation, supported in part by private philanthropy and in part by U.S. government grants. Clinical trials were done at publicly supported institutions such as the Free Hospital for Women in Brookline, Mass., and the Family Planning Association of Puerto Rico (Segal, 1987). The early generation of pills contained progestin and 100 micrograms or more of estrogen. Low-dose pills today contain only 30–35 micrograms of estrogen, along with a reduction in the progestin content.

The birth-control pill is coitus independent, highly effective, and in many countries does not require a medical prescription. Its price is highly variable, but when purchased in large quantities, for example, by the U.N. Family Planning Association or U.S. Agency for International Development, it is relatively inexpensive. Commercial firms have invested heavily in marketing of the pill, at least in part because a user must obtain supplies monthly. (See Figure 6 for the developing countries with the highest proportion of users of hormonal methods.)

4. *Injectable contraceptives.* This method has attracted a great deal of attention during the past decade, but it is used by significant proportions of women of reproductive age in only a few countries, for example, Thailand, Indonesia, and Jamaica. Depo-Provera, one injection of which provides protection for 3 months, has the advantages of providing protection against pregnancy for a moderately long period and at a relatively low cost. A major constraint to its use is the decision of the U.S. Food and Drug Administration (FDA) not to approve it as a contraceptive method. Many governments have been reluctant to include the injectable as a program method because of the negative decision of the FDA. Figure 7 shows those countries with the highest proportion of users of injectable contraceptives.

5. *Condom.* The principal criticisms of condoms, aside from the fact that they require action at the time of coitus, have been that they tend to tear or develop holes through which semen can pass, that they are so thick that they greatly reduce sensitivity, and that their dryness causes some discomfort. Thus, attention has been given to controlling their quality, decreasing their thickness, and packaging them with a lubricant. These changes have resulted in their being more acceptable than previously, and the protection they afford against acquired immune deficiency syndrome (AIDS) has recently increased their use.

6. *Abortion.* Vacuum aspiration during the first trimester of pregnancy has greatly reduced the risks associated with abortion, and has also reduced the severity of side effects. Abortions can now be performed on an outpatient basis.

EFFECTS ON PROGRAM EXPANSION

Rates of population growth increased greatly during the 1950s, with the result that a number of countries adopted policies to reduce fertility and rates of population growth. The invention of the pill and the IUD greatly stimulated the creation and implementation of family planning programs in the 1960s. Subsequent improvements in

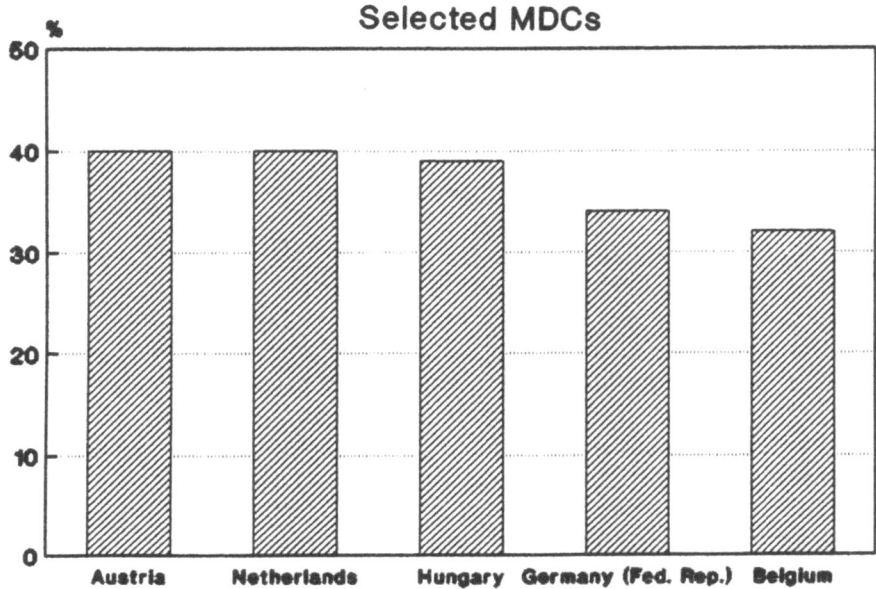

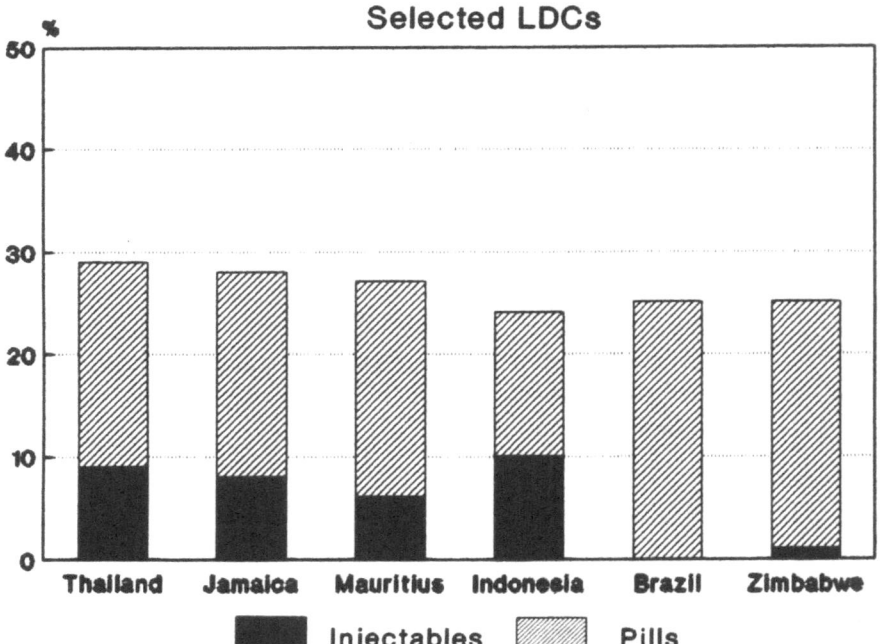

FIGURE 6   Percentage of couples using hormonal contraception in selected MDCs and LDCs in 1985.

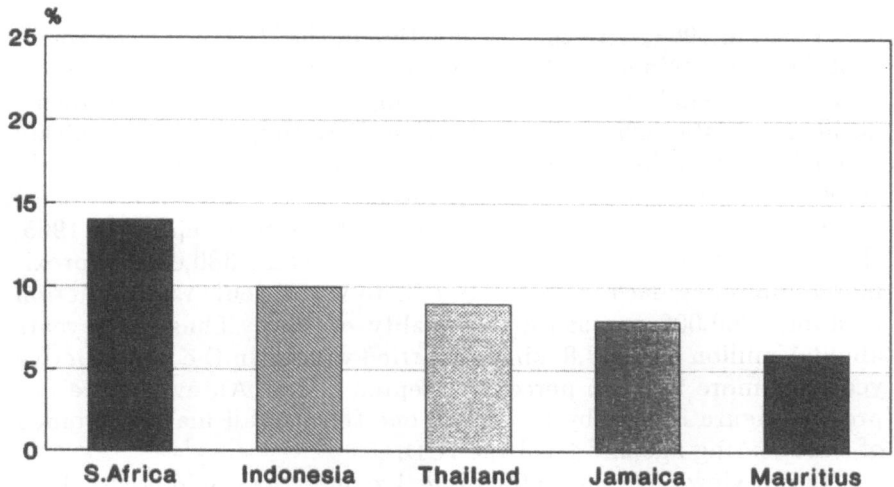

FIGURE 7   Percentage of couples using injectable contraceptives in selected MDCs and LDCs in 1985.

these and other methods of fertility control have also helped in the development and implementation of national programs.

As Freedman and Berelson (1976:12) have pointed out: ". . . any method that extends acceptability through its intrinsic attractiveness is obviously a valuable adjunct, and particularly when it is able to generate its own programmatic activity or delivery system expansion. . . ." This double advantage of new methods—their acceptability and their appeal to administrators—led to the introduction of additional methods in many programs.

A case in point is the Republic of Korea (Kim, Ross, and Worth, 1972), which is particularly interesting because it had a program at the health center level before the introduction of IUD technology. A program and a policy were established in late 1961; and during the next 2 years the program provided vasectomy, with about 20,000 procedures per year, which is a very low acceptance rate. It also distributed large quantities of foams, spermicides, and condoms. These were distributed quite liberally, partly for publicity purposes, to establish that the new program was under way. However, the numbers of acceptors were quite moderate.

Then, in 1964, with the introduction of the IUD, the government (not just the Ministry of Health and Social Affairs but also the Economic Planning Board and the highest levels of government) decided to establish a comprehensive IUD program, and quickly expanded the national program by training and assigning 1,473 field workers at the myun, or township, level.

In the first year more than 100,000 IUDs were accepted; in 1965, the second year, 225,000; and in the third year, 380,000, approximately doubling each year. In 1967 there was a deliberate reduction to about 300,000 to ensure the quality of care. Thus, in 4 years about 1 million out of 3.8 million married women in the reproductive years, or more than 25 percent, accepted IUDs. An even more impressive figure is that by late 1969, one-third of all married women of childbearing age had tried the IUD.

In our view any reasonably objective observer would credit these results to the introduction of a new technology in a strong family planning program. The IUD had a strong appeal to individuals and to the government, stimulating it to greatly increase the numbers of program personnel and service points (largely through an arrangement with private doctors using a coupon system with a small reimbursement). At that time, per capita income was about $80, and again, few observers would argue that in such a short span of time socioeconomic progress would have been sufficient to produce similar results.

The Korean history continued, giving further evidence on the importance of technology. The pill was introduced in 1968 for IUD dropouts only, and then it was introduced for everyone in 1969. It produced yet another program expansion, with distribution extended down to village depots and mother's clubs. Thus, in this second phase it exemplified the observation of Freedman and Berelson (1976).

The number of acceptances of birth-control pills was quite large, as Kim, Ross, and Worth (1972) document, with their being continued substantial percentages of women using the IUD. Simultaneously, some 150,000 couples per month were using conventional contraceptives, mainly condoms.

Simplified sterilization procedures were introduced in the mid-1970s. This in turn led to many more service points, as laparoscopic equipment (through donors) was dispersed widely throughout the country. A steady growth in the number of sterilizations done followed. The simplified technology included both laparoscopes and minilaps, permitting outpatient sterilization to be performed with local anesthesia and at many more locations than before. The response was appreciable, and when added to that for the other methods, it resulted in very rapid increases in the proportions of couples adopting and using contraception. Another boost was given to the number of sterilizations in about 1982, when incentives for acceptances were greatly increased.

The experience in Thailand also demonstrates the ability of a new method to set off a program expansion. A careful study there demonstrated that auxiliary midwives, using a checklist for contraindications, could safely prescribe oral contraceptives (Rosenfield, 1971; Rosenfield and Limcharoen, 1972). The Ministry of Public Health then authorized birth-control pill distribution by those personnel, who were posted throughout the country, and so added over 4,000 service points, leading to 1,748,000 birth-control pill acceptors (over 30 percent of married women of reproductive age) through 1975. As in South Korea, a new method meant a radical change in the program's scope and in contraceptive use.

AVAILABILITY OF THE NEW TECHNOLOGIES

In 1973 five methods of fertility control were included in national family planning programs around the world: IUDs, oral contraceptives, condoms, sterilization, and abortion. Table 3 summarizes method availability in 1973 and 1982 based on estimates of population specialists familiar with family planning programs in each of the countries shown in the table. There has been a significant increase in the availability of methods to populations in many countries, but it is also evident that in most countries availability is still quite limited. One indication of the importance of multiple methods is that the correlation between the number of methods available and the total fertility rate (TFR) is 0.70; thus, one-half (49 percent) of the variance in the TFR is associated with the number of contraceptive methods available. Similar data are available for 1987 (Ross et al., 1988).

Availability is affected by many factors, including laws and regulations, national policies, cultural beliefs, the health care infrastructure, and costs. Sterilization is illegal in a number of countries, particularly Muslim countries. India was very slow to include birth-control pills in the national program because of concern about costs and, perhaps more important, apprehension about side effects.

TABLE 3 Number of Contraceptive Methods Readily Available to More Than Half the Population of Various Countries, 1973 and 1982

Number of Methods, 1973	Number of methods, 1982:					
	5	4	3	2	1	0
5	China South Korea					
4	Singapore Taiwan Thailand					
3	Colombia	Jamaica Philippines Hong Kong	Egypt Sri Lanka		Venezuela Trinidad and Tobago	
2	Tunisia	Dominican Republic Malaysia[a]	Indonesia El Salvador	India Pakistan		Nepal
1		Mexico	Mauritius Morocco		Guatemala	Iran
0			Bangladesh			Ghana Kenya Laos Turkey
Not rated	Cuba Panama	Brazil	North Korea Vietnam Fiji		Zimbabwe Lebanon	

[a]Male sterilization is not readily available in Tunisia, Brazil, the Dominican Republic, Trinidad and Tobago, North Korea, or Malaysia.

Japan also was resistant to the introduction of birth-control pills; some say this was because of objections by the medical fraternity, which worried that birth-control pills would lead to fewer abortions, and thus reduce the incomes of many doctors. In sharp contrast to this is the experience in Thailand, where, as noted above, a policy decision opened up an entire national network of paramedical service points. Other countries have also permitted paramedical personnel to prescribe birth-control pills, and some have permitted the purchase of birth-control pills without a prescription. A new contraceptive technology is the implant, that is, NORPLANT®. A major constraint to its introduction is the long process required for submission to, and clearance by, the FDA and the high up-front costs.

SELECTION AMONG TECHNOLOGIES

Many technologies have been introduced that have been displaced or never accepted by significant numbers of people. There have been many versions of IUDs—four sizes of the Lippes loop, the Margulies spiral, the Birnberg Bow, the Dalkon Shield, several Multiloads, the Gräfenberg, the Ma and Ota rings, three major variations of the Copper T, the Copper 7, and so on. More than 200 types and modifications have been tested clinically (Hawkins and Elder, 1979). Similarly, there have been many variations of the pill, including experimentation with different chemicals; different combinations of chemicals; changes in dosage; 21-, 22-, and 28-day regimens; and supplementation with vitamin, iron, or placebo tablets. Foam tablets, intravaginal pills, vaginal rings, and scores of "local" contraceptives have been introduced but have not found a significant place in the market or in large-scale programs.

Over the years a winnowing out process has been at work among these many variations, with there being the "survival of the fittest" in some sense. The determinants of which contraceptives win are quite diverse and go beyond the scope of this paper.

One determinant, however, is the role of the donors. The first IUD to be widely used was the loop, which, as mentioned above, was invented by Dr. Jack Lippes with financial support from the Population Council, a tax-exempt research organization. Lippes required that the licensing company, Ortho Pharmaceuticals, recognize the council's role in the loop's development by providing to the council rights to provide the loop to the public sector of developing countries, including the right to license the manufacturing of it by others for that sector. This served to make the loop available in developing countries at a very low cost and permitted its rapid spread. The decisions of donor agencies to supply large, free quantities of oral contraceptives, condoms, sterilization equipment, and injectable contraceptives have advanced their distribution and removed serious barriers of costs and foreign exchange. The large Indonesian pill program, for example, which services about 5 million women monthly, has until recently relied entirely on contributed supplies.

Donors have also been important for training medical personnel in each new method. In Taiwan, particular care was taken to involve the medical community in the training and introduction of the IUD. We have noted above the role of donors in training and supplying equipment such as the laparoscope, and the careful studies in Thailand that guided the training of paramedical personnel to determine whether potential users of the pill had any of a specific list of contraindications to its use.

ADDITIVE EFFECTS

No single technology serves all subgroups of the population. When several methods are made available, the typical pattern is coexistence, each one being adopted by couples of somewhat different interests and needs. Therefore, the addition of a new method in the past has not appeared to simply replace others, among the five principal ones considered here. In Taiwan each new method added another layer of use to the existing practice. In Thailand the large increase in birth-control pill use at the end of the 1960s was additive; adoption of the IUD and sterilization continued to increase. In India the condom added another layer of use to that achieved by sterilization and the IUD. An exception was Hong Kong; with relatively easy logistics, there was a deliberate programmatic decision to substitute the pill for the IUD as the method of choice (Freedman and Berelson, 1976:11). In general, the more methods offered among the five described here, the higher the prevalence of contraceptive use.

THE PUBLIC SECTOR ROLE

We have stressed that the new technologies created the possibility of mass programs with tangible administrative objectives. In 1965 national family planning programs were in their infancy, and therefore the public sector provided only a small proportion of all users with contraceptive supplies and services. In the developing world that has changed dramatically as many countries have adopted population policies and programs designed to reduce rates of population growth. It is estimated that more than three-quarters of contraceptive users receive supplies and services from the public sector (Figure 8); nearly all of this is composed of modern methods. Some writers have hypothesized that as programs mature and the levels of contraceptive prevalence increase there will be a shift away from

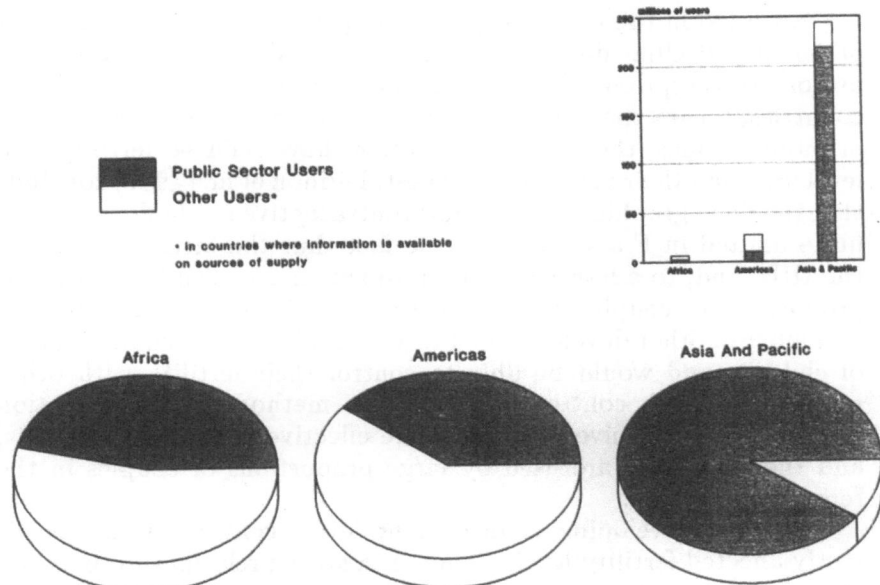

FIGURE 8   Source of supply for contraceptive users in developing countries in 1985.

dependence on the public sector to increased reliance on the private sector. Data are available for more than one time period for 16 developing countries. What is the trend over time within these countries? If one considers that a shift of 5 or more percentage points in the proportions receiving supplies, services, or both from the public sector is significant, eight countries show an increasing dependence on the public sector, five countries show a decreasing dependence, and three countries show no change. These limited data do not give a clear indication of the likely trends in the future. Indonesia embarked on a program of self-reliance beginning in 1988 and is developing a scheme designed to shift suppliers of contraceptives for large proportions of contraceptive users from the public to the private sector. As of now, however, as Figure 8 shows, very large proportions of users in developing countries rely on public programs.

As noted in the beginning of this paper, the primary instrument of fertility decline during the past several decades has been the use of contraception, primarily the modern methods. In developed countries, where the desired family size has been quite low for two or more decades, the new contraceptives have reduced fertility to a level less than their usage may suggest. Leridon et al. (1987) conclude that the demographic effects of new contraceptive methods have been quite limited in France, despite the fact that the birth-control pill, the IUD, and, to a lesser extent, sterilization are used by significant proportions of couples of reproductive age. In France, as well as in a number of other developed countries, couples desire small numbers of children and would be able to control their fertility with other methods of birth control. The modern methods of contraception are simply more convenient and more effective than older methods, and therefore they are used by large proportions of couples in the reproductive years.

In most developing countries, however, contraception has directly affected fertility levels. There is a strong relationship between the percentage of couples who use contraception and the level of fertility (the TFR). The R^2, or coefficient of determination, between these two variables is 0.84 in developing countries, but is only 0.06 in developed countries. If the analysis is limited to modern methods, the correlation coefficient is trivially lower for LDCs (0.82) but is appreciably higher for MDCs (0.50). An important factor accounting for the weaker relationship between the level of fertility and the use of modern methods of contraception in MDCs as compared with that in LDCs is the widespread use of abortion in a number of developed countries. Another factor is the relatively high rates of use of rhythm and withdrawal in developed countries. Indeed, there is a positive relationship between the level of use of traditional methods and fertility in developed countries; this is because fertility is slightly higher in those developed countries with a relatively high use of traditional methods of contraception.

CONCLUSION

From an experimental design viewpoint, much of the historical experience falls nicely into place. Interventions have occurred in situations in which acceptance rates and prevalence could be monitored. Program expansions, stimulated in part by the new methods, could also be traced. Changes in these indicators in many cases were very rapid and large. Concurrent influences (modernization) on prevalence changed far too little in the same periods to offer competing explanations. Over the longer run, the new technologies have continued to dominate, as have program services and supplies.

A final observation concerns minor versus major breakthroughs. When only one or two modern methods are offered, the addition of another method may considerably raise the prevalence of overall contraceptive use. If all five major methods are easily available, the addition of a new one is less likely to have a large net effect, unless it meets the needs of a large subgroup considerably better than any current method does. Thus, minor incremental improvements in the present methods, or new methods lacking very strong advantages, cannot be expected to matter greatly in developing countries. Therefore, the scientific search should be directed to inventions that offer a major advantage over some current method, and that do so for some substantial subgroup of the population. Past experience shows the low probability of discovering such methods unless research is sustained, is well-funded and staffed, and is conducted in several centers.

Technology has made a major difference in the acceptance and use of contraception, and it has stimulated both the creation and the expansion of mass programs. It is not the only determinant: good programs must implement new methods well, through dispersed service points, worker training, medical backup, and activities intended to provide information to the public. At the heart of a strong family planning program, however, is ready access by the public to several methods of birth control that are simple, safe, low cost, and effective.

REFERENCES

Brady, N.C.
    1988   The role of the Agency for International Development in technology transfer to developing countries. In R. Magarick and R. Burkman, eds., *Reproductive Health Education and Technology: Issues and Future Directions.* Baltimore, Md.: The Johns Hopkins Program for International Education in Gynecology and Obstetrics.
Burkman, R.T., R.H. Magarick, and R.S. Waife, eds.
    1980   *Surgical Equipment and Training in Reproductive Health.* Baltimore, Md.: The Johns Hopkins Program for International Education in Gynecology and Obstetrics.
Forrest, J.D., and R.R. Fordyce
    1988   U.S. women's contraceptive attitudes and practice: How have they changed in the 1980s?. *Family Planning Perspectives* 20(3):112–117.

Freedman, R., and B. Berelson
    1976   The record of family planning programs. *Studies in Family Planning* 7(1):1–40.
Hawkins, D.F., and M.G. Elder
    1979   *Human Fertility Control: Theory and Practice.* Boston: Butterworth.
Himes, N.E.
    1936   *Medical History of Contraception.* Baltimore, Md.: The Williams & Wilkins Co.
Kim, T., J.A. Ross, and G.C. Worth
    1972   *The Korean National Family Planning Program.* New York: The Population Council.
Leridon, H., Y. Charbit, P. Collomb, J.P. Sardon, and L. Toulemon
    1987   *La Seconde Révolution Contraceptive: La Régulation des Naissances en France de 1950 à 1985.* Travaux et Documents, Cahier n. 117. Paris: Institut National d'Etudes Démographiques, Presses Universitaires de France.
Levin, H.L.
    1966   Distribution of contraceptive supplies through commercial channels. In B. Berelson, et al., eds., *Family Planning and Population Programs.* Chicago: The University of Chicago Press.
Mauldin, W.P.
    1965   Fertility studies: Knowledge, attitude, and practice. *Studies in Family Planning* 1(7):9.
Mauldin, W.P., and S.J. Segal
    1988   World trends in contraceptive use. *Studies in Family Planning* 19(6).
Rosenfield, A.G.
    1971   Family planning: An expanded role for paramedical personnel. *American Journal of Obstetrics and Gynecology* 110:1030.
Rosenfield, A.G., and C. Limcharoen
    1972   Auxiliary midwife prescription of oral contraceptives. *American Journal of Obstetrics and Gynecology* 114:942.
Ross, J.A., M. Rich, J.P. Molzan, and M. Pensak
    1988   *Family Planning and Child Survival: 100 Developing Countries.* New York: Center for Population and Family Health, Columbia University.
Segal, S.J.
    1987   The development of modern contraceptive technology. *Technology in Society* 9:277–282.

Part II
Consequences for Fertility

The Demographic Impact of Changes in Contraceptive Practice in Third World Populations

CHARLES F. WESTOFF, LORENZO MORENO, AND
NOREEN GOLDMAN

One of the persistent questions in the population field relates to the potential impact of improved contraceptive practices on the level of fertility. This improvement can take several forms: (1) increases in the adoption of contraception by nonusers, (2) increases in the use of the more effective methods, (3) reduction of discontinuation rates, and (4) introduction of new contraceptive technologies. In a recent analysis of European and U.S. data, a methodology to explore several of these questions was developed that can now be applied (with modifications) to Third World countries. We pose two broad questions: (1) What is the implication for future fertility of the prevailing rates of unwanted fertility? and (2) What unwanted births are associated with the nonuse of contraception and with the different methods currently in use, and what would the birth rates be if the mix of methods was improved or if a new method was introduced?

UNWANTED FERTILITY

Unwanted births are defined as those births occurring after the last wanted birth; these are births that, in theory, would never have occurred if their conception had been avoided by the practice of contraception or by methods with lower failure rates. Since these births, in principle, are completely preventable, they would have a direct and commensurate effect on the fertility rate. We measured this impact by partitioning the age-specific fertility rates into wanted and unwanted components and summing each series to the total fertility rate (TFR) for the past 5 years of experience. Thus, we can divide the TFR into its wanted and unwanted components and estimate what the TFR would be in the absence of unwanted births. (The methodology for this kind of decomposition was developed for marital fertility by Westoff [1981]).

The data used for this analysis are derived from the recent Demographic and Health Surveys (DHS) Project and are based on the surveys completed in eight countries between 1986 and 1987. These countries include some representation of the three continents of the developing world: four have experienced rapid declines in fertility (Dominican Republic, Colombia, Trinidad and Tobago, and Sri Lanka), two are in the middle of the transition (Ecuador and Peru), one has recently begun the transition (Guatemala), and one has not yet begun the transition (Burundi).

For all but one of these countries (Burundi), the estimates of unwanted fertility pertain to the 5 years preceding the interview—a period extending from 1981 or 1982 to 1986 or 1987. For Burundi, the estimate is based on the preceding 12 months.[1] For each birth during this period, a question was asked about whether the child had been wanted then, or whether the respondent had wanted to wait until later or wanted no more children at all. The last category—births to women who had wanted no more children at all—is the basis for the unwanted birth classification. All other births, regardless of whether they represented a timing failure with some contraceptive method, are classified as wanted. The denominator for these rates is all women, regardless of marital status.[2]

The basic results are given in Table 1 and Figure 1. The TFRs range from a low of 2.8 in Sri Lanka to a high of 7.3 in Burundi. The lowest proportion of unwanted births is found in Burundi, where the norm of fertility control has yet to spread; the highest proportion is found in Peru, where more than one-third of all births are reported as unwanted.

The potential impact on the TFR of preventing all unwanted births is considerable in all countries except Burundi. In Peru, where the effect would be greatest, the TFR would be 2.9 instead of 4.5,

---

[1] In Burundi, the question on unwanted births was asked only about the last birth. In order to derive an unbiased estimate of fertility, only information pertaining to fertility during the 12 months preceding the interview could be used.

[2] In Sri Lanka, only ever-married women were interviewed. However, the household survey screening data provided information on the ages of the never-married women.

TABLE 1 Total and Wanted Fertility Rates and the Percentage of Births Unwanted for 5 Years Preceding the Interview

Country	Total Fertility Rate	Wanted Fertility Rate	Percent Unwanted Births
Burundi[a]	7.3	6.8	7.4
Guatemala	5.6	4.9	12.1
Peru	4.5	2.9	35.6
Ecuador	4.3	3.6	17.1
Dominican Republic	3.8	2.8	26.0
Colombia	3.3	2.8	15.0
Trinidad and Tobago	3.1	2.6	18.5
Sri Lanka	2.8	2.3	16.2

[a]Rates for Burundi are for the preceding 12 months only.

SOURCE: Demographic and Health Surveys.

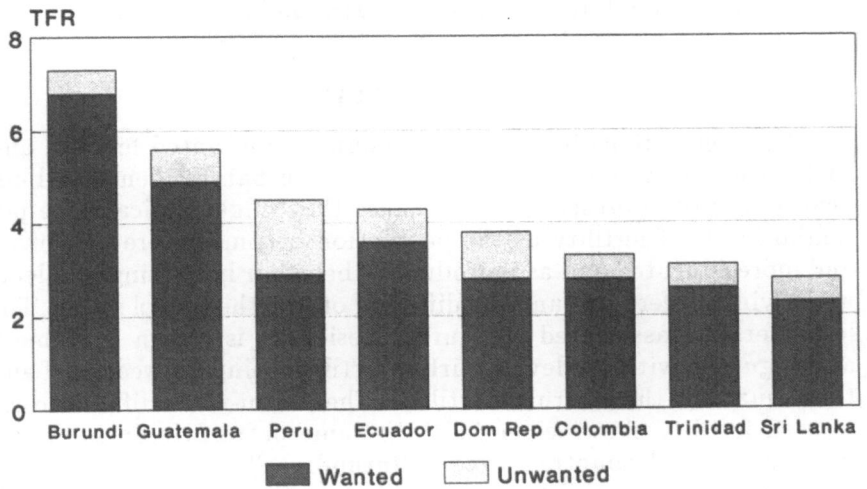

FIGURE 1 Total fertility rates by reproductive intention. Source: Demographic and Health Surveys.

TABLE 2 Wanted and Unwanted Fertility Rates for the 5 Years Preceding the
Interview, by Residence

Country	Total Fertility Rate		Wanted Fertility Rate		Percent Unwanted Births	
	Urban	Rural	Urban	Rural	Urban	Rural
Burundi	5.5	7.4	4.9	6.8	10.6	7.3
Guatemala	4.1	6.5	3.5	5.8	13.0	11.6
Peru	3.3	6.9	2.3	4.1	29.8	40.8
Ecuador	3.5	5.5	2.9	4.5	16.4	17.7
Dominican Republic	3.2	5.1	2.5	3.5	22.0	30.5
Colombia	2.8	4.9	2.4	3.9	11.1	20.0
Trinidad and Tobago	3.0	3.2	2.5	2.6	15.9	20.0
Sri Lanka	2.2	2.9	1.9	2.4	15.5	17.0
(Estates)		3.4		3.2		5.1

SOURCE: Demographic and Health Surveys.

and in Colombia and the Dominican Republic, it would 2.8. In Sri
Lanka, the effect would be more modest, reducing the TFR from 2.8
to 2.3 (the same relative impact as in Trinidad and Tobago).

DIFFERENTIALS

The connections between the amount of unwanted fertility and
such socioeconomic indicators as rural and urban residence and education are of interest, in part because they might indicate the potential levels of fertility as the population becomes more urbanized
and more educated and as reproductive behavior increasingly reflects
underlying preferences and the diffusion of a birth-control norm. The
lower fertility associated with urban residence is shown in Table 2
and Figure 2, with the level of urban fertility being between half and
three-quarters that of rural fertility. The urban-rural difference for
wanted fertility shows essentially the same pattern, reaching quite
low levels in all countries except Burundi. The most pronounced
difference is in Peru, where the urban wanted fertility rate is 2.3,
compared with the national TFR of 4.5 (see Table 1). In Sri Lanka,
the rate for wanted fertility in the urban population is estimated
at only 1.9. There is little difference in fertility between urban and
rural areas in Trinidad and Tobago, probably because of the size

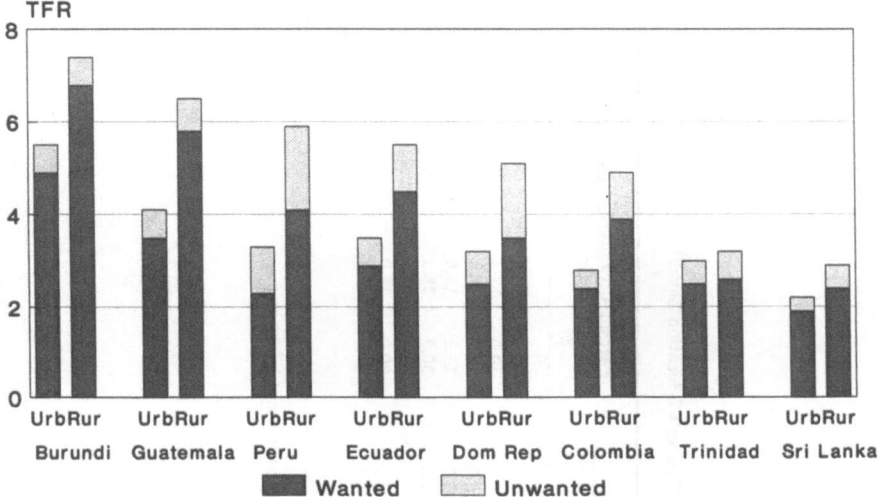

FIGURE 2   Total fertility rates by reproductive intention and residence. Urb, urban; Rur, rural. Source: Demographic and Health Surveys.

of the country. With the exception of Burundi and Guatemala, the proportion of the TFR attributable to unwanted births is lower in the urban than in the rural areas, no doubt reflecting greater use of effective contraception.

The unwanted component of the TFR also declines with an increase in women's education in these countries (Table 3 and Figure 3). The mechanics of the fertility transition are suggested in these educational differentials. The use of contraception and the reduction of unwanted births will have a greater marginal effect on the fertility of less educated women, but as the persistence of a negative relationship between education and wanted fertility suggests, increases in education play an important role in reaching low fertility.

CONTRACEPTION AND FERTILITY RATES

Having estimated the potential demographic significance of the prevention of unwanted births, we focus on the birth rates associated with the different methods and the nonuse of contraception. Several methodological issues need to be mentioned here.

TABLE 3 Wanted and Unwanted Fertility for the 5 Years Preceding the Interview, by Woman's Education Level[a]

Country	Total Fertility Rate				Wanted Fertility Rate				Percent Unwanted Births			
	None	Primary	Secondary	Higher	None	Primary	Secondary	Higher	None	Primary	Secondary	Higher
Burundi[b]	7.5	6.8	5.4		6.9	6.1	5.0		6.9	10.7	7.7	
Guatemala	7.0	5.6	3.9	2.7	6.2	4.9	3.2	2.5	10.9	12.4	17.8	7.4
Peru	7.4	5.4	3.0	2.1	4.2	3.4	2.3	1.6	42.7	36.7	23.3	26.6
Ecuador	6.4	5.2	3.1	2.3	5.4	4.2	2.8	2.2	16.1	19.0	10.3	3.5
Dominican Republic	5.6	4.4	2.9	2.2	3.9	3.2	2.5	2.0	30.7	28.1	12.9	8.1
Colombia	5.4	4.2	2.5	1.5	4.3	3.5	2.3	1.4	20.0	16.0	7.5	3.0
Trinidad and Tobago	4.0	3.6	3.1	2.3	3.0	2.9	2.6	2.1	23.7	20.1	16.3	9.9

[a]Data for Sri Lanka were omitted because information on education was not collected for never-married women.
[b]For Burundi, data on only three levels of education were collected.

SOURCE: Demographic and Health Surveys.

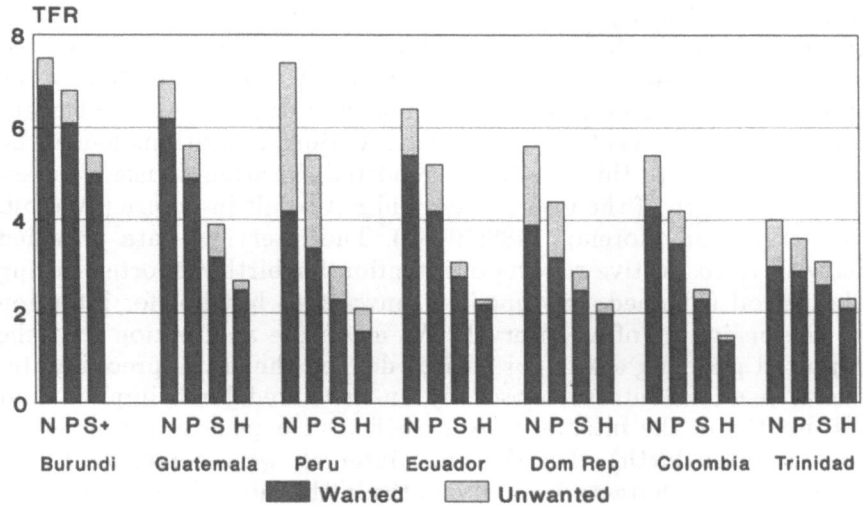

FIGURE 3 Total fertility rates by reproductive intention and education. N, None; P, completed primary school; S, completed secondary school; H, completed higher education. Source: Demographic and Health Surveys.

It is important to keep in mind that we are estimating birth rates, not conception rates. Information on abortion (induced or spontaneous) was not collected in the DHS, mainly because past survey experience has repeatedly demonstrated that such information is seriously underreported. Thus, the rates estimated are, to an unknown extent, underestimates of the failure of methods to prevent conception. The underestimate may not be too serious among women selected for this part of the analysis, which is limited to those who are currently married.[3]

As in the first part of this presentation, the data assembled for this analysis are for the 5 years preceding the interview. In order to calculate the desired birth rates from the data collected in the DHS surveys, various imputations and modifications of reported information were required. For example, we needed to classify each

---

[3]Some early premarital exposure is a greater potential source of unreported abortions. The limitation to the currently married is because of the need for information on reproductive intentions, which is not determined for unmarried respondents.

of the 60 months of exposure by use or nonuse of contraception, by the method used, by intention, and by the planning status of the conception (Westoff et al., 1987; Laing et al., 1985). To classify the type of exposure, we relied on the reported durations of contraceptive use within recent birth intervals. Various algorithms had to be devised to locate this use if the reported duration of use was less than the length of the interval and did not result in failure (Westoff, Goldman, and Moreno, 1988:79–88). The interview data provided us with retrospective reports of intention for births reported during the period (planned, mistimed, or unwanted) but not for intention at the beginning of an interval. We made the assumption that the reported planning status for a birth defined the entire preceding interval (e.g., an interval closed by an unwanted birth implied that all months in the interval were classified as exposure to the risk of an unwanted birth). For the open interval, we assumed that current intention characterized all months in the interval. Various other algorithms too numerous to describe here were devised to estimate missing data.

The sample for these calculations consists of all currently married women ages 15 to 49. However, the premarital exposure of women who married during the 60-month interval is included if they reported a date of first sexual intercourse prior to the date of first marriage.

The output of this analysis is a set of birth rates specific for intention and for type of exposure. Each of the 60 months was classified as a month in which the intention was to become pregnant, postpone becoming pregnant until some later time, or avoid pregnancy permanently. Each month was also classified as one in which contraception was used or not used, and if it was used, by type of method. Each birth was classified by the woman's report as planned, mistimed, or unwanted. Three types of birth rates can be calculated for each exposure category: rates of mistimed births, rates of unwanted births, and the combination of these (labeled rates of unintended births).

It is important to note that these rates are neither life table calculations nor Pearl rates, both of which take the duration of contraceptive use into account. They are period birth rates, specific for type of exposure and for intention. Since the ultimate goal of this analysis is to evaluate the demographic potential of particular mixes of contraceptive practice, not to estimate the comparative efficacy of particular methods for counseling or other purposes, a cross-sectional sample of a period of time (with all durations of use represented as they exist in the cross-section) is the appropriate methodology. The rates are calculated per woman-month of exposure for the 60-month observation period and then converted to annual form.[4]

BIRTH RATES BY METHOD AND INTENTION

Because it has the highest rate of unwanted fertility of the eight countries examined, we use Peru to illustrate the implications of different contraceptive methods for the reduction of fertility. We focus on the unwanted births that comprise over one-third of the total fertility rate in the period from 1981 to 1986 in Peru (Table 1). This is not to deny the potential demographic significance of reducing the rate of mistimed births, which, by lengthening interbirth intervals, would increase the age at maternity and reduce the length of the generation even in the absence of any reduction of completed fertility. A delay in childbearing would also reduce the period of risk of an unwanted birth. Our focus is confined to unwanted births, because the demographic effect is more readily demonstrable. In order to incorporate the simultaneous impact of reducing mistimed fertility, one would have to estimate the magnitude of the additional time for the preferred birth interval. Since the women who reported that they wanted another child but became pregnant sooner than they wanted were not asked how much longer they would have preferred to wait, such estimates would have to be hypothetical.[5] In addition, there are other issues involving the implications of improvements in the control of birth timing for the reduction of exposure to the risk of an unwanted birth. The birth rates for both types of exposure are shown in Table 4 to highlight the considerable differences in the magnitudes of the rates. The denominators for the rates are months of exposure to the risk of either a mistimed or an unwanted birth aggregated over the 5-year period. The rate is the number of births per 100 women-years of exposure over the last 5 years by type of exposure to risk. If abortions and current pregnancies were included, the pregnancy rates would be higher than the birth rates shown here.

The results in Table 4 show the expected pronounced difference in the rates for mistimed and for unwanted births. The former are three times the magnitude of the latter, a ratio that is fairly consistent regardless of type of exposure. This contrast reflects differences

---

[4]We set 2,500 months as the minimum number on which to base a rate.

[5]One could use the preferred length of the next birth interval as a proxy for the interval closed by the current pregnancy, but many women would be in the category of not wanting another child.

TABLE 4 Birth Rates by Type of Exposure and Intention,
Peru, 1981–1986

Type of Exposure	Mistimed Birth Rates	Unwanted Birth Rates
Pill	5.2	2.0
IUD	1.6	0.9
Sterilization	NA	0.1
Rhythm	31.2[a]	12.1
Withdrawal		5.4
Other	17.9	5.3
All use [b]	18.3	5.5
Nonuse[b]	53.0	18.5
Total exposure[b]	34.3	12.4

NOTE: NA = Not applicable.

[a]Fewer than 2,500 months.
[b]Excludes months of gestation.

SOURCE: Demographic and Health Surveys.

in the age and duration of marriage of women at risk of a mistimed compared with an unwanted birth. Thus, in addition to the
greater motivation to control fertility when exposed to the risk of an
unwanted birth, there are implicit differences in fecundability and
coital frequency.

Sterilization, the intrauterine device (IUD), and the pill show
the lowest unwanted birth rates. Collectively, these methods have an
annual rate of less than 1 per 100. Withdrawal and other methods
together have a rate just above 5, while the rhythm method has the
highest rate at 12. The unwanted birth rate for exposure with the
use of no method at all is 18.5. The rate for unwanted births for
all methods together is 5.5. The total unwanted birth rate—use and
nonuse together (excluding gestation)—is 12.4.

PATHS TOWARD THE REDUCTION OF FERTILITY

There are two possible routes for the reduction of unwanted
fertility in Peru: an increase in general prevalence or a shift away from
the rhythm method to more reliable methods of contraception. We
can also include the possibility of a new (unidentified) method. There

TABLE 5 Hypothetical Improvements in Contraceptive Practice and Their Fertility Implications for Peru

Type of Exposure	Rate of Unwanted Births (1981-1986)	Percent Distribution of Married Women Exposed to Risk of Unwanted Birth				
		1986	I	II	III	IV
Pill	2.0	6	9	11	13	7
IUD	0.9	7	10	12	15	8
Sterilization	0.1	8	12	14	17	9
Rhythm	12.1	14	0	14	28	14
Withdrawal	5.4	5	8	10	11	6
Other	5.3	5	8	10	11	6
New method	1.0					25
Nonuse	18.5	43	43	21	0	18
Pregnant		11	10	8	6	7
Total	11.3	100	100	100	100	100
Implied unwanted birth rate	11.3	10.3	9.1	7.0	4.7	6.1
Percent reduction of current rate (from 1986)			12.0	32.0	54.0	41.0
Implied total fertility rate		4.0	3.8	3.6	3.4	3.5

NOTE: Totals do not add to 100 because of rounding.

SOURCE: Demographic and Health Surveys.

are many scenarios that can be hypothesized, but we confine the exercise to only a few, which are primarily intended to illustrate the implications of certain changes. For example, if all women exposed to the risk of an unwanted birth were to adopt the rhythm method and its failure rate were to remain unchanged, the unwanted fertility rate for all women would remain essentially unchanged. The rhythm method is significantly better than no method at all (a birth rate of 12.1 compared with 18.5), but it is appreciably less effective than all other methods combined (2.3), and in the hypothetical situation in which all women use rhythm, the improvement over nonuse is counterbalanced by the loss of the more effective methods. If use of the rhythm method dropped to 0, nonuse remained the same, and the 14 percent of women currently using the rhythm method were redistributed proportionately among other methods, the reduction of unwanted fertility would be only 12 percent (model I in Table 5).

Only modest gains can be realized without reducing the extent of nonuse, which currently makes up 43 percent of all exposure among women at risk of an unwanted birth.[6]

Suppose that nonuse were reduced by half of its current level to 21 percent, that the percentage of women using the rhythm method remained constant, and the balance was redistributed proportionately among the other methods, the result would be a 32 percent reduction in unwanted fertility. This distribution is shown in model II in Table 5.

An extreme version is depicted in model III in Table 5, which is designed to illustrate the effect of eliminating nonuse completely and redistributing the exposure proportionately among all other methods, including the rhythm method (which increases from 14 to 28 percent from model II to model III). The effect would be a 54 percent reduction in unwanted births.

A different picture can be imagined if a new contraceptive method were to be introduced, say with a 1 percent annual birth rate (about the average rate for the birth-control pill, IUD, and sterilization combined, as currently observed in Peru among women at risk of an unwanted birth). Suppose that this new method were to attract 25 percent of exposed women, all of whom were drawn from nonusers. In this scenario (model IV in Table 5), the practice of all other methods would remain as it is. The result would be a 41 percent reduction in unwanted births. If the effectiveness were a birth rate of 1 per 1,000 rather than 1 percent, the reduction of the unwanted birth rate would rise to 43 percent.

---

[6]It should be noted that this nonuse exposure includes sterility (but not contraceptive sterilization), which is, of course, reflected in the estimated birth rate for that exposure. It is also noteworthy that one-third of the nonuse exposure is accompanied by breastfeeding. This component of nonuse shows a birth rate of 12.5 per year compared with 21.5 per year in the absence of breastfeeding.

Gestation months are included in Table 5 in order to represent *all* months of exposure and conform more closely to the concept of a birth rate. Gestation is assigned a birth rate of 0 because all births have been assigned to the appropriate exposure at the time of conception. The proportion of exposure classified as gestation in the different projections is estimated from the current proportion reduced by the rate of reduction of the unwanted birth rate.

The final calculation in Table 5 (bottom row) shows the TFR implied by each hypothetical reduction in unwanted fertility,[7] assuming a constant wanted fertility rate. This calculation simply reduces the unwanted birth component of the TFR for 1986 (Goldman et al., 1988:Table 4)[8] by the rate of decline estimated for each scenario. The greatest reduction would be from the TFR in 1986 of 4.0 to 3.4 in model III, in which all nonuse would be redistributed proportionately. The questionable assumption implicit in such a calculation is that the proportion of women exposed to the risk of unwanted fertility would remain the same. In fact, the adoption of more effective contraception could in some measure increase the proportion of women wishing to avoid further births. Since these calculations do not take into account any increase in the proportion of women who want no more births, they could underestimate the decline in fertility, although this might be minimal in Peru (Fisher and Way, 1988:Table 3).[9]

There is an important caveat that applies to these hypothetical calculations. When we redistribute women from using one method to using another, we make the implicit assumption that the method-specific birth rate remains unchanged, thereby ignoring any selectivity involved in method choice. It seems highly likely that women will stay with the methods that they use successfully and will discontinue those with which they fail. Differences in fecundability may also play a role: Women who take a long time to become pregnant may be less likely to adopt contraception. We have no choice but to make the assumption that these rates remain constant, but it is important to recognize its unrealistic nature.

TRENDS IN CONTRACEPTIVE PRACTICE

The analysis thus far has focused on recent contraceptive experience in Peru and the implications for the reduction of unwanted

---

[7]Since our estimates of method-specific birth rates are necessarily confined to data for currently married women (because information on reproductive intention is only available for married women), it would be more appropriate to relate these hypothetical reductions to marital fertility rather than to the TFR. It turns out that the same conclusions apply to the marital fertility rate because in Peru very few births occur outside of marriage.

[8]The TFR for 1986 was estimated at 4.0. The proportion of this rate classified as unwanted births is 0.312 (Instituto Nacional de la Estadistica, 1988).

[9]The proportion of married women wanting no more children is higher in Peru (77 percent) than that in any other country reported so far in the DHS.

TABLE 6 Distribution of Women Who Want No More Births, by Current Contraceptive Practice (in percent)

Method	1976-1977	1981	1986	1991[a]
Pill	3.6	4.5	6.2	8
IUD	1.2	4.9	7.3	9
Sterilization	4.5	4.5	8.4	12
Rhythm	12.2	20.2	13.8	12
Withdrawal	3.2	3.1	5.5	5
Other	7.3	6.5	5.5	6
No use	54.6	45.9	42.6	39
Pregnant	13.3	10.4	10.6	9
Percent total	100.0	100.0	100.0	100
Implied unwanted birth rate	12.2	11.6	10.3	8.7

NOTE: Totals do not add to 100 because of rounding.

[a]Estimated.

SOURCES: Distributions for the 1976-1977 and 1981 periods tabulated, respectively, from the Contraceptive Prevalence Survey and the World Fertility Survey data tapes.

fertility of various hypothetical distributions of improved contraceptive practice. Again assuming that the birth rates estimated for the different types of exposure remain unaltered by shifts in the distribution of contraceptive use, we now add the further assumption that these method-specific birth rates have remained unchanged over time. This permits us to trace the trend in the unwanted birth rate since 1976–1977 and project the distribution of use and the implied unwanted birth rate in the future. We limit the projection exercise to 5 years beyond the most recent survey (1991).

What will the contraceptive profile among women who want no more births look like in Peru 5 years later? There is obviously some guesswork, but we have some clues. We know that contraceptive practice in general has been increasing in Peru from our comparisons of the World Fertility Survey (WFS) (1971–1977), the Contraceptive Prevalence Survey (CPS) (1981), and the DHS (1986) (Table 6). We observe also that the use of the most effective methods (birth-control pill, IUD, and sterilization) has increased, while the use of less effective methods has leveled off or declined. We also know that contraceptive practice has increased rapidly throughout Latin America.

The projection begins with the percentage of women not using any method of contraception among those who want no more births. The percent not using in 1976–1977 was 54.6, whereas in 1981 it was 45.9, a decline of 16 percent. By 1986, nonuse had declined to 42.6 percent, a decline of 7 percent over those 5 years. On the (conservative) assumption that the same rate of decline would continue unchanged for the next 5 years, the percentage of nonusers would be close to 39 percent by 1991. Since we are projecting an increase in the use of the more effective methods, we show a decline in the percentage of women who are currently pregnant (from 10.6 to 9 percent).

The 47 percent of women who use contraception are then projected by method to 1991, roughly following the assumption that the pattern of change in the last 5 years would continue and taking into account the methods preferred by nonusers who say that they intend to use contraception. This further increases the proportion who use the more effective methods. Application of the failure rates observed for the last 5 years to this projected distribution for 1991 yields an estimated rate of unwanted births of 8.7, a reduction of 15 percent since 1986. However, this would reduce the 1986 TFR of 4.0 to only 3.8, which considerably exceeds the TFR of 2.8 that would have been obtained for that year if only wanted births had occurred.

SUMMARY AND CONCLUSIONS

We posed two questions in this analysis: (1) How much would fertility decline if unwanted births were totally prevented? and (2) How much would unwanted fertility decline if contraceptive practice improved?

To answer the first question, we estimated the proportion of the total fertility rate that comprises unwanted births of eight Third World countries participating in the Demographic and Health Surveys project. The lowest proportion of unwanted births was observed for Burundi and the highest proportion was observed for Peru. In Peru, the TFR would be one-third lower if all unwanted births were avoided. In Sri Lanka, the TFR would be near replacement if only wanted births occurred. We also examined wanted and unwanted fertility rates for rural and for urban areas and for those by education of the mother. With a few exceptions, unwanted fertility rates were highest in rural areas. Both wanted and unwanted fertility rates declined with increasing education.

To answer the second question, we selected Peru, which has a high unwanted fertility rate, and estimated birth rates specific for the main contraceptive methods used. Several hypothetical distributions of improved contraceptive practice were explored. The greatest potential improvement requires radical decreases in nonuse of contraception. The rhythm method, the most popular method in Peru, has a birth rate associated with it roughly equal to the observed total birth rate, implying that if everyone used that method, the birth rate would remain at its current level. The implications of the use of a new method were also explored.

The final analysis examined trends in contraceptive practice in Peru, based on data from previous surveys, and estimated the contraceptive method distribution for 1991. On the assumption that existing method-specific birth rates persist, the decline in the unwanted birth rate would be on the order of 15 percent below its current level.

In addition to exploring the situation for Peru, this paper develops a methodology appropriate for the general objective of determining the effect on fertility of improvements in contraceptive practice. It is a potentially useful tool for estimating reductions in an important component of the unmet need for family planning services (Westoff, 1988).

There also seem to be several policy implications in the exercise described here. The first is that unless wanted fertility declines, the opportunity to reduce total fertility is largely limited to the extent of unwanted fertility in the population. Even in Peru, where as many as one-third of all births are reported as unwanted, the potential for reducing total fertility by increasing contraceptive use and reducing contraceptive failure is fairly limited. Even eliminating nonuse of contraception completely among women at risk of an unwanted birth theoretically reduces the TFR from 4.0 to only 3.4—not a negligible effect, but one that does require an extreme assumption.

A second apparent lesson is that the introduction of a new method, even one with extremely high effectiveness that would be used by as many as half of the women (at risk of unwanted fertility) currently not using any method, would reduce the TFR from 4.0 to only 3.5, which is not much different than the TFR of 3.6 estimated from simply redistributing half of the nonusers to other methods.

There are, of course, other worthwhile objectives of developing new, improved contraceptive technologies, including the reduction of abortion, health considerations, and women's general status. The demographic potential seems limited, however, at least in a population like that of Peru, with other methods currently in use. One would have to argue that a new method would promote greater acceptance by nonusers rather than simply substituting for other existing methods. Or a new method might accelerate the process of adoption, thereby increasing the prevalence rate to a higher level in a shorter period of time than would be experienced otherwise. Finally, there is also the potential that a new method might have characteristics that would reduce the rate of discontinuation of methods, a subject that was not addressed here, although its impact is implicitly reflected in the prevalence rate.

ACKNOWLEDGMENTS

The authors acknowledge the Demographic and Health Surveys project of the Institute for Resource Development, Westinghouse Corporation, which is responsible for the data collection. We also acknowledge with thanks the careful reading and suggestions of Anrudh Jain of the Population Council and Amy Tsui of the Carolina Population Center, University of North Carolina.

REFERENCES

Fisher, Andrew W., and Ann A. Way
    1988   The Demographic and Health Surveys Program: An overview. *International Family Planning Perspectives* 14(2).
Goldman, Noreen, et al.
    1988   *Full vs. Five-Year Maternity History Data for Fertility and Child Measures.* Seminar on Collection and Processing of Demographic Data. Santiago, Chile: International Union for the Scientific Study of Population.
Instituto Nacional de Estadistica
    1988   *Encuesta Demográfica y de Salud Familiar (endes 1986).* Lima, Peru: Instituto Nacional de Estadistica.
Laing, John E.
    1985   Continuation and effectiveness of contraceptive practice: A cross-sectional approach. *Studies in Family Planning* 16(3):138–153.
Westoff, Charles F.
    1981   Unwanted fertility in six developing countries. *International Family Planning Perspectives* 7(2):43–52.
    1988   The potential demand for family planning: A new measure of unmet need and estimates for five Latin American countries. *International Family Planning Perspectives* 14(2).

Westoff, Charles F., Noreen Goldman, and Lorenzo Moreno
    1988   *Peru Experimental Survey Results.* Advance Report of Demographic
            and Health Surveys. Columbia, Md.: Institute for Resource Develop-
            ment, Inc./Westinghouse.
Westoff, Charles F., C. R. Hammerslough, and L. Paul
    1987   The potential impact of improvements in contraception on fertility
            and abortion in Western countries. *European Journal of Population*
            3:7–32.

Effects of Demographic Factors on the Use and Effectiveness of New Contraceptive Technologies

WILLIAM R. GRADY AND JOHN O.G. BILLY

INTRODUCTION

Understanding the ways in which demographic factors will affect the use and effectiveness of new contraceptive technologies is a challenging task. A logical course of action is to first classify new methods according to the characteristics they share with existing methods and then use the theory and research as to how individual factors affect current methods to inform the discussion of the new technologies. This is the general strategy adopted in this paper. There are, however, two problematic aspects of this strategy that make this task especially difficult. First, a firmly established and well-specified conceptual framework that relates demographic characteristics to the use and effectiveness of contraceptive devices does not exist. Instead, partial and rather ad hoc explanations for why a particular characteristic affects an individual's or couple's use of a method are typically found. Second, most of the existing research on contraceptive use and effectiveness has serious shortcomings that limit its usefulness for understanding the effects of demographic factors. Most notable among these shortcomings are measurement and study design problems that negate these studies' ability to adequately address the issue.

In line with our overall objective and the two problems noted above, this paper is divided into three sections. In the first section, we provide a general conceptual model by which we might better understand how individual characteristics affect contraceptive efficacy.

73

In doing so, we partition efficacy into its three components and establish the causal operators through which demographic factors may affect each component. Our model is admittedly rudimentary and is intended only as a framework to guide our subsequent discussion. The second section addresses the specific inadequacies of previous research for providing information about the effects of demographic factors on the use of current or future contraceptive technologies. Our intention is not to cast dispersions on this body of literature. Rather, our aim is to make clear its limitations for understanding the processes that are the focus of this paper. The third section deals with the primary task at hand. Using the conceptual framework developed in the first section and drawing upon relevant pieces of the empirical literature, we discuss the likely effects of a set of demographic characteristics on the use and effectiveness of new contraceptive technologies.

DIMENSIONS OF CONTRACEPTIVE EFFICACY

The utility of a contraceptive method for preventing unintended pregnancy is a function of three factors: the likelihood of adoption, the risk of discontinuation, and effectiveness during use. In addition to the availability of the method, the likelihood of adoption depends on the couple's evaluation of its attractiveness relative to other method types. The criteria for this evaluation include perceptions about such factors as effectiveness, health effects (risks and benefits), convenience (including ease of use and conflict with religious or cultural values), and cost. The risk of discontinuation depends on the couple's satisfaction with the use of the method. That is, discontinuation will occur if the couple's actual experiences with the method conflict with its original perceived attractiveness, or when a change in life circumstances (e.g., a change in marital status) alters the types of characteristics that are desirable in a method. Use-effectiveness has two dimensions: the effectiveness of the technology when used under ideal conditions (method effectiveness) and the accuracy with which it is used. Accuracy of use varies according to the characteristics of the method (e.g., whether it is coitus-independent and easy to use), but is also related to user motivation and knowledge.

Adoption and discontinuation decisions, as well as use-effectiveness, are affected by a wide range of demographic characteristics including age, parity, socioeconomic status (SES), marital status, and frequency of intercourse. With respect to the effects of these factors on the adoption decision, it is important to note first that the marketing of certain technologies, either by manufacturers or family planning service providers, may be directed at population subgroups with these specific characteristics. Assuming no external marketing influences, however, these factors may be presumed to operate primarily by determining the salience of the various dimensions, described above, on which methods are evaluated. For example, age, parity, and marital status may be related to the salience of the health dimension. The birth-control pill has greater negative health implications for older women; the association of the intrauterine device (IUD) with pelvic inflammatory disease (PID), and thus possible sterility, may be more important to low-parity couples who have not completed their family building; and single individuals may derive greater benefit from methods, such as the condom, that provide some protection against sexually transmitted diseases. These and other factors (e.g., SES) that are associated with the cost of an unintended pregnancy or unwanted birth may also affect adoption via the method effectiveness dimension. Marital status and frequency of intercourse may determine the salience of method convenience. Single individuals and those with high frequencies of sexual intercourse may be less able to plan sexual encounters and may thus find coitus-independent and easy-to-use methods more acceptable. Finally, couples occupying different socioeconomic positions may differentially adopt a particular method on the basis of relative cost.

Whereas the adoption decision reflects the *perceived* acceptability of a method, the discontinuation decision reflects the situation in which *actual* acceptability is lower than *perceived* acceptability with respect to the performance of the method on the salient dimensions. The lack of correspondence between perceived and actual performance, which leads to dissatisfaction and method abandonment, has three major sources: incorrect initial information about the method, new information acquired from use of the method or from outside sources, and errors in the assessment of the information. Characteristics of the couple or individual may affect the risk of discontinuation, then, by giving rise to differential sources of information about method characteristics, ability to correctly interpret the information, and motivation or ability to use the method correctly, which affects method experiences. For example, sources of information are probably related to age, marital status, and SES. Ability to understand the information about a contraceptive method or to reevaluate it on the basis of new information may be related to such factors as age and SES. Motivation to use the method correctly may be associated with all of the demographic characteristics mentioned above.

When considering the impact of demographic factors on contraceptive discontinuation, it is also important to remember that some characteristics change over the lifetime of the individual and may alter the salience of the dimensions on which methods are evaluated. For example, as persons age, achieve their ultimate parity, or change marital statuses, they may reassess their contraceptive choice and change methods. Thus, the effects of changes in demographic characteristics are also important to consider.

The use-effectiveness of methods is also affected by most of the demographic characteristics considered here. Age, parity, marital status (through consistency of exposure to intercourse), and frequency of intercourse are related to fecundability and thus affect the risk of method failure even when used accurately. SES may also affect fecundity to the extent that nutrition and access to health care are related to social standing. Accuracy of use is affected by such factors as age, parity, marital status, and SES that influence the value placed on children and thus the motivation for avoiding an unintended pregnancy. Many of these characteristics, most notably age and SES, also affect accuracy of use by limiting or facilitating an individual's ability to understand and follow method-use instructions.

In the above few paragraphs, we have briefly highlighted how demographic characteristics may affect each of the primary components of contraceptive efficacy. To summarize, demographic factors may be expected to affect method adoption by influencing the salience of one or more evaluative criteria. Characteristics of the couple or individual may affect the risk of discontinuation by giving rise to differential sources of information about method characteristics, ability to correctly interpret the information, and motivation to use the method correctly. Discontinuation may also occur when changes in demographic factors alter the salience of the evaluative criteria. Method use-effectiveness is a function of two factors: inherent method effectiveness and accuracy of use. Demographic characteristics may influence use-effectiveness by affecting fecundability (and thus the maximum effectiveness of the method), motivation, and ability to use the method accurately. Before applying this general framework to a discussion of the likely effects of demographic factors on the use and effectiveness of new contraceptive technologies, we next consider the ability of previous research literature to inform us about this issue.

MEASUREMENT ISSUES

Method Adoption

Ideally, a study of the effects of demographic characteristics on the method adoption process should have three primary attributes. First, it should separately examine couples who are engaged in each type of method adoption (e.g., initial adoption, after a pregnancy termination, and after discontinuing a previous method). Second, it should be based on a longitudinal study so that the causal effects of such variables as frequency of intercourse can be ascertained. Finally, it should identify the sources and accuracy of information that the woman has received about each type of contraceptive method. This last consideration is necessary to identify how demographic characteristics affect the evaluation of methods as opposed to how they affect sources of information about the methods. To date, no study has approached this ideal.

Examinations of the effects of demographic factors on the type of method adopted have taken one of two general approaches. The most common class of analysis is the examination of contraceptive use (or nonuse) at a single point in time, usually at the time of the survey on which the analysis is based. These studies of contraceptive prevalence are typically regarded as analyses of contraceptive choice because individuals are assumed to be engaged in a continuous selection process. That is, individuals are viewed as constantly assessing their current method and making choices about continuing use of that method or of changing method types (cf. Steven, Rindfuss, and Bean, 1987).

More accurately, current contraceptive status is an outcome of a multidimensional process involving method adoption (e.g., first method of birth control used or method at first intercourse), method discontinuation (e.g., change from one method of birth control to another or no method), pregnancy (which removes the woman from method use), and method readoption (e.g., adoption of a method after a pregnancy termination or after discontinuing a previous method). Contraceptive prevalence, then, captures both the adoption and discontinuation decisions without distinguishing the effects of either.[1] As such, these studies provide very limited information about the effects of demographic characteristics on either process. Further, because of the nature of a prevalence measure, many of the adoption decisions that produced the current method distribution of the population may have occurred long before the survey. This is particularly problematic if the effects of demographic characteristics on the adoption process have changed over time.

The other class of demographic studies of contraceptive choice comprises analyses of actual method adoption. These are primarily examinations of the adoption of the first method or method at first intercourse (Zelnik and Kantner, 1977, 1979, 1980; Zelnik and Shah, 1983; Dawson, 1986) but also include adoption of the first method following a pregnancy termination (Margolis et al., 1974; Taffel and Placek, 1980), following the discontinuation of use of a previous method (Grady et al., 1989; Tsui et al., 1988; Reboussin et al., 1989), or at the time of a family planning visit (Gorosh, 1982; Higgens et al., 1986; Sivin et al., 1983; Shaaban et al., 1983; Satayapan, Kanchanasinith, and Varakamin, 1983; Marangoni et al., 1983; Meade et al., 1984; Basnayake, Thapa, and Balogh, 1988). These analyses provide more accurate information about the effects of demographic characteristics on the method adoption process than the prevalence studies because they observe method use at a common stage of the method selection and redistribution process.

Even these studies, however, have fallen short of the ideal. All of the population-based studies, for example, have used cross-sectional surveys, meaning that detailed information about dates of method use and first intercourse and covariate information (e.g., marital status and frequency of intercourse) was obtained retrospectively. As a consequence, the information may be less reliable, more limited in scope, and less useful in establishing causality. For example, we know that women who adopt more effective contraceptive methods have a higher frequency of intercourse (Trussell and Westoff, 1980),

---

[1] For example, among married women in the United States, birth-control pill use has experienced a substantial decline, while sterilization has become the most prevalent contraceptive method (Bachrach, 1984). This has occurred despite the fact that the birth-control pill remains the first method most likely to be adopted by women (Mosher and Bachrach, 1987) and is the method most often chosen by married women who stop to change methods (Grady, Hayward, and Florey, 1988). The rise of sterilization and the decline of birth-control pill use is therefore more a function of discontinuation rates than adoption rates. Very few sterilizations are reversed, but about 44 percent of married women discontinue pill use within 2 years of adoption.

but we do not know whether the elevated level of intercourse is a cause or a consequence of the adoption decision. Such information can only be obtained from prospective or longitudinal studies with detailed information about method adoption. However, even the clinic-based studies that could have obtained information on such factors as frequency of intercourse at the time of method adoption have typically not done so. Further, causality would still be difficult to establish because, as discussed below, provider inputs may affect the observed relationships between a woman's characteristics and her method choice.

Studies of method adoption have also failed to identify completely the sources and accuracy of information about contraceptive methods that an individual has received. As noted above, such identification is important so that the effects of demographic characteristics on the evaluation of methods can be distinguished from their effects on the sources of information about the methods. Since method adoption is a function of perceived acceptability, it is highly subject to the influence of information sources.[2] Certain population subgroups have increased access to or are targets for such information. That is to say, information sources may partly determine the effects of demographic characteristics on the method adoption process. Consider, for example, the providers of family planning services. Trussell, Faden, and Hatcher (1976) find that the accuracy of information about methods provided by clinicians depends on their subjective assessments of those methods. Moreover, their assessment of the appropriateness of a method for a given woman may depend, in part, on the woman's characteristics. When examining method adoption patterns, then, it is important to remember that any observed group differences in method selection may be partly due to external influences. This confounding factor may be especially acute for clinic-based samples. Hence, drawing valid conclusions about the effects of demographic factors on method adoption from studies using clinic samples is problematic.

---

[2]As an illustration, media attention on the possible adverse health effects of the pill and IUD certainly reduced the rate of adoption of those methods. Similarly, the focus on the acquired immune deficiency syndrom (AIDS) epidemic and advertising for the condom has probably raised the adoption rate for that method.

Method Discontinuation and Use Failure[3]

A major shortcoming of much of the existing literature on contraceptive failure and discontinuation is the types of measures used. For example, the earliest studies of contraceptive failure, as well as some more recent studies, utilize a measure known as the Pearl Index (Pearl, 1932). This measure is based on the simple ratio of events (i.e., unintended pregnancies) to women-years of exposure. It is much easier to calculate than life table measures and has less restrictive data requirements, an advantage for studies based on surveys conducted in developing countries where detailed histories of contraceptive use and exposure to intercourse are usually not obtained. However, Trussell and Kost (1987:239) note that the Pearl Index is "seriously flawed as a summary measure of contraceptive failure because failure rates typically decline with duration of use." Thus, the higher the duration of use observed in a study, the lower the failure rate estimated by the index. Because the duration of use may be different for each population subgroup, this feature is particularly unattractive for estimating effects of demographic characteristics on use failure. The failure rates may differ even if the underlying risk of failure is the same for each category of a group characteristic. Further, even if duration of use is truncated at the same duration for each subgroup (which overcomes the major limitation of the measure), it will still be affected by the pattern of discontinuation caused by competing risks (Trussell and Kost, 1987).

The preferred methodology for estimating contraceptive failure rates is the life table. Life table measures are not subject to the problem of duration dependence found in the Pearl Index because they are based on ordinal month-specific risks, which are used to calculate cumulative proportions experiencing the event of interest within a given number of months since the beginning of exposure. In some studies women are allowed to exit the life table for multiple reasons (i.e., multiple-decrement life tables are used). In such tables, however, the estimated failure rate is inversely related to the magnitude of the competing risks (e.g., discontinuation), and any group differences in these competing risks would thus affect comparisons of contraceptive

---

[3]Since contraceptive discontinuation and contraceptive use failure share many of the same conceptual and methodological issues and are estimated in much the same way, they will be discussed together. Trussell and Kost (1987) provide an excellent review of these issues, most of which are relevant to the examination of population subgroup differences in these events. Much of the following discussion is therefore based on their review.

failure rates.[4] The effects of demographic characteristics on the risks of contraceptive failure, then, must be based on comparisons of gross rates calculated from associated single-decrement life tables (Tietze and Lewitt, 1973; Potter, 1966; Trussell and Menken, 1980). In these life tables, women who exit for reasons other than unintended pregnancy are censored at the month of exit, and the estimated rate of failure is that which would be obtained in the absence of competing risks.

An examination of the effects of demographic characteristics on contraceptive discontinuation should also be based on gross rates obtained from associated single-decrement life tables. All of the considerations mentioned above for contraceptive failure also hold for discontinuation, only the type of event that is the focus of the analysis is different.

Even among those studies based on the calculation of gross rates, however, conflicting results may be obtained because of definitional differences. Trussell and Kost (1987) note that some studies of contraceptive failure (e.g., Ryder, 1973) attribute unintended pregnancies to a method even if use had stopped prior to conception. Analyses of these extended-use failure rates would be not comparable to those restricted to examining failure during an interval of use (use failure) because the former measure incorporates the risk of abandoning method use. Further, some studies do not include unintended pregnancies resulting from improper use of the method. Trussell and Kost (1987) argue that this is both a conceptual and methodological error. Discontinuation may also be defined differently across studies. For example, some researchers include stopping all method use as the only reason for discontinuation (e.g., Hammerslough, 1984), while others include stopping to change methods as a reason (e.g., Grady et al., 1983). To the extent that demographic characteristics differentially affect the risk of each type of discontinuation, the estimated effects would vary across studies for definitional reasons alone. From the standpoint of understanding method acceptability, including both reasons for discontinuation is probably preferable since both are indicators of method dissatisfaction.

Another caution about the calculation of life table measures of contraceptive failure and discontinuation is the way in which exposure is counted. In many surveys, month-by-month information

---

[4] For an illustrative example of this relationship, see Trussell and Kost (1987).

about exposure to intercourse is not obtained. Thus, some studies have examined the proportion failing or discontinuing by months since method adoption, regardless of whether the woman was having intercourse during each of those months. In these analyses, the observed effects of demographic factors on the risk of interest is confounded by their effects on consistency of exposure to intercourse.

Also having implications for our understanding of how demographic characteristics operate is whether the studies of contraceptive use failure and discontinuation are based on clinic- or population-based samples. Population-based surveys draw a representative sample of the population and are thus well-suited for analyses of the effects of demographic characteristics. Clinic-based samples are limited to subsets of the population, and the characteristics of the sample depend on the nature of the clinic or, in prospective studies, the purpose of the study. For example, a sample drawn from a family planning clinic will reflect the target population of the clinic (e.g., low income), and a sample chosen for a clinical trial of a specific method may be selected for characteristics thought to be associated with consistent or accurate use of the method. Thus, the sample may have certain unreported or unmeasured characteristics that have an impact on any reported effects of demographic characteristics. It is also important to note that the results of clinical trials seldom report the effects of such characteristics.

An important problem common to both types of samples is selectivity with respect to the type of method used. Trussell and Kost (1987) point out, for example, that women who are highly motivated to avoid pregnancy are probably more likely to select one of the more effective methods. To the extent that this is true, the effects of demographic characteristics that are related to motivation to avoid unintended pregnancy will be expressed in the type of method selected and not in the use failure rate of methods. This problem could be overcome if such motivation could be measured and included in the statistical model used to examine failure or discontinuation. To date, no study has attempted to do so. As noted earlier, frequency of intercourse is a characteristic that is probably related to the selection of a method type. Since it is highly variant over time and difficult to measure accurately, it, too, is not typically included in an analysis. As a consequence, the observed effects on failure and discontinuation of factors such as age and marital status that are associated with frequency of intercourse will be biased.

,Selectivity may be exacerbated in clinical trials by clinician bias. Further, women sampled from a clinic will probably be underrepresentative of women who are successful, long-term users of a contraceptive method, since they are likely to be enrolled at a clinic for the purpose of obtaining a new method. The bias resulting from clinician assignment of women to a method, rather than having women randomly select a method, may be particularly acute in developing countries where the type of methods dispensed may be determined by organizational or governmental policy.

Both clinic- and population-based samples also suffer from the exclusion of certain subjects from observation. In clinical trials, "it is not uncommon for 15 percent of women to simply disappear from the trial" (Trussell and Kost, 1987:242) without the investigators being able to determine their contraceptive or pregnancy status at the time of departure. Further, these women are typically coded as not experiencing the event of interest, biasing the effects of characteristics associated with this loss to follow-up. A comparable problem exists in population-based surveys. The typical assumption is that women omitted from the survey or omitted from the study because of missing data items have the same contraceptive experiences as women with similar measured characteristics who are included in the study. There is, however, no evidence to support this assumption.

We must emphasize that regardless of the nature of the sample, the independent effects of demographic characteristics on contraceptive failure and discontinuation can only be ascertained using a multivariate life table model. Even when such an approach is used, however, the omission of crucial variables such as frequency of intercourse will leave in doubt the nature of the relationships among the remaining variables. Further, comparison of results across studies is limited when different subsets of variables are included in the statistical models. For example, the effects of marital status on contraceptive use failure will undoubtedly differ according to whether or not marital status differences in frequency of intercourse are controlled.

To summarize, we can characterize the literature on contraceptive failure and discontinuation as follows. Much of this research focuses on method differences in the risk of failure or discontinuation and does not investigate how the risk varies across population subgroups. This is particularly true of studies based on clinical trials. The remaining studies all suffer to some degree from problems of selectivity and the omission of crucial variables from the analyses. Further, to our knowledge, only the National Survey of Family Growth, a U.S. population-based survey, has sufficiently detailed information on contraceptive use and exposure to intercourse to allow the construction of true life table measures of failure and discontinuation. The state of our knowledge about the effects of demographic factors on use failure and discontinuation of current contraceptive methods, then, is at a very rudimentary level. Moreover, there is little information that is useful in extrapolating the current method experiences of women to new contraceptive technologies. In our subsequent discussion of new method types, we will therefore rely mostly on the theoretical linkages between demographic characteristics and contraceptive behavior developed in the first part of this paper.

EFFECTS OF DEMOGRAPHIC FACTORS ON THE NEW METHODS

In this section we focus on the likely effects of demographic characteristics on the use and effectiveness of the new contraceptive technologies. To provide order to this discussion, the new methods are categorized into groups that are fairly homogeneous with respect to important characteristics. The discussion of each group of new methods follows a standard format. We indicate the characteristics that the new methods share with existing methods. Applying our conceptual framework and extending previous research on those current methods that are most similar to the new technologies, we then discuss the possible effects of a core set of demographic factors on the adoption, discontinuation, and use-effectiveness of the new methods.

Implants

The first group of new methods to be discussed is implants. Since some types of implants are already available in a number of countries, this discussion is aided by recent research pertaining directly to their use. Implants also share some characteristics with both the oral contraceptive (OC) pill and the IUD, and thus, research on these methods types is also relevant. For example, like the OC pill and the IUD, implants are a highly effective, coitus-independent, low-cost, reversible female contraceptive method with some potential negative health impacts. It is also important to note that implants are more like the IUD in some ways and more like the OC pill in other ways.

In terms of adoption and discontinuation, the implant is like the IUD in that it requires an outpatient medical procedure but does not require daily user action. On the other hand, it is more like the OC pill than the IUD in the types of health consequences it may generate because it is steroidal and is not associated with PID. These differences and similarities must be taken into account in extending the research on the OC pill and the IUD to the possible effects of demographic characteristics on method adoption and discontinuation and the use-effectiveness of implants.

With respect to the adoption of an implant, the effects of age and parity are unclear. Since age is positively related to the costs of an unintended pregnancy, we might expect these factors to be positively related to the adoption of this highly effective method type. Older and higher-parity couples, however, may also be more likely to adopt a method as a long-term means of preventing future births, rather than for shorter-term use in spacing intended births. Thus, they may be more concerned about possible health effects implied by use for long durations. To the extent that health concerns arise similar to the much-publicized negative effects associated with OC pill use, then, age and parity may negatively affect the adoption of an implant. This relationship would be enhanced by the competing risk of sterilization, which women adopt at older ages after their childbearing is completed.

Evidence on the effects of age and parity on the adoption of the NORPLANT® implant are mixed. For example Sivin et al. (1983) find that age and parity are both positively related to its adoption in Chile but have very different effects in the Dominican Republic and Finland. In the Dominican Republic, age is negatively related and parity is positively related to the acceptance of the implant. In Finland, age displays a positive relationship and parity shows a negative relationship with adoption. Findings of research set in other countries leads to further confusion. Studies based in Egypt (Shaaban et al., 1983), Thailand (Satayapan, Kanchansinith, and Varakamin, 1983), Ecuador (Marangoni et al., 1983), and Sri Lanka (Tsui et al., 1988) all show generally negative relationships between age and method acceptance; but the effect of parity varies across countries. In Sri Lanka, the effect of parity is curvilinear, peaking at a parity of two.

The conflicting results have several possible sources. First, the focus of each study is on the acceptability and efficacy of the method itself and not on the effects of demographic characteristics. Thus, certain restrictions were applied to the study populations. In particular, only women who had demonstrated fertility and no contraindications for steroidal contraception were enrolled in the studies. These selection criteria could easily influence the age and parity profiles of acceptors. In addition, the acceptors were drawn from clinic populations, and as discussed earlier, clinician bias might therefore be a confounding factor. For example, if sterilization was offered and encouraged as a contraceptive option, this might markedly affect the age and parity profile of acceptors of other methods. Finally, none of these studies uses a multivariate statistical technique to determine the independent effects of the characteristics. The interrelationships of age, parity, and other characteristics may thus confound the observed bivariate relationships.

In general, given the kinds of contraindications for use of a steroidal contraceptive,[5] it is likely that the major use of implants will be for the spacing of pregnancies among younger women. Thus, the adoption patterns of this method, with respect to age and parity, will probably be similar to that of the OC pill, which has some of the same side effects and similar contraindications. This may especially be the case to the extent that implants are viewed by potential adopters as a method that is similar to the OC pill, but with a different mode of administration. Hence, we might expect generally negative effects of age and parity on adoption. Similar to Grady, Hayward, and Florey's (1988) findings on OC pill switching, we might expect that as women reach their ultimate parity and end their family building they will switch to other methods, such as sterilization, for long-term prevention.

The coitus-independent nature of the implant, together with its high effectiveness, makes it a method likely to be adopted by women with a high coital frequency. Independent of differences in frequency of intercourse, however, these same characteristics should appeal to single women who may have less regular exposure to sexual intercourse and for whom the costs of an unintended pregnancy are high. This follows from the pattern of OC pill use found in the United States. The OC pill is most likely to be the first method adopted by never-married women (Mosher and Bachrach, 1987), most likely to be adopted after discontinuing another method type among both never-married and postmarried women (Grady et al., 1987a,b), most

_____

[5]Important contraindications include thromboembolic disease, PID, cancer, liver disease, jaundice, sickle-cell anemia, and herpes gestationis.

likely to be adopted after an abortion among single women (Margolis et al., 1974), and most likely to be switched to in the event of a marital separation (Bumpass and Rindfuss, 1984).

SES is expected to be positively related to the adoption of the contraceptive implant because of the greater opportunity costs associated with an unintended birth among high-status women, especially highly educated women. As noted by (Callahan, 1970), education provides employment opportunities and the chance to achieve status as well as encouraging "a rational more purposive attitude toward fertility" (p. 296). This prediction is further strengthened by noting that there is a positive relationship between SES and OC pill use among U.S. women choosing their first contraceptive method (Mosher and Bachrach, 1987), among both U.S. (Grady et al., 1989) and Malaysian (Reboussin et al., 1989) women adopting a new method after discontinuing another method type, and among method adopters in a clinic in Sri Lanka (Basnayake, Thapa, and Balogh, 1988). However, it should also be noted that a negative relationship between SES and OC pill use is found among method acceptors in clinic studies based in Thailand (Satayapan, Kanchanasinith, and Varakamin, 1983) and Indonesia (Lubis et al., 1983).

Little information exists regarding the effects of demographic characteristics on the discontinuation of implants.[6] Existing studies of the NORPLANT® implant largely examine how side effects are related to discontinuation. A study by Lubis et al. (1983), however, does show that termination for menstrual problems is positively related to age but that the overall discontinuation rate for non-pregnancy-related reasons is negatively related to age. This overall negative age relationship is not surprising given that it has been found for all contraceptive methods in the United States (Vaughan et al., 1980; Hammerslough, 1984; Grady et al., 1983; Grady, Hayward, and Yagi, 1986). The types of side effects evidenced by the implant, then, are only expected to somewhat mitigate the general negative effect of age.

The expected effect of parity is less clear. In multivariate analyses of contraceptive discontinuation among women in the United States, Hammerslough (1984) finds that the risk of stopping all

---

[6]Here, as well as in our discussion of other method types, our consideration is limited to discontinuation after an interval of continuous use. Readoption of the method after a pregnancy termination or after a period of no method use is not considered, since we regard these behaviors to be part of the method adoption process.

method use is negatively related to parity, but Grady, Hayward, and Florey (1988) find no effect of parity on either stopping all method use or stopping use to change methods. Declines in discontinuation with increased age and parity, however, are consistent with the notion that the costs of an unintended birth are higher for older, higher-parity women who are more likely to have completed their family building. These women would therefore be expected to be more consistent method users. Further, they are probably more experienced method users who have identified the characteristics they want in a method and thus experience less dissatisfaction during its use.

Marital status may evidence countervailing effects on the risk of discontinuation. If the costs of an unintended birth are higher for single than for married women, the risk of discontinuation of the highly effective implant should be lower for the former group. Single women who experience less consistent exposure to intercourse may also value its coitus-independent feature and therefore be unlikely to discontinue use. On the other hand, this more sporadic exposure to intercourse may lead single women to choose not to continue exposing themselves to the potential side effects of the method when they are not in a sexual relationship, but this would be reduced by the fact that removal of the method is a medical procedure. Further, the high degree of effectiveness and the coitus-independent nature of the implant should be important features for married women who typically have higher coital frequencies. Overall, then, we expect discontinuation rates to be lower among single women than among married women of the same age, but the difference should not be large.

Some previous research on contraceptive discontinuation indicates that the risk of discontinuation increases with SES (e.g., Vaughan et al., 1980; Grady et al., 1983; Keller et al., 1981; Hammerslough, 1984). Vaughan et al. (1980) and Hammerslough (1984) demonstrate that this relationship results from the greater likelihood of women of a high SES to switch method types; they are actually *less* likely to stop all method use. The usual explanation for this finding is that women of a high SES have greater access to information about various alternative methods and their characteristics and may be more likely to discontinue use of a method if they experience any dissatisfaction with it. In contrast, Grady, Hayward, and Florey (1988) find that during the period from 1979 to 1982, there was an overall negative relationship between SES and discontinuation, and that SES had no significant effect on the risk of stopping to change method types. They explain their findings by suggesting that the opportunity costs of an unintended birth are higher for women of a high SES, and thus, they may be more consistent method users. The divergent and general conclusions about the effect of SES on the discontinuation of any method type allows us to speculate only about this factor's likely effect on the implant. However, given the implant's high effectiveness, convenience, and limited number of side effects, it may be that the opportunity cost explanation takes precedence over the dissatisfaction explanation. If so, we might therefore expect a negative, albeit small, relationship between SES and the risk of discontinuing the implant.

Because the implant is coitus independent and requires only very infrequent actions on the part of the user, demographic characteristics should affect the risk of use failure through fecundity. Because of their relationship with fecundity, we would therefore expect age and parity to negatively affect the risk of unintended pregnancy with use of the implant. Frequency of intercourse would clearly be positively related to the risk of use failure, but marital status should have no effect except through exposure to and frequency of intercourse. SES would be positively related to the risk of use failure of the implant via its effects on nutrition, access to health care, life-style, and other factors that increase fecundity. The strength of this relationship, however, may vary markedly across societies.

Biodegradable Capsules and Vaccines

From the consumer's standpoint, biodegradable capsules and vaccines have similar characteristics. Their durations of effectiveness are roughly equivalent—1 to 2 years for the vaccines and about 1.5 years for the capsules. Although the vaccine is administered via injection and the capsules are implanted, both require a clinic visit for adoption. Further, both are limited with respect to the time at which they can be discontinued. After the first-month booster, the vaccine can only be discontinued at the end of its effective life; the biodegradable capsules can only be removed within the first 6 months of implantation. In most other respects these methods are very similar to the implants. As such the effects of demographic characteristics on method adoption, discontinuation, and use-effectiveness will probably be very similar to those described above for that method type. Thus, only the expected exceptions are discussed below.

The limited times at which these methods can be discontinued may make these methods less acceptable as a means of spacing births. If so, we would not expect age and parity to negatively affect their adoption. That is, their lack of flexibility for spacing births would be expected to limit use among younger, low-parity women, but potential side effects associated with long-term use may have an equally depressing effect on use among older, higher-parity women who have completed their childbearing. If any decline in adoption with age is evidenced, it will probably be only at the oldest ages as women adopt sterilization.

In terms of method discontinuation, the major departure from the patterns described above for the implants may be an elevated rate of discontinuation at the time of entry into marriage, at least among women in their childbearing years. This would follow from the lack of flexibility of the methods for birth spacing. It is also possible that the requirement of a 1-month booster shot for the vaccine will allow demographic factors to operate on method use-effectiveness through accuracy of use. That is, some women, perhaps those who are young or of a lower SES, may be late in getting the booster or not get it at all. However, since only one follow-up is required at such a short interval after adoption, we would expect these effects to be very minor.

Injectables, the Vaginal Ring, and the Vaginal Pill

Couples will probably view injectables, the vaginal ring, and the vaginal pill as very similar to the OC pill. The only major perceived difference between these methods and the OC pill is likely to be the mode of administration, with injections given every 1 to 3 months, the vaginal ring self-inserted periodically (at 1 or more months of duration), and the vaginal pill inserted daily. Unless providers of these method types make a strong effort to differentiate them from the OC pill, then, the effects of demographic factors on their use and effectiveness should be very similar to those currently affecting pill use.

Like the pill, we might expect younger and lower-parity women who are spacing their births to adopt these nonpermanent methods.[7]

---

[7]It should be noted that three clinic-based studies offer evidence that conflicts with this hypothesis. A study in the United States (Higgens et al., 1986) finds that switching to depot-medroxy progesterone acetate (DMPA) from other method types is slightly positively associated with age, in contrast to a negative

They also will probably appeal to single women because of their effectiveness and coitus independence. For similar reasons, independent of marital status, they should be more likely to be adopted by women with high coital frequencies. A positive relationship between adoption of the vaginal ring and vaginal pill and SES is expected for the same reasons as discussed above in connection with the implants. However, the effect of SES on adoption of the injectables may be negative. High-status women may be less willing to incur the opportunity costs associated with a monthly clinic visit for an injection. They also may be less willing to endure the discomfort associated with an injection because of greater knowledge about and access to alternative methods.

The effects of demographic factors on discontinuation of the vaginal ring and vaginal pill are expected to be very similar to those found for the OC pill in previous research. However, we might expect variations from those patterns in the case of injectables. Since the injectable is administered less frequently than the OC pill and cannot be discontinued between injections, temporary discontinuation because of intermittent exposure to sexual intercourse could not occur. This would tend to reduce or eliminate marital status differences in the risk of discontinuation. Unlike the OC pill, we might also expect a strong, positive effect of SES on the discontinuation of the injectable. As noted above, the opportunity costs associated with clinic attendance may be higher for high-status women. Further, these women probably have more information about and greater access to alternative method types and may thus be less willing to endure the discomfort and inconvenience of periodic injections.

Because periodic user actions are required by these contraceptive technologies, accuracy of use becomes an important consideration in the risk of use failure. For any population subgroup, the use failure

---

association with the adoption of the pill and IUD. A study in Lagos, Nigeria, finds that adopters of DMPA, the OC pill, and the IUD are all negatively related to age; but adopters of DMPA do not evidence the decline in acceptance at the highest parity (five or more) that was found for the other two methods. Finally, a study of norethisterone enanthate, whose subjects came from a clinic in rural Mexico, shows a negative effect of age but a positive effect of parity on adoption (Meade et al., 1984). The findings from these clinic studies must be viewed with caution. It is impossible to know what kinds of information were given to the clinic clients about each method type, and in none of the clinics was the sample representative of the population of the entire society. Further, in the study based in Mexico, the subjects were selected on the basis of a lack of contraindications, no comparisons were made with adopters of other method types, and the age and parity profiles of all clinic users were not reported.

rates of the injectables and vaginal ring should be lower than those for the OC pill or vaginal pill because less frequent actions are required. Nevertheless, the effects of demographic factors on the use failure of these methods are probably very similar.

Studies of use failure based on U.S. data show that age is consistently negatively related to the risk of use failure (Vaughan et al., 1980; Grady et al., 1983; Grady, Hayward, and Yagi, 1986). Part of this relationship is undoubtedly due to the fact that frequency of intercourse (not measured in any of the studies) declines with age. However, net of frequency of intercourse, the relationship is expected to be maintained because age is negatively related to fecundity and positively related to the cost of an unintended birth.

Parity has sometimes been found to be positively related to the risk of use failure (Grady et al., 1983; Grady, Hayward, and Yagi, 1986), despite the fact that fecundity declines with parity. However, in these studies intent to have another birth, which is highly related to parity, has been included as a control variable. Since women preventing a birth have demonstrated consistently lower use failure rates than women delaying a birth (Vaughan et al., 1980; Schirm et al., 1982; Grady et al., 1983; Grady, Hayward, and Yagi, 1986), and since high-parity women are more likely to be preventing a birth, it is clear that high parity is associated with low failure rates. This is consistent with the low discontinuation rates of high-parity women (Grady, Hayward, and Florey, 1988) and is probably related to the costs of an unintended birth.

Frequency of intercourse will surely be positively related to the use failure of these methods. However, this relationship may be somewhat mitigated by the fact that women with a higher frequency of coitus are likely to be more accurate contraceptive users because of their higher risk of pregnancy. Single women have been shown to have lower risks of use failure than married women (Grady, Hayward, and Yagi, 1986), no doubt because the former group has less exposure to sexual intercourse. Controlling for coital frequency, single women would be expected to be more likely to experience a use failure with the methods considered here.

High SES is expected to be associated with low use failure rates for three reasons. First, it is positively related to the opportunity costs of an unwanted birth. Second, it is probably positively related to the ability to obtain and understand the information necessary for accurate use of a method. Finally, it may be associated with a more rational and purposive attitude toward fertility.

Barrier Methods

The barrier methods considered here are the antiviral condom, the female condom, and the disposable diaphragm. These methods are discussed together because they are of intermediate effectiveness, require an application of the technology at each coital act, and have either no health implications or have health benefits.

Because it offers protection from sexually transmitted diseases (STDs), we would expect the antiviral condom to be adopted almost exclusively by young, single individuals who have multiple sex partners. This prediction of a young, never-married profile of acceptors of this method follows from research on the adoption of the currently available condom. Bumpass and Rindfuss (1984) show that women who experience a marital dissolution are likely to abandon the condom and are unlikely to adopt that method. Further, in Grady et al.'s (1987a) study of contraceptive switching among postmarried women, so few of these women switched to this method that the risks of adoption cannot be estimated. Bumpass and Rindfuss (1984) suggest that the unpopularity of the male condom among postmarried women stems from a lack of trust and cooperation between partners. Among these women, the female condom may be particularly important because it affords protection from STDs and is a female method. We might therefore expect the female condom to appeal to single women of all ages; however, to the extent that intercourse with multiple partners is characteristic of younger women, it too may exhibit a negative age profile of use.

Both the antiviral and female condoms will probably also tend to be used by low-parity, unmarried women, to the extent that the presence of children reduces the opportunities for finding sex partners. Independent of marital status, use of both methods should be negatively related to frequency of intercourse because of their coitus-intrusive nature. Further, as with findings on adoption of the traditional condom (Bachrach, 1984; Reboussin et al., 1989), use of these methods should probably be more prevalent among high-SES men and women. This relationship is expected because high-SES individuals probably have both a greater awareness of the level of risk of STD transmission during unprotected intercourse and a greater sense of personal efficacy that would extend to the effort to control that risk.

Since both types of condoms are more special-use (primarily disease prevention) methods rather than methods intended for general fertility regulation, the effects of demographic variables on their discontinuation and use-effectiveness are very difficult to predict. Discontinuation probably increases with age and parity because of the probable effects of these two factors on the nature of sexual relationships. It probably also increases with frequency of intercourse, because the methods are coitus intrusive and decline with SES for the reasons mentioned above in the discussion of method adoption. Further, discontinuation may be higher among married than among single individuals because disease prevention will be of less concern for the former group.

In terms of use-effectiveness, the effects of demographic factors will probably parallel those found for the traditional condom. The risk of use failure should decline with age, parity, and SES; increase with frequency of intercourse; and be higher among single than among married women (net of differences in frequency of intercourse).

In developed countries like the United States, where disposable products are very popular, the disposable diaphragm will probably be viewed as little more than a convenient substitute for the durable diaphragm. If so, the effects of demographic characteristics on the adoption, discontinuation, and use-effectiveness of this new method will probably parallel those found for the older method. In developing countries, there is little information on diaphragm use since most studies do not differentiate it from other barrier methods. However, cost is likely to be a more salient evaluative criterion for the majority of couples in those countries, especially if government- and private group-sponsored family planning programs do not offer the method as an alternative.

Because the disposable diaphragm does not have the side effects associated with hormonal and steroidal methods, it is suitable for long-term use and use among older women. Thus, positive associations between method adoption and age and parity are expected. However, as is the case for the current diaphragm, a decline in use at the oldest ages among married women might be expected because of switching to sterilization. In the United States, net of the effects of age and parity, single women are more likely to use the diaphragm than married women, except at the youngest ages (Bachrach, 1984). This probably occurs because sterilization is a less viable option among single women and because there are few alternative acceptable methods for long-term use. Thus, despite its coitus-intrusive nature, the disposable diaphragm may be expected to exhibit higher adoption rates among single women unless concern about STDs promotes increasing acceptability of the condom or such new methods as implants gain acceptance among members of this group. Other things being equal, adoption of the disposable diaphragm should be negatively related to frequency of intercourse. Finally, adoption of the current diaphragm is positively related to SES. An even stronger positive effect of this factor will probably be obtained for the disposable diaphragm because of its higher cost.

Paralleling the findings for the current diaphragm, discontinuation of the disposable diaphragm is expected to be negatively related to age, parity, and SES and positively related to coital frequency. It may also be higher among single women who are less likely to be consistent method users and more likely to be contraceptive risk-takers (Grady and Hayward, 1987). The effects of demographic factors on the use failure rates of the disposable diaphragm are expected to be the same as those identified above for the antiviral and female condoms.

Postovulatory Methods

The postovulatory methods will probably serve as special purpose methods. That is, they are likely to gain their largest acceptance as methods to be used when a woman believes she has a high risk of already being pregnant, such as after an episode of unprotected intercourse or when there is reason to believe that her primary method has failed (because of improper use or failure of the technology itself).

The abortifacient nature of the postovulatory methods will clearly have dramatic effects on their acceptability, and thus on adoption and discontinuation. Objections to abortion are grounded in cultural, religious, and political beliefs. Some of the demographic factors considered here may exhibit effects on the adoption of these methods because their categories represent individuals with different beliefs about abortion. For example, younger women are the most likely to obtain a legal abortion in the United States (Henshaw, 1987). This may partially reflect a more liberal attitude toward abortion on the part of the young. Further, contraceptive risk-taking and contraceptive use failure are both highest among younger women. Given a more liberal attitude and a predisposition toward greater risk-taking, we might expect a negative effect of age on the adoption of postovulatory methods.

As another example, consider the likely effect of SES on the adoption of these methods. In the United States antiabortion activists are predominately of lower SES (Luker, 1984). Further, Luker

(1984) suggests that low-SES women in general are more likely to be against abortion because they have less chance to achieve status outside the home and therefore define their importance in terms of the family and their role as a mother. In contrast, high-SES women probably have a more rational, purposive attitude toward fertility and probably experience greater opportunity costs when they have an unwanted birth. For these reasons, then, we might expect a positive relationship between SES and adoption of the postovulatory methods.

To the extent that these methods are used only rarely and for accidental pregnancies, rather than as a primary method, contraceptive discontinuation is not an issue. In addition, the chances of use failure will probably be very small, given the high motivation of all adopters, the medical prescription and supervision required, and the fact that steroids are taken orally for only 3 days together with a prostaglandin vaginal suppository. The major source of use failure, other than failure of the technology itself, would be a lack of understanding of the instructions received. Understanding of the instructions may be positively affected by age and SES.

Male Methods

The last group of methods to be discussed consists of the male methods. These include the gossypol pill, luteinizing hormone-releasing hormone (LHRH) + androgen (injection and possibly oral supplement), and percutaneous vas occlusion (sterilization). All of these methods are highly effective and coitus independent but vary according to the frequency of user action and reversibility. The gossypol pill requires the most frequent application, with daily pills taken for the first 3 months after adoption followed by one pill twice a week. Even though it requires frequent action on the user's part, a major possible side effect is possible irreversibility. In contrast to the gossypol pill, the sterilization technique requires only a single application. It, too, is irreversible. The LHRH + androgen method will probably require monthly injections of peptide and periodic supplemental injections or orally taken steroids. The possible side effects of this method are as yet undetermined. However, its cost is expected to be high.

The irreversibility of the sterilization technique means that its appeal would probably be limited to older and higher-parity men who have completed their family-building careers. The possible side effects resulting from long-term use of LHRH + androgen or the gossypol pill would probably result in a negative effect of age on adoption, but the effect of parity may differ for each. The possible irreversibility of the gossypol pill would make it unsuitable as a method for spacing births and lead to higher adoption rates among higher-parity men. In contrast, the LHRH + androgen method is the only male method considered here that is suitable for use in spacing wanted births. It may therefore evidence a negative association with parity because as men achieve their desired family size they would be likely to switch to a less costly method without the side effects associated with long-term use.

All of these methods may have limited appeal to single men who are not in stable, long-term relationships. This is expected to occur for one of two reasons. First, for the gossypol pill (which is potentially irreversible) and sterilization, men who are unable to have children may be disadvantaged in their search for a marital relationship. Second, all three methods may be unattractive to the partners of men in short-term, uncommitted relationships. That is, it is possible that women in such relationships may have limited confidence that their male partner is actually using contraception or is sterile until some level of mutual trust has been established.

Because of their coitus-independent nature and their high effectiveness, all of these methods would be more attractive to men who have a high frequency of sexual intercourse. They are also more likely to be adopted by men of high SES because these males would incur higher opportunity costs in the event of an unwanted birth.

The effects of demographic factors on the discontinuation of those male methods that can be stopped or reversed are expected to parallel the patterns anticipated for women who use similar methods. Discontinuation is expected to be lower among men who are older, of higher parity, and who have a higher frequency of coitus. Higher discontinuation is anticipated among single men, who may have more intermittent sexual relationships, and among higher-status men. The latter relationship is expected because, like higher-status women, these men would probably be more likely to change method types in the event of dissatisfaction, given a greater knowledge of and access to alternative methods.

The use failure rates of the gossypol pill and LHRH + androgen are expected to be negatively related to age and SES because the opportunity costs associated with an unwanted birth are probably higher for older and higher-status men. Further, we anticipate that single men will demonstrate higher use failure rates than married men because of less consistent exposure to sexual intercourse. That is, single men may sometimes not consistently use their method during periods when they are not sexually active. Since the injectable requires infrequent user action, however, this relationship may not be as great for this method type. SES is expected to have a negative effect on that risk. High-status men, as noted above, probably have higher opportunity costs associated with an unwanted birth but may also be better able to acquire and use information about accurate method use and fertility in general.

SUMMARY AND CONCLUSIONS

The objective of this paper has been to develop some under-standing about how selected demographic factors might affect the adoption, discontinuation, and effectiveness of new contraceptive technologies. To accomplish this objective, we have attempted to extend to the new technologies findings from research on existing method types that share important characteristics with the new methods. The result of this effort is summarized in Appendix A, which presents expected relationships, for each new method type, between demographic variables and each dimension of contraceptive use and effectiveness.

It is important to note, however, that in the course of preparing this paper it has become apparent that our knowledge of the ways in which demographic factors affect the use and effectiveness of existing methods is so rudimentary that extrapolation to new methods is very difficult. Our lack of understanding stems from a number of sources. Among the most important of these is measurement problems. For example, the adoption and discontinuation processes have seldom been examined separately. Most studies of method choice or accept-ability have instead focused on contraceptive prevalence, providing little information about how demographic characteristics are related to the underlying adoption and discontinuation processes.

A major reason for the focus on contraceptive prevalence is that an examination of either method adoption or discontinuation re-quires detailed information about sexual, contraceptive, and marital behaviors. Such information is typically not obtained in most sur-veys, particularly in developing countries. Our knowledge about how demographic factors affect contraceptive failure is limited for the same reasons. Because of data limitations, most population-based studies of contraceptive failure have relied on a measure known as the Pearl Index that has been likened to a "rubber yardstick."

Even those studies that have explicitly focused on adoption or discontinuation and have used life table measures of discontinuation and use failure have fallen far short of the ideal. Crucial variables, such as frequency of intercourse, have been omitted from all of the analyses. Further, the analyses of discontinuation and use failure all suffer from severe problems of selectivity. Some of these problems could be overcome in clinic-based studies, where prospective information is obtained, but they also are subject to selectivity biases and usually do not examine or report the effects of demographic characteristics.

Another major reason for our lack of understanding about contraceptive behaviors is that cultural context may have very important effects on the use and acceptability of various methods and that multiple cultural contexts may exist within even a single society. Given the primitive level of our understanding of the very complex demographic processes within any single society, the task of understanding how cultural context creates differences across societies quickly becomes overwhelming. Further, the effects of both demographic factors and cultural context on each of the contraceptive behaviors examined here may also vary according to the type of method considered and the types of alternative methods available.

The final major problem, and perhaps the most important one, is that there are no fully developed conceptual models of how demographic factors may affect contraceptive behavior. Although some models, primarily psychological and economic, have been applied to the examination of contraceptive choice or contraceptive risk-taking, they often omit demographic characteristics from the model, and there has been no attempt to incorporate the three highly interrelated behaviors (adoption, discontinuation, and use failure) considered here into a single model.

In summary, our current understanding of the demographic processes underlying the adoption, discontinuation, and use failure of current methods is incomplete. Thus, the expected demographic relationships identified in this paper should be regarded as more speculative in nature than as a set of firm predictions.

ACKNOWLEDGMENT

The authors acknowledge the assistance of Mary Kay Dugan in the preparation of this manuscript.

REFERENCES

Bachrach, C.A.
  1984   Contraceptive practice among American women, 1973–1982. *Family Planning Perspectives* 16(6):253–259.
Basnayake, S., S. Thapa, and S.A. Balogh
  1988   Evaluation of safety, efficacy, and acceptability of the Norplant® implants in Sri Lanka. *Studies in Family Planning* 19(1):39–47.
Bumpass, L., and R.R. Rindfuss
  1984   The effect of marital dissolution on contraceptive protection. *Family Planning Perspectives* 16:271–274.
Callahan, D.
  1970   *Abortion: Law, Choice and Morality.* London: Collier-Macmillan.
Dawson, D.A.
  1986   The effects of sex education on adolescent behavior. *Family Planning Perspectives* 18:162–170.
Gorosh, M.
  1982   Patterns of contraceptive use among female adolescents: Method consistency in a clinic setting. *Journal of Adolescent Health Care* 3:96–102.
Grady, W.R., and M.D. Hayward
  1987   *Contraceptive Discontinuation Among Women in the United States: January 1, 1979–July 1, 1982.* Seattle, Wash.: Battelle Memorial Institute.
Grady, W.R., M.D. Hayward, and F.A. Florey
  1988   Contraceptive discontinuation among married women in the United States. *Studies in Family Planning* 19(4):227–235.
Grady, W.R., M.D. Hayward, and J. Yagi
  1986   Contraceptive failure in the United States: Estimates from the 1982 National Survey of Family Growth. *Family Planning Perspectives* 18:200–209.
Grady, W.R., M.D. Hayward, J.O.G. Billy, and F.A. Florey
  1987a   *Contraceptive Switching among Post Married Women in the United States.* Seattle, Wash,: Battelle Memorial Institute.
  1987b   *Contraceptive Switching among Never Married Women in the United States.* Seattle, Wash.: Battelle Memorial Institute.
  1989   Contraceptive switching among married women in the United States. *Journal of Biosocial Science.* Forthcoming.
Grady, W.R., M.B. Hirsch, N. Keen, and B. Vaughan
  1983   Contraceptive failure and continuation among married women in the U.S., 1970–1975. *Family Planning Perspectives* 14(1):9–19.
Hammerslough, C.R.
  1984   Characteristics of women who stop using contraceptives. *Family Planning Perspectives* 16(1):14–18.

Henshaw, S.K.
  1987   Characteristics of U.S. women having abortions, 1982–1983. *Family Planning Perspectives* 19(1):5–9.
Higgins, J.E., I-Cheng Chi, L.R. Wilkens, and R.A. Hatcher
  1986   Patterns of Depo-Provera use in a large family planning clinic in the United States. *Journal of Biosocial Science* 18:379–386.
Keller, A., R.A. Jiminez, J.G. Figuero, and A.R. de Rodriguez
  1981   Limitations of life table analysis: Empirical evidence from Mexico. *Studies in Family Planning* 12(10):341–345.
Lubis, F., J. Prihartono, T. Agoestina, B. Affandi, and H. Sutedi
  1983   One-year experience with Norplant® implants in Indonesia. *Studies in Family Planning* 14(6/7):181–183.
Luker, K.
  1984   The war between women. *Family Planning Perspectives* 16(3):105–110.
Marangoni, P., S. Cartagena, J. Diaz, and A. Faundes
  1983   Norplant® implants and the TCu 200g IUD: A comparative study in Ecuador. *Studies in Family Planning* 14(6/7):177–180.
Margolis, A., R.R. Rindfuss, P. Coghlan, and R. Rochat
  1974   Contraception after abortion. *Family Planning Perspectives* 6:56–60.
Meade, C.W., L.P.M. Casarin, M.A. Diaz, A.G. Aquado, L.S. Zacaris, S. Holck, P. Diethelm, and J. Annus
  1984   A clinical study of norethisterone enanthate in rural Mexico. *Studies in Family Planning* 15(3):143–148.
Mosher, W.D., and C.A. Bachrach
  1987   First premarital contraceptive use in the United States: Determinants and trends, 1960s–1982. *Studies in Family Planning* 18(2):83–95.
Pearl, R.
  1932   Contraception and fertility in 2000 women. *Human Biology* 4:363–407.
Potter, R.G., Jr.
  1966   Application of life table techniques to measurement of contraceptive effectiveness. *Demography* 3(3):297–304.
Reboussin, D., J. Da Vanzo, E. Starbird, T.B. Ann, and S. Abdullah
  1989   Contraceptive method switching over women's reproductive careers. *Journal of Biosocial Science.* Forthcoming.
Ryder, N.B.
  1973   Contraceptive failure in the United States. *Family Planning Perspectives* 5:130–141.
Satayapan, S., K. Kanchanasinith, and S. Varakamin
  1983   Perceptions and acceptability of Norplant® implants in Thailand. *Studies in Family Planning* 14(6/7):170–176.
Schirm, A., J. Trussell, J. Menken, and W.R. Grady
  1982   Contraceptive failure in the United States: The impact of social, economic, and demographic factors. *Family Planning Perspectives* 14:68–80.
Shaaban, M.S., M. Salah, A. Zarzour, and S.A. Abdullah
  1983   A prospective study of Norplant® implants and the TCu 380g IUD in Assiut, Egypt. *Studies in Family Planning* 14(6/7):163–169.

Sivin, I., S. Diaz, P. Holma, F. Alaverez-Sanchez, and D.N. Robertson
   1983
        A four-year clinical study of Norplant® implants. *Studies in Family Planning* 14(6/7):184–191.
Steven, E.H., R.R. Rindfuss, and F.B. Bean
   1987   Racial differences in contraceptive choice. *Demography* 25(1):53–70.
Taffel, S.M., and P.J. Placek
   1980   Postpartum sterilization in cesarean and noncesarean deliveries: 1970–1975, United States. *NCHS Working Paper Series* 2:1–14.
Tietze, C., and S. Lewitt
   1973   Recommended procedures for the statistical evaluation of intrauterine contraception. *Studies in Family Planning* 4(2):35–42.
Trussell, J., and K. Kost
   1987   Contraceptive failure in the United States: A critical review of the literature. *Studies in Family Planning* 18(5):237–283.
Trussell, J., and J. Menken
   1980   The calculation of gross rates of continuation for contraceptive methods: Single and multiple increment life tables. In *Contraceptive Efficacy Among Married Women Aged 15–44 Years. Vital and Health Statistics*, Series 23, No. 5. National Center for Health Statistics. Washington, D.C.: U.S. Government Printing Office.
Trussell, J., and C.F. Westoff
   1980   Contraceptive practice and trends in coital frequency. *Family Planning Perspectives* 12:246–249.
Trussell, J., R. Faden, and R.A. Hatcher
   1976   Efficacy information in contraceptive counseling: Those little white lies. *American Journal of Public Health* 66(8):761–767.
Tsui, A., V. De Silva, D. Hamill, and S. Thapa
   1988   Contraceptive method change in rural Sri Lanka. *Journal of Biosocial Science* 18(5):237–283.
Vaughan, B., J. Trussell, J. Menken, E.F. Jones, and W.R. Grady
   1980   *Contraceptive Efficacy Among Married Women Aged 15–44 Years. Vital and Health Statistics*, Series 23, No. 5. National Center for Health Statistics. Washington, D.C.: U.S. Government Printing Office.
Zelnik, M., and J.F. Kantner
   1977   Sexual and contraceptive experience of young unmarried women in the U.S., 1976 and 1971. *Family Planning Perspectives* 9(2):55–71.
   1979   Reasons for nonuse of contraception by sexually active women aged 15–19. *Family Planning Perspectives* 11:289–296.
   1980   Sexual activity, contraceptive use and pregnancy among metropolitan-area teenagers: 1971–1979. *Family Planning Perspectives* 12:230–237.
Zelnik, M., and F.K. Shah
   1983   First intercourse among young Americans. *Family Planning Perspectives* 15:64–70.

APPENDIX A

APPENDIX A Expected Effects of Selected Demographic Characteristics on the Adoption, Discontinuation, and Use Failure Rates of New Contraceptive Technologies

Method Types and Event	Demographic Characteristics				
	Age	Parity	Marital Status	Coital Frequency	SES
Implants					
Adoption	-	-	S > M	+	+
Discontinuation	-	-	S < M	-	-
Use failure	-	-	0	+	+
Vaccines and biodegradable capsules					
Adoption	0	0	S > M	+	+
Discontinuation	-	-	S < M	-	-
Use failure	-	-	0	+	+
Injectables, vaginal ring, and vaginal pill					
Injectables					
Adoption	-	-	S > M	+	-
Discontinuation	-	-	0	-	-
Use failure	-	-	S > M	+	-
Vaginal ring and pill					
Adoption	-	-	S > M	+	+
Discontinuation	-	-	S > M	-	-
Use failure	-	-	S > M	+	-
Barrier methods					
Antiviral and female condoms					
Adoption	-	-	S > M	-	+
Discontinuation	+	+	S < M	+	-
Use failure	-	-	S > M	+	-
Disposable diaphragm					
Adoption	+	+	S > M	-	+
Discontinuation	-	-	S > M	+	-
Use failure	-	-	S > M	+	-
Post-ovulatory methods					
Adoption	-	+	S > M	+	+
Discontinuation	n.a.	n.a.	n.a.	n.a.	n.a.
Use failure	-	0	0	0	-
Male methods					
Percutaneous sterilization					
Adoption	+	+	S < M	+	+
Discontinuation	n.a.	n.a.	n.a.	n.a.	n.a.
Use failure	n.a.	n.a.	n.a.	n.a.	n.a.
Gossypol pill					
Adoption	-	+	S < M	+	+
Discontinuation	-	-	S > M	-	-
Use failure	-	-	S > M	+	-

APPENDIX A--Continued

Method Types and Event	Demographic Characteristics				
	Age	Parity	Marital Status	Coital Frequency	SES
LHRH + androgen injectable					
Adoption	-	-	S < M	+	+
Discontinuation	-	-	S > M	-	-
Use failure	-	-	S > M	+	-

NOTE: + = Positive effect; - = negative effect; 0 = no effect; S = single; M = married; n.a. = not applicable.

Programmatic Factors in Contraceptive Use-Effectiveness: Lessons Learned from Operations Research

INTRODUCTION: SYSTEMS PERSPECTIVE ON THE SUPPLY OF CONTRACEPTIVES

Family planning programs are organized efforts to provide individuals and couples with information, supplies, and services to control their fertility. Given the high theoretical effectiveness of most modern methods, the introduction of a new contraceptive technology provides only marginal gains in effectiveness. Major impacts, however, are possible in extending appropriate use, through greater continuation and wider acceptance (Berelson, 1976). The principal operational goals for a new contraceptive technology, then, are greater acceptance and use-effectiveness, taking into account all the deficiencies in the ways that a method is delivered and actually used.

The significance of this issue is evident when analyzing the failure to successfully introduce the intrauterine device (IUD) in India. The IUD was an inexpensive, reversible, and effective method that could be inserted either by physicians or trained auxiliaries. It appeared to fit every requirement and was quickly introduced. Nevertheless, the success was short-lived, as inadequacies in screening, poor follow-up, complications, and exaggerated rumors led to high discontinuation rates and a 7-year slump in insertions. The program had quite simply been rushed through without the organizational preparation needed to deal with user's realistic concerns (Soni, 1983).

Based on these experiences, more recent introductory efforts, for example, NORPLANT® and the vaginal ring, have specifically attempted to manage method delivery. Emphasis has been placed on

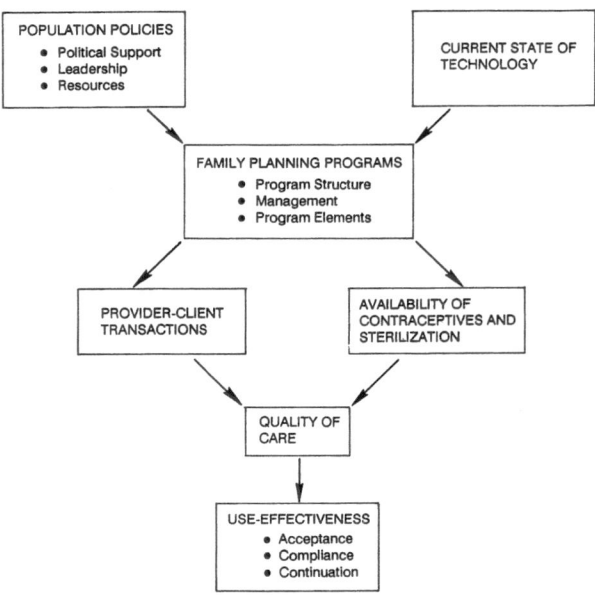

FIGURE 1   Supply-side elements of family planning effectiveness.

training providers, preparing information materials for clients and providers, and counseling (Population Council, 1987). However, contraceptive introduction does not depend only on providers and users. A National Research Council report (Simmons and Lapham, 1986) characterized family planning programs as systems with many interrelated parts and complex relationships with the social, economic, and political environment as well as with users. Essentially, the successful introduction of a new contraceptive technology is contingent on the existence of favorable conditions in many parts of the system.

For example, Figure 1 illustrates how elements of supply influence use-effectiveness. Both population policies and the current state of contraceptive technology contribute to the ways that programs are structured and how management mobilizes program elements to provide methods to users. By increasing the availability of contraceptives and improving the quantity and quality of provider-client transactions, overall quality of care is enhanced and use-effectivness (i.e. acceptance, compliance, and continuation) is improved (Jain, 1988).

This paper examines the lessons that have been learned from operations research projects as the empirical basis for informed speculation on how program variables can affect the acceptability and efficacy of new methods.

THE DATA BASE ON PROGRAMMATIC FACTORS

Empirical work on the nature of programs and their effects is limited (Simmons and Lapham, 1986). The use of methods has been analyzed extensively in major sample surveys (e.g., knowledge, attitude, and practice [KAP] Surveys, the World Fertility Survey [WFS], and the Demographic and Health Surveys [DHS]). The focus has been on individual acceptors, however, and has largely ignored method use as a product of organized service delivery (Finkle and Ness, 1985). The principal source of information on programmatic factors is the data base on operations research, including about 200 studies supported by the U.S. Agency for International Development (U.S. AID) and the World Health Organization (WHO) since the early 1970s (Gallen and Rinehart, 1986). Other health care services research is more qualitative in nature and examines program successes and shortcomings from a user's perspective (Ainsworth, 1985; Bruce, 1987).

Recent operations research has been experimental in nature, systematically examining the impact of changes in specific program components. Yet, in the absence of a coherent theory of program operations, the research has focused on resolving the specific service delivery problems faced by managers and less on testing, in a systematic fashion, hypotheses about overall program operations. Less emphasis is currently placed on collecting data on use-effectiveness and continuation; and more emphasis is placed on contraceptive prevalence, couple-years of protection provided and cost-effectiveness, variables that are more often used in program management. Operations research provides a wealth of experience, and lessons have been learned that can be applied to the introduction of new methods in family planning programs.

PROGRAMMATIC FACTORS AS DETERMINANTS OF USE-EFFECTIVENESS: MANAGERS

Family planning managers are the critical link between policy and contraceptive technology. They are the gatekeepers to the successful introduction and supply of new or underutilized methods.

While some decisions on introduction are based on legal and political considerations (e.g., the status of the abortifacient RU-486 in countries where abortion is illegal), others are often entirely in the hands of the manager. Their political acumen and personal style can make a significant difference in program operations. For example, in Malaysia a program director decided not to offer IUDs out of concern for the religious sensitivities of Muslim women, by interpreting the rule of cleanliness in prayer as a proscription against the presence of an IUD in the body during prayer (Finkle and Ness, 1985). In contrast, in rural Bas Zaire, a single physician was responsible for two-thirds of modern method use by providing surgical contraception for women with elevated reproductive risk (Bertrand et al., 1985).

Effective program managers are prepared to make adjustments routinely in their programs to accommodate new information and new technology, whether it be computers or contraceptive methods (Roper, 1987). Because managers are able to manipulate program delivery systems, it is within these systems that the successful introduction of contraceptive methods occurs.

CHARACTERISTICS OF METHODS AND DELIVERY SYSTEMS

Although nearly 30 contraceptive products or leads are in the development process, the 16 methods that will be available before the year 2000 are relatively simple to characterize. Three-fourths (12 methods) of the methods are designed for females, and nearly two-thirds (10 methods) are provider-dependent, most of which (6 methods) require medical staff. One method, RU-486, is not really a contraceptive but is an abortifacient. Many of the methods are really not new but, rather, are adaptations of existing methods (e.g., implants, condoms, IUDs, and injectables).

Most of these methods have improved on the effectiveness and safety of their earlier presentations. Yet, irregular bleeding remains a highly unacceptable side effect of the long-acting steriods, which account for more than half (7 methods) of all new methods for women. Also, half of the methods are either coitus related (e.g., condom) or require that females touch their genital organs (e.g., vaginal suppository, vaginal pill, and vaginal rings), both of which are characteristics of less acceptable methods.

TABLE 1 Relative Method Appropriateness to Delivery Systems

New Methods	Hospital or Clinic Delivery	Community-Based Distribution	Commercial or Social Marketing
Female methods			
Steroids			
Implants (two methods)	A,A	I,I	I,I
Injectables (two methods)	A,A,	A,A	A,A
Medicated vaginal rings (two methods)	LA,LA	A,A	A,A
Medicated IUD	A	I	I
Vaginal pill	LA	A	A
Postovulatory, RU-486	A	I	I
Vaccine, anti-human chorionic gonadotropin	A	I	I
Vaginal			
Female condom	LA	A	A
Disposable diaphragm	A	I	I
Male methods			
Antiviral condom	LA	A	A
Gossypol pill	LA	A	A
LHRH[a], injectable	A	I	I
Vasectomy, percutaneous	A	I	I

NOTE: A = appropriate; LA = less appropriate; I = inappropriate.

[a]LHRH = Luteinizing hormone-releasing hormone.

SOURCE: Adapted from Hutchings and Saunders (1985).

Nevertheless, the analysis of new technology is not complete without consideration of the corresponding service delivery mechanisms (Bruce, 1987). Table 1 illustrates the relative method appropriateness for different delivery systems. It suggests that 10 of the methods are more appropriate for hospital or clinic delivery systems, and 6 are less appropriate (i.e., the oral, condom, and medicated vaginal ring methods). Half of the methods are appropriate for community-based and commercial distribution systems; only the injectables are appropriate for all three delivery systems.

The choices of delivery systems and providers are important, as each strategy has strengths in reaching different segments of the population. Most hospitals and clinics offer limited accessibility, provide services largely for mothers and children, and are burdened with high operational costs. Postpartum programs may, however, reach a sizable proportion of users (e.g., in social security systems) and offer a unique opportunity to influence maternal and child health. Community-based distribution (CBD) programs are more accessible, but they serve mostly rural and poor urban populations and are faced with the problem of continuing recruitment and training of community health care workers. Commercial and social marketing systems, even those that are subsidized, rely on existing commercial distribution channels and target a paying public.

Regardless of the delivery system, the most effective strategy to increase prevalence is to concentrate on recruiting a manageable number of acceptors and providing high-quality care to ensure their continuation (Berelson, 1976; Jain, 1988). For this reason, it is important not to focus on the continuation of a particular method but, rather, to be concerned about the aggregate contraceptive behavior of couples. This recognizes the practice among users of switching between methods to conform to their different needs, ages, and lifestyles. Programs must be flexible enough to allow for changing preferences, as well as to provide quality support once methods are selected.

PROGRAM ELEMENTS

Program elements are components of delivery systems whose configurations can be manipulated by managers. Aspects of each major element are reviewed here to show its role in improving use-effectiveness.

Availability of and Access to Contraceptive Methods

The essence of availability is increasing the quantity of contact between providers and clients, as well as providing them with a broad range of contraceptive options from which to choose. The assumption is that programs that offer a full range of contraceptive technologies will be more able to provide methods that are acceptable to a large number of users.

Much of the early work on the impact of CBD programs has demonstrated that availability leads to greater use (McGuire, 1984). In the early CBD programs, the median impact on contraceptive use prevalence was approximately 20 percentage points (range, 3–47 percentage points), with the increase largely being attributable to the greater use of oral contraceptives. More recently, a number of studies on medical backup services to CBD programs suggest that use of the IUD, when effectively offered in urban CBD programs, can also be increased significantly. In Peru, the number of IUDs inserted increased from 125 to 1,387 in a CBD program experimental area within 1 year, largely because of referrals from promoters. Moreover, IUD insertions increased linearly with increased frequency of clinic sessions, up to four a month (Ramos et al., 1986).

It is important to realize that the more subtle forms of limited access (e.g., waiting time, weak referral links, fewer hours devoted to the provision of a given method, less well prepared staff, and unnecessarily restrictive admission requirements) negatively influence the number of clients who select a particular method, as well as their willingness to continue use (Bruce, 1988). Fortunately, improving access is almost always easier and less costly for managers to achieve than increasing the number of delivery systems or service points. For example, in Mexico merely moving condoms from the shelves of a supermarket to the display space next to the cashiers nearly doubled the number of condoms sold per month, as well as reduced pilfering (De la Macorra, Roca, and Townsend, 1987).

Expanding the choice of methods contributes significantly to increased use. Because offering users a choice of methods is central to the quality of care, the addition of one method to those available may produce an increase of about 12 percent in the use of contraceptives (Jain, 1988). The experience in Matlab, Bangladesh (Figure 2), demonstrated that broadening the choice of available methods increased overall prevalence: Household provision of injectables raised contraceptive prevalence from 7 to 20 percent in 1977, the introduction of sterilization services contributed to the addition of 10 percentage points in prevalence in 1978, and the household insertion of IUDs raised the prevalence further in 1981 (Phillips et al., 1987).

Choice is also important for continuation of contraceptive use. The WHO study (1980) on method choice concluded that when women are given balanced information and a genuine choice of contraceptive methods, their preference of method often differed from that used previously. Moreover, in a study in Indonesia, 85 percent of the women who were denied the method they originally requested discontinued use of the method they did receive within a year, whereas only 25 percent of those who received the method they requested discontinued use (Pariani et al., 1987).

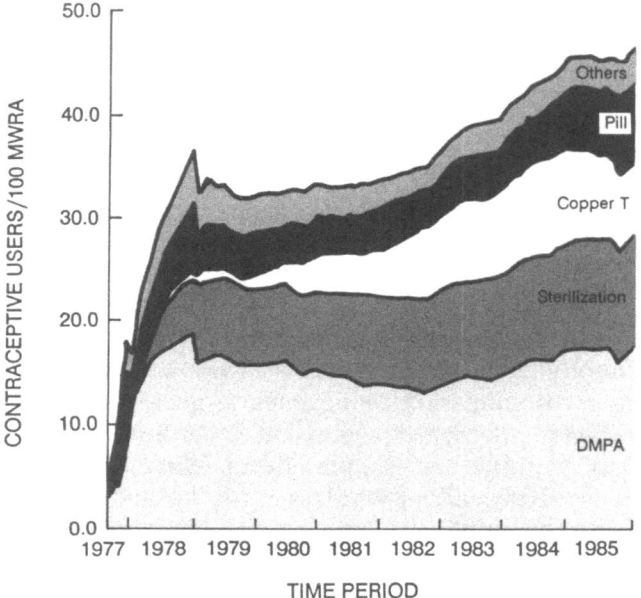

FIGURE 2   Time trend in Matlab, Bangladesh, treatment area. Contraceptive use prevalence among currently married women by method, 1977–1985. Source: Phillips (1987).

Efforts to increase choice should not be limited only to the more effective methods. Evidence indicates that combining methods, each with a relatively low level of effectiveness (e.g., natural family planning and condoms), may lead to levels of use-effectiveness comparable to those obtained with oral or injectable methods (Thapa, 1988).

Selection, Training, and Supervision of Personnel

From the client's perspective, contraceptive technology cannot be separated from the delivery system or the individual providers. The issue of personnel selection—who should be the provider—has been much debated. Studies in a number of countries have demonstrated that community health care workers can safely provide oral contraceptives, condoms, and injectable contraceptives and that paramedical personnel (i.e., nurses and midwives) can successfully insert IUDs (Treiman and Liskin, 1988). Certainly, in the countries where competency-based training is available, one would expect that the same personnel would be able to insert implants, fit diaphragms, and perform other relatively simple service tasks often solely reserved for medical personnel.

There is considerable support for the principle that females are more acceptable providers of most family planning services for females (Repetto, 1987). Although in a Moroccan household delivery project male and female workers proved to be equally able to recruit new users of contraception, projects in Bangladesh (Phillips, 1987), Ecuador (Salvador et al., 1987), and Nigeria (Lapido et al., 1985) have demonstrated that females are more acceptable deliverers, particularly in providing information to women about oral and barrier methods. In the introduction of new methods for women, females may also be more responsive to users' concerns for information. There is some debate about whether males are also more acceptable providers of contraceptive services for males.

While efforts to design more safe and effective IUDs have been made over the past 20 years, the quality of care that IUD users receive (e.g., counseling and insertion technique) may make more of a difference to IUD performance than the design of a specific IUD. The health care providers' practical training and experience, particularly with respect to insertion technique, are especially important for continuation of use, given that 24-month continuation rates for both the TCu-200 and TCu-380A IUDs vary from 50 to 90 percent among programs (Treiman and Liskin, 1988).

In areas of Sri Lanka where doctors and public health midwives received refresher training that emphasized insertion technique, counseling, and followup, rates of termination caused by expulsion or complications were significantly lower than in those areas where there was no special training (Figure 3) (Fisher and De Silva, 1986). Furthermore, where the trained midwives worked alone or with satisfied users, the number of new IUD acceptors recruited was significantly higher than that in the no-treatment comparison areas (Figure 4).

Competency-based training is becoming an increasingly important issue for CBD programs as well. A number of research projects with successful community-based programs in Latin America have

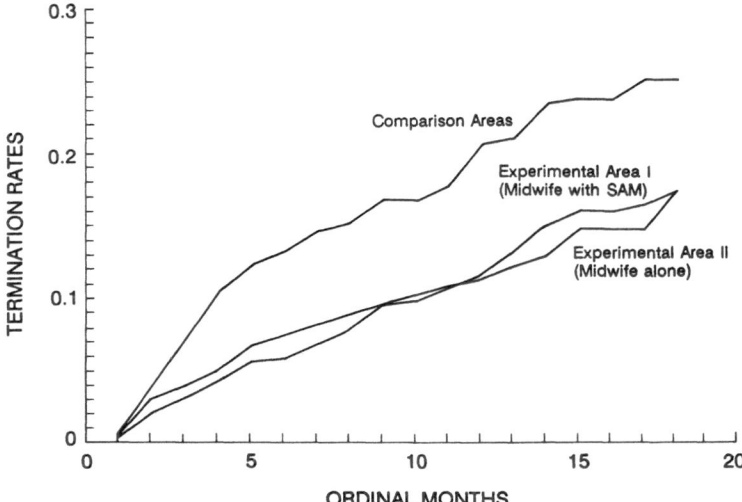

FIGURE 3   Age-standardized cumulative gross IUD termination rates for study areas in Sri Lanka. SAM = Satisfied acceptor motivator. Source: Fisher and De Silva (1986).

highlighted serious problems with compliance on the part of users of oral contraceptives. In addition, providers have been found to be deficient in their knowledge of how to identify women with contraindications, deal with side effects, and explain how to use the method appropriately (Bertrand et al., 1980; Potter et al., 1987; Townsend and Ojeda, 1985). If health care workers were more skilled at providing information on how to use self-administered methods, use-effectiveness would undoubtedly be improved.

Most important, for performance to be maintained at acceptable levels, periodic supervision is essential. Supervision should improve workers' knowledge of indications, contraindications, as well as practical instructions on how to use a method. For example, when nurse-midwives in Turkey were evaluated after at least 1 year of field work, 68 percent of those who had been visited by a supervisor since training performed adequately. In contrast, only 40 percent of those who had not been visited by a supervisor performed adequately (WHO, 1986). Other results from Colombia suggest that supervision that includes on-the-job training may be the most cost-effective mechanism for improving CBD programs distributors' knowledge about the use of oral contraceptives, the IUD, and natural family planning (Vernon and Ojeda, 1988).

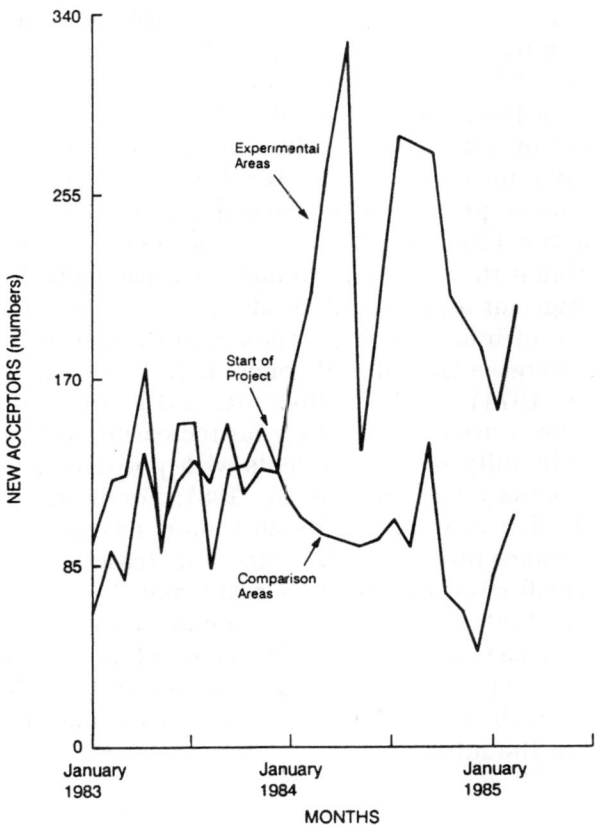

FIGURE 4   New IUD acceptors in study areas in Sri Lanka from January 1983 through January 1985. Source: Fisher and De Silva (1986).

Information, Education, and Communications

The basic proposition of information, education, and communications is that people who are well informed will use the method better. Information, education, and communications help to ensure that clients are satisfied, will return for services, and will recommend the method to others (Gallen and Lettenmaier, 1987). Service providers who helped users understand and manage use-related side effects were able to positively affect use, continuation, and satisfaction. A study in Mexico found a strong relationship between the receipt of accurate information about methods, including possible side effects, and the client's continuation of use and ability to resist negative, ill-founded rumors (Keller, 1973).

Compliance with instructions for correct use is a major concern. In a program in Bangladesh, 1 month after users received a booklet about the use of oral contraceptives, 83 percent of the recipients could correctly remember when to start taking oral contraceptives as opposed to only 16 percent in the control group, which received only verbal instruction (Haffey, Zimmerman, and Perkin, 1984).

Advertising is the approach employed for user education in social marketing programs and is a potentially powerful tool. For example, the simple use of information pamphlets in drugstores was able to significantly increase the sales of condoms in Colombia (Bailey and De Zambrano, 1974). Radio, billboards, and mass print media advertising has been used as a strategy for increasing public awareness about the availability of new methods with positive results, particularly for vasectomy (Bertrand et al., 1987; Foreit, De Castro, and Franco, 1989). For example, in Brazil a short advertising campaign in men's magazines produced a 58 percent increase in vasectomies in the PRO-PATER clinic (Foreit, De Castro, and Franco, 1989). Some would contend that public education about the risks and benefits associated with new methods should begin before large-scale introduction is begun (International Women's Health Coalition and the Population Council, 1986). This issue certainly should be examined more closely in the future.

Logistics

There have been very few empirical investigations on how the performance of logistics systems can be measured, how and why performance varies, and what impact these systems have on users (Simmons and Lapham, 1986). This is because much of the effort in logistics has been limited to the development of normative procedures and the training of personnel in their execution, rather than in research on the operation of logistics systems (Centers for Disease Control, 1986; Management Sciences for Health, 1982).

When new methods are introduced, supply channels are often ill defined. Introduction may be delayed as stocks of old methods are slowly depleted, as is currently the case with the new TCu-380 IUD and the old Lippes IUD. Similarly many couples never initiate use or use methods incorrectly because they are simply not available on a reliable basis.

New methods are less likely to be used by large populations immediately. Programs should therefore develop flexible strategies to request supplies as demand increases and program periodic checks within the pipeline to ensure the quality of the products supplied. Methods also lose their effectiveness when they are subjected to long periods of improper storage in the supply pipeline (e.g., condoms stored in hot tropical warehouses or exposed to ultraviolet light). This is particularly true for methods that must be ordered in large lots and are not utilized in volume (e.g., barrier methods).

Running out of stocks undoubtedly has a negative effect on method continuation and user satisfaction. In the Dominican Republic, for example, nearly 8 percent of discontinuers indicated that they stopped using oral contraceptives because they could not find their accustomed brand (Green, 1988). This problem is exacerbated by large donors changing brands in procurement arrangements, leaving users without continued supplies of preferred brands (Altman and Piotrow, 1980). In rural areas, the problems of running out of stock are even more severe. For example, a recent evaluation of the supply system of the Ministry of Health of Honduras found that 51 percent of rural posts did not have condoms and 57 percent did not have vaginal spermicides (Correu et al., 1988). Similar experiences are common in rural health posts throughout the world.

Costs to the User and the Program

Costs affect both the user and the service delivery program. With respect to costs to the consumer, too high a price for hormonal contraceptives discourages use, or at least shifts demand to subsidized sources or traditional methods. Beyond the price of the product, consumers also face the opportunity costs of waiting and travel time and futile trips to closed or overextended family planning services. On the other hand, free oral contraceptives do not appear to attract a greater number of users than do similar, modestly priced items when they are both accessible to households (Lewis, 1985). In controlled experiments, free services only appeared to affect acceptance rates when prices were reduced in an established program. Thus, free commodities are probably unnecessary, perhaps even detrimental, given the low acceptance for free services; but in many countries the commercial price for hormonal contraceptives can be too high for the average household (Lewis, 1985). Fees for service are also important for program sustainability. For example, in Cameroon, a $2,000 grant in 1980 added injectables to the services of a local hospital in Yaounde, but user fees have since made possible their continued resupply (S. Huber, personal communication, 1983).

The costs of training and logistics are also a factor in a manager's decisions to introduce or adequately promote the use of a new method. Although procurement costs, of course, vary depending on quantity, timing of purchase, delivery schedule, exchange rates, and other factors, some methods are generally more expensive than others. For example, Hutchings and Saunders (1985) examined relative method costs per couple-years of protection amortized over the average lifetime of the method. Using estimates of product and provider costs, they concluded that the most cost-effective methods for providers were the IUD, vasectomy, and female sterilization, each of which was about half the cost of oral contraceptives for the same protection. At the other extreme were vaginal spermicides and implants, which were about twice as expensive as oral contraceptives for the same level of protection.

However, funds to cover the costs of the introduction of new methods may come from more efficient delivery systems. For example, in India, a clinic program interested in increasing the use of temporary methods paid women to use oral contraceptives for a 6-month period. Although it cost the program $2.30 per user per month, savings were accrued by reducing the personnel and transportation costs of sterilization promoters (Stevens and Stevens, 1988). More important, it produced an increase from 30 percent to nearly 65 percent in contraceptive prevalence in 1 year and increased the use of temporary methods among younger women. Other studies in India suggest that acceptor incentives may contribute to increased levels of overall contraceptive acceptance (Satia and Maru, 1986). In Colombia and Jamaica, incentives for distributors dramatically increased the sales of temporary methods, more than would have been expected by simply adding another salesperson (Townsend and Ojeda, 1985; Westinghouse Health Systems, 1977). In many social marketing programs, however, the introduction of new methods may require the help of salespersons, as distributors give lower priority in promotion to low-volume merchandise.

IMPLICATIONS FOR THE INTRODUCTION OF NEW METHODS

Program Elements

Program elements, then, as expressed in terms of quality of care, logistics, and costs, seem to influence the method acceptance, the continuation, and the use-effectiveness of contraceptive methods. Relying on informed speculation, Table 2 provides an illustration of the expected direction and magnitude of the effects of these program elements on use-effectiveness. Improvements can be observed in acceptance, continuation, or both and can be expressed in percentage point or rate increases over baseline levels. With the exception of costs, improvements in each of the elements (i.e., the availability of methods; the selection, training, and supervision of personnel; efforts to communicate with users; and logistics) should improve the use-effectiveness of new methods.

The largest improvements in use-effectiveness should be observed in most temporary self-administered methods (e.g., vaginal meth-

TABLE 2 Effect of Programmatic Factors on Use Effectiveness

Factors	Direction of Effect	Magnitude of Effect
Availability		
Increased choice	+	Moderate
New delivery systems	+	Moderate-Large
Training/supervision		
Competency training	+	Moderate
Frequent supervision	+	Small-Moderate
IE&C[a]		
Couseling users	+	Moderate
Use of media	+	Small-Moderate
Logistics		
Removing barriers to service	+	Small-Moderate
Continuing stocks	+	Small-Moderate
Cost		
High cost to consumer	−	Moderate
Charging moderate fee	0/−	Small

[a]IE&C = Information, education, and counseling.

NOTE: Small--5 percent or less; moderate--6-15 percent; large--more than 15 percent.

ods, including rings, pills, condoms, and diaphragms). Although marginal improvements in any one of these elements may produce small increases in acceptance (e.g., 3–5 percent in prevalence over a 1-year period) and continuation (5–10 percent increase in use at 1 year), when introduced in combination with other elements managers should expect moderate to large changes. However, when program management is weak, contraceptive prevalence is low, and field operations are lethargic, a more comprehensive strategy for program improvement may be necessary. Under these conditions, marginal changes in program elements would probably have little effect.

Program Managers

Program managers exercise considerable control over the supply of methods and, in turn, can influence both the level and quality of use of specific methods. Therefore, a priority for any introduction program must be the demonstration of the benefits of a new contraceptive technology to program managers. Some skeptics would contend that once three or more methods are available, new methods simply contribute to a switch to the new method. Operations research on method introduction must respond to the concerns of directors and managers, who must decide whether to include new methods in their programs. A strategy for achieving this is to support the network of program directors who understand program research and the benefits and potential risks of program innovations. They have experience in dealing with important user concerns, as well as a feeling for the cultural acceptability of proposed changes in service delivery components.

Managers can stimulate innovation by fostering the development of an environment for introduction. By focusing on choice and quality, managers can motivate staff to respond to the demand for improvements in services. A potential benefit for managers is that innovations often focus attention on strengthening the program elements required for introduction (e.g., counseling and logistics). An introduction program can serve to mobilize field operations or can provide the opportunity to critically review service policies and procedures. In a number of countries, strategies to effectively promote underutilized methods already on the market (e.g., copper IUDs and condoms) are adopting a similar systems approach.

If an introduction program is to be successful, however, overall program sustainability must be considered in planning. If new methods create a greater dependence for the service agency, there is small likelihood that services will continue without external funding. Managers may not be willing to trade off marginal gains in effectiveness for a technological package that ultimately places in jeopardy their ability to serve large populations. One way to ensure program continuity while introducing new methods is to select institutions and training centers that have efficient delivery systems or that can mobilize their own funds to sustain introduction activities.

Researchers

There is a tremendous need to improve theory in the area of organizational change and develop models for the operation of service delivery programs. Research on program operations is a high priority, with special emphasis needed on specific program elements and the quantity and quality of transactions between clients and providers.

Because quality of care is a central feature of efforts to introduce new methods, researchers should develop and integrate quality of care indicators into management information systems. This will provide both program managers and policymakers with information about the probability of success of any method introduction effort.

Researchers should also look for opportunities to examine the operation of logistics systems, including storage requirements and conditions, transportation arrangements, and strategies for decision making in commodities requests. There is a paucity of research in this area. In part, this is because donors have been willing to accept weak systems as long as methods were moving through the pipeline. As more focus is placed on the leaks in the pipeline, however, the need and demand for research becomes stronger.

As the marginal benefits of new technology become smaller, researchers should develop better estimates of the costs and consequences of introducing new methods. One way of doing this is to develop simulation models of introducing existing technologies (e.g., NORPLANT® , TCu-380, and diaphragms) into countries where their use is limited and apply these models to the introduction of the expected technologies.

CONCLUSION

Operations research makes a substantial difference in the performance, quality, and cost-effectiveness of family planning service delivery systems. Use of this approach to improve the introduction of new and/or underutilized contraceptive methods will both improve services for users and contribute positively to the social impact of family planning programs. In the future, managers, researchers, and users must work together to ensure that the experience of the introduction of the IUD in India is not repeated.

ACKNOWLEDGMENT

This work was supported by contract no. DPE-3030-C-00-4074-00 from the U.S. Agency for International Development.

REFERENCES

Ainsworth, M.
   1985   *Family Planning Programs: The Clients' Perspective.* Washington, D.C.: World Bank.
Altman, L., and P. Piotrow
   1980   Social marketing: Does it work? *Population Reports* Series J, no. 21.
Bailey, J., and M.C. De Zambrano
   1974   Contraceptive phamplets in Colombian drugstores. *Studies in Family Planning* 5(6):178–182.
Berelson, B.
   1976   The impact of new technology on population. Pp. 115–121 in B. Berelson, J. Ross, and F. Mauldin, eds. New York: Springer-Verlag.
Bertrand, J.T., R.A. Pineda, R. Santiso, and S. Hearn
   1980   Characteristics of successful distributors in the community-based distribution of contraceptives in Guatemala. *Studies in Family Planning* 11(9–10):274–285.
Bertrand, J.T., N. Mangani, M. Mansilu, and E. Landry
   1985   Factors influencing the use of traditional versus modern family planning methods in Bas Zaire. *Studies in Family Planning* 16(6):332–341.
Bertrand, J.T., R. Santiso, S.H. Linder, and M.A. Pineda
   1987   Evaluation of a communications program to increase adoption of vasectomy in Guatemala. *Studies in Family Planning* 18(6):361–370.
Bruce, J.
   1987   User's perspectives on contraceptive technology and delivery systems: Highlighting some feminist issues. Pp. 359–383 in G. Zeidenstein, ed., *Technology in Society*, Vol. 9, nos. 3, 4. Fairview Park, N.Y.: Pergamon Journals.
   1988   Fundamental elements of quality of care: A simple framework. New York: The Population Council. August. Mimeo.
Centers for Disease Control
   1986   *Training Materials for Family Planning Logistics.* Altanta, Ga.: Centers for Disease Control.
Correu, S., G. Ojeda, J.S. Nuñez, C. Salmon, and C. Belcher
   1988   Evaluation of the Family Planning Program. Ministry of Health, Tegucigalpa, Honduras.

De la Macorra, L., R. Roca, and J.W. Townsend
  1987   *Marketing of Condoms in Supermarkets: Cash Registers Versus Regular Shelves as Point of Sales.* Final report to the Population Council. Queretaro, Mexico: PROFAM.
Finkle, J.L., and G.D. Ness
  1985   *Managing Delivery Systems.* Final report to the AID Office of Population. Ann Arbor: University of Michigan.
Fisher, A., and V. De Silva
  1986   Satisfied IUD acceptors as family planning motivators in Sri Lanka. *Studies in Family Planning* 17(5):235–242.
Foreit, K., M. De Castro, and E. Franco
  1989   Growth versus maintenance in voluntary sterilization programs: The impact of mass media advertising. *Studies in Family Planning* 20(2):107–116.
Gallen M., and C. Lettenmaier
  1987   Counseling makes a difference. *Population Reports* Series J, no. 35.
Gallen, M.E., and W. Rinehart
  1986   Operations research: Lessons for policy and programs. *Population Reports* Series J, no. 31.
Green, E.C.
  1988   A consumer intercept study of oral contraceptive users in the Dominican Republic. *Studies in Family Planning* 19(2):109–117.
Haffey, J., M.C. Zimmerman, and G.W. Perkin
  1984   Communicating contraception. *Populi* 11(2):35.
Hutchings J., and L. Saunders
  1985   *Assessing the Characteristics and Cost-Effectiveness of Contraceptive Methods.* PIACT Paper Ten. Seattle, Wash.: PIACT.
International Women's Health Coalition and the Population Council
  1986   The Contraceptive Development Process and Quality of Care in Reproductive Health Services. Report of a meeting held in New York. The Population Council, New York.
Jain, A.
  1988   Assessing the fertility impact of quality of family planning services. *International Programs Working Paper No. 22.* New York: The Population Council.
Keller, A.B.
  1973   Patient attrition in five Mexico City family planning clinics. In J.M. Stycos, ed., *Clinics, Contraception and Communication.* New York: Meredith Corp.
Lapham, R.J., and W.P. Mauldin
  1985   Contraceptive prevalence: The influence of organized family planning programs. *Studies in Family Planning* 16(3):117–137.
Lapido, O.A., E.M. Weiss, G.E. Delano, J. Revson, M.O. Onadeko, and O. Ayeni
  1985   Community-based distribution of low-cost family planning and maternal and child health services in rural Nigeria. Pp. 371–381 in Wawer, M., S. Huffman, D. Cebula, and R. Osborn, eds., *Health and Family Planning in Community-Based Distribution Programs.* Boulder, Colo.: Westview Press.

Lewis, M.A.
  1985   Pricing and Cost Recovery Experience in Family Planning Programs.
          World Bank working paper no. 684. Washington, D.C.: World Bank.
Management Sciences for Health
  1982   *Managing Drug Supply.* J. Quick, P. Hume, and R. O'Conner, eds.
          Boston: Management Sciences for Health.
McGuire, E.S.
  1984   Family Planning Operations Research: A Decade of Experience.
          Paper presented at the National Center for International Health
          Eleventh Annual International Health Conference, Arlington, Va.
Pariani, S., D.M. Heer, and M.D. Van Arsdol
  1987   Continued Contraceptive Use in Five Family Planning Clinics in
          Surabaya, Indonesia. Paper presented at the American Public Health
          Association Annual Meeting, New Orleans, La.
Phillips, J.F.
  1988   Two projects in Bangladesh. *Asia Pacific Population Journal* 2(4):3–
          28.
Phillips, J.F., R. Simmons, M.A. Koenig, and J. Chakraborty
  1987   Determinants of Reproductive Changes in a Traditional Society: Ev-
          idence from Matlab, Bangladesh. Center for Policy Studies Working
          Paper no. 135. New York: The Population Council.
Population Council
  1987   Guidelines for Programmatic Introduction of NORPLANT® Con-
          traceptive Subdermal Impacts (draft). New York: The Population
          Council.
Potter, L., D. Berrio, S. Wright, P. Suarez, R. Pinedo, and Z. Castañeda
  1987   Oral Contraceptive Compliance in Rural Colombia: Daily Use, Per-
          sonal and Provider Characteristics. Paper presented at the American
          Public Health Association Annual Meeting, New Orleans, La.
Ramos, M., J.R. Foreit, E. Mostajo, J. Garcia-Niñez, R. Monge, L.M. Aller,
and R. Iparraguire
  1986   An Experiment to Improve an IUD Insertion and Medical Back-up
          Component of a CBD Program in Lima, Peru. Paper presented at
          the American Public Health Association Annual Meeting, Las Vegas,
          Nev.
Repetto, R.
  1977   Correlates of field-worker performance in the Indonesian family plan-
          ning program: A test of the homophily-heterphily hypothesis. *Studies
          in Family Planning* 8(1):19–21.
Roper, L.E.
  1987   The management of family planning programs: Profamilia's experi-
          ence. *Studies in Family Planning* 18(6):338–351.
Salvador, L., T. de Vargas, J. Foreit, L. Orozco, and S. Heredia
  1987   Delivering Family Planning and Health Services to Indigenous Com-
          munities in Ecuador. Paper presented at the American Public Health
          Association Annual Meeting, New Orleans, La.
Satia, J.K., and R.M. Maru
  1986   Incentives and disincentives in the Indian family welfare program.
          Studies in Family Planning 17(3):136–145.

Simmons, G., and R.J. Lapham
  1986   Family Planning Program Effectiveness. Report prepared for the Committee on Population, National Research Council, Washington, D.C.
Soni, V.
  1983   Thirty years of the Indian family planning program: Past performance, future prospects. *International Family Planning Perspectives* 9(2):35–45.
Stevens, J., and C. Stevens
  1988   Description of Tamil Nadu incentive program for temporary methods. Memo to the Agency for International Development, Bureau for Science and Technology, Office of Population.
Thapa, S.
  1988   Summary of preliminary results of a project on improving the use-effectiveness of NFP: Indonesia. Presentation at the 1988 National Center for International Health Conference, Washington, D.C.
Townsend, J.W., and G. Ojeda
  1985   Community distribution of contraceptives in rural areas: Final narrative report. The Population Council, New York. 191 pages. July. Mimeo.
Treiman K., and L. Liskin
  1988   IUDs—A new look. *Population Reports* Series B, no. 5.
Vernon, R., and G. Ojeda
  1988   *Private Sector Community Based Distribution and Commercial Social Marketing Strategies in Colombia.* Final report to the Population Council. Bogota, Colombia: PROFAMILIA.
Westinghouse Health Systems
  1977   *Contraceptive Retail Sales Program: Jamaica.* Columbia, Md: Westinghouse.
World Health Organization
  1980   User preferences for contraceptive methods in India, Korea, the Philippines, and Turkey. *Studies in Family Planning* 2(9–10):267–273.
  1986   The use of female school teachers and imams as motivators in family planning services in rural Turkey. Special Programme of Research, Development and Research Training in Human Reproduction. In *Research in Human Reproduction, WHO.* Biennial Report, 1986–1987. Geneva: World Health Organization.

Psychosocial Factors in Contraceptive Efficacy

SUSAN PHILLIBER

INTRODUCTION

It is not yet clear what the most accurate psychosocial model of contraceptive adoption should be. Indeed, it seems likely that any model predicting the initial adoption of contraception may not be adequate for predicting continuation or effective use.

There are several reasons for the slow progress in building psychosocial models of contraceptive use. The first is the relative infrequency with which psychologists and social psychologists become interested in fertility and contraceptive-related topics. The second problem is that these variables are intensely culture-specific. If locus of control is much studied in some settings, the variable is unknown and unthought of in others. If attitudes toward genital touching are paramount among some women, they are quite irrelevant among others. In other words, identifying which particular psychosocial variables are important in predicting contraceptive use must be specific to countries, cultures, or at least, regions.

This problem is related to another one: the difficulty of measuring these variables. The most advanced attitude theorists and researchers are routinely baffled by how to successfully tap these predispositions in all their nuances, a problem compounded when the predictive task is cross-cultural.

If it is not possible, then, to produce a comprehensive catalog of exactly how each psychosocial variable affects contraceptive use in various countries, it is possible to enumerate the kinds of variables commonly found to be important. After reviewing selected research, this paper also reviews the theoretical frameworks currently being used to guide these studies and suggests what this research portends for the adoption of new contraceptive technologies. Finally, directions for future research are suggested.

KNOWLEDGE OF CONTRACEPTIVE METHODS

Whether or not it is a psychosocial variable, it is necessary to have knowledge of the possibility of fertility control, of the available fertility-control methods, and of the sources of these methods. These are often not sufficient conditions for birth-control use, however. Moreover, specific knowledge of how to use each method and any changes that may occur because of its use are also related to effective and continuing use.

While there are still areas of the world and subgroups within nations for whom this information is lacking, such a situation is not the rule but the exception. In most of the 19 countries included in a World Fertility Survey comparative study, for example, over 90 percent of the population knew of the existence of at least one method of birth control (Vaessen, 1980).

Researchers in India have noted that while knowledge seems to be increasing, the actual information necessary to use most methods correctly is still absent (Khan and Prasad, 1985). Many people in India still lack the knowledge of anything but permanent methods of contraception (Basu, 1984). In the Marshall Islands, knowledge of all birth-control methods except sterilization appears low (Levy et al., 1988). In Kenya, incorrect information regarding method costs and risks is prevalent (Dow and Werner, 1983). Other similar examples of uneven or incorrect information can be found in many other countries.

In the United States, while 9 out of 10 black teenagers had heard of modern methods of birth control, two-fifths of these teenagers thought that condoms and pills were equally effective, and over half thought that they needed a prescription to get condoms in a drugstore (Clark, Zabin, and Hardy, 1984). There are many such studies in the United States documenting inadequate knowledge among teenagers and those with little education (e.g., Kisker, 1985; Morrison, 1985; Zelnik and Kantner, 1979).

Knowledge deficits also affect contraceptive use-effectiveness in the expected ways, since incorrect use of any method can have serious consequences. However, the lack of early knowledge about the potential side effects of a particular method apparently has negative impacts on method continuation as well. Contraceptive users who have substantial knowledge about method side effects before these effects occur are apparently less likely to be unnerved by even rather dramatic bodily changes (Zetina-Lozano, 1983).

Overall, then, it is reasonable to conclude that those who wish to introduce new contraceptive methods will have to overcome general ignorance of the possibility of fertility control in some areas, will have to disseminate knowledge about the new technology and how to use it correctly, and will need to include education about potential side effects or bodily changes if these methods are to be adopted and continually used.

APPROVAL OF CONTRACEPTIVE USE

General approval of regulating the number of children one has is another necessary but not sufficient condition for the adoption of any contraceptive method. Many authors have mentioned the importance of holding this attitude (Ainsworth, 1985; Bogue, 1983; Kar, 1978, 1981–1982) and have pointed out that general social disapproval of contraception exacts a substantial cost to potential users. Indeed, the whole tradition of KAP studies has been sensitive to the measurement of such attitudes.

While there are still those who would assert that no method of fertility regulation is ever acceptable under any circumstance, in most countries this is not the majority opinion. For example, over 27 percent of rural Kenyan women report that they do not approve of family planning (Dow and Werner, 1983). While Bangladesh, Costa Rica, and Colombia are cited as countries where substantial numbers still disapprove of birth-control use, the actual percentage of individuals holding this view ranges from 15 to 22 (Nair and Smith, 1984). Nor is this a situation commmon only to developing countries. In a 1982 survey of women in the United States aged 18 to 44, 16 percent of the nonusers of birth control said they did not believe in this practice (Forrest and Henshaw, 1983).

It is difficult to tell from the available data how real or deeply held such convictions may be. It is possible that, confronted with the general unpleasantness associated with obtaining or using current methods of birth control, men and women rationalize their failure to endure these costs by asserting philosophical objections. The correlation of parity with effective use of birth control seems to suggest that these convictions are vulnerable to other considerations as family size increases (Grady et al., 1983; Jones, Paul, and Westoff, 1980).

Overall, however, like lack of knowledge, an attitude unfavorable to fertility regulation in general can affect the reception of even the most attractive and effective methods. Such attitudes exist and must be gauged at each potential distribution site.

ATTITUDES TOWARD CONTRACEPTION-RELATED ISSUES

It is well-known that attitudes and motivations about issues other than contraception itself are clearly related to contraceptive use. A substantial body of literature has demonstrated that attitudes toward family size and the desired sex of children influence contraceptive use. In Egypt, for example, the number of sons was found to be directly related to both the adoption of contraception and 9-month continuation rates (Gadalla, McCarthy, and Campbell, 1985). While there is some question about the strength of these relationships (Karki, 1988; Cleland, Verrall, and Vaessen, 1983), their existence is easy to document.

There are other psychosocial attitudes, however, that are also related to contraceptive use. Three of these that have received attention in the literature are mentioned here. These are attitudes toward sex roles, sexuality, and one's body and its functions.

Attitudes Toward Sex Roles

In developed countries there has been much recent study of attitudes toward male and female roles; of role orientations; of masculine, feminine, and androgenous attitudes; and the like. When these variables are related to the use of birth control, the results are rather consistent. Traditional attitudes are negatively related to use, while more egalitarian or nontraditional attitudes are positively related to both adoption and continuation (Fox, 1977; MacCorquodale, 1984; Miller, 1986; Rosen and Ager, 1981). On the family level, a similar finding emerges wherein couples with less traditional family structures are more consistent users of fertility-control methods (Beckman et al., 1983).

Also in this research tradition, studies of males find that when they have more egalitarian sex role preferences, they are more likely to state their willingness to use male birth-control pills, if they were available (Marsiglio, 1985).

The closest parallel to these findings in developing countries is that women with more modern attitudes or exposure to more Western influences are more likely to adopt contraception. Feminist discussions of the relative power of men and women in the developing world have also noted the importance of traditional structures in inhibiting contraceptive use (Bruce, 1987).

Attitudes Toward Sexuality

In developed countries, there has been a recent spate of research on attitudes toward sexuality and how these have an impact on contraceptive use. Researchers have reported that erotophilia, or positive affect toward sexuality, is positively related to clinic use, contraceptive use, condom use, and other variables, while erotophobia, or negative affect toward sexuality, is negatively related to these behaviors (Fisher, 1984; Fisher et al., 1979).

In addition, a variable called sex guilt has been shown to be negatively related to the use of reliable contraceptives (Keller and Sack, 1982), negatively related to the use of pills and the intrauterine device (IUD) (Mosher and Vonderheide, 1985), and negatively related to the consistent use of birth control (Herold and Goodwin, 1981). Sex guilt is also related to failure to use birth control at first intercourse, and to embarrassment about clinic attendance to receive a birth-control method (Berger et al., 1985).

Other sexuality variables are also apparently related to the use of birth control. For example, anxiety about sexuality is negatively related to contraceptive use among male teens (Gold and Berger, 1983), and poor sexual functioning among Swedish couples apparently leads to the use of male methods of birth control (Nettelbladt and Uddenberg, 1984).

Research suggests that in the United States, and perhaps elsewhere, the notion still exists that females should neither plan for nor enjoy sex, attitudes which in turn lead to failure to use contraception (Cassell, 1984; Kisker, 1985). These are attitudes that appear to be more prevalent among young unmarried women than others.

Research of this kind in developing countries is sparse by comparison. However, it has been historically noted that Moslems believe that sexuality should be enjoyed (Kirk, 1966), an attitude that may lead to fewer problems with contraceptive adoption and use. A related suggestion is that in many developing countries, use of birth control is problematic if it requires conversation about sex between spouses. Bogue (1983) argues that this is one of the major current costs of contraception in these nations.

Overall, when introducing new contraceptive methods, general attitudes toward sexuality should be assessed with the anticipation that groups in which attitudes are traditional or in which sex is a taboo subject for discussion or enjoyment may be the least receptive. Similarly, methods requiring sexual partners to discuss and cooperate in contraceptive use may be the most negatively received.

Attitudes Toward One's Body and Its Functions

There is a growing body of literature, often contributed by medical anthropologists, on yet another set of subtle and often unnoticed attitudes that influence contraceptive use. These attitudes are a collection of feelings, beliefs, and expectations about bodily image, or functioning, which affect how women judge both the side effects that may accompany contraceptive use and how the method is delivered or administered.

Currently, one of the most well-known of these is the reluctance of some women to manipulate their genitals in order to use contraceptive methods (Bogue, 1983; Kelley, 1979). It also appears, however, that women have definite ideas about how long their menses should last and what their volume of bleeding should be (World Health Organization, 1981). Prolonged bleeding is inconvenient and can result in restrictions from sexual intercourse and religious functions, while amenorrhea creates fear of pregnancy (Shaaban et al., 1983).

A 10-country World Health Organization study (1981) recommended that preferred contraceptive methods would (1) not result in amenorrhea; (2) not change the amount of blood loss; (3) keep bleeding regular and short; (4) permit women to predict when they will bleed; and (5) not change the consistency or color of the blood loss. If bleeding patterns must change, it appears that methods which create less bleeding are not as bothersome as those which create more bleeding (Mauldin, 1979; Satayapan, Kanchanasinith, and Varakamin, 1983).

These guidelines about menstruation are related to considerations about modesty. In countries where women must manage menstrual flow by using washable rags, the public laundering made necessary by increased flow can be a deterrent to adopting a contraceptive method that produces this result (Bruce, 1987).

Caldwell and Caldwell (1988) have recently argued that the abhorrence of barrenness in African cultures will keep sterilization procedures from being very popular on that continent. If this is so, changes in sterilization delivery systems will have little impact.

There are other variables of this kind about which we know precious little. For example, while women in the United States complain bitterly of any method that they believe produces weight gain, women in the Dominican Republic were pleased with the increase in body weight that they thought was associated with use of the vaginal ring (Hardy et al., 1983). However, these same women complained about inserting something that looked "dirty" into their vaginas after the ring became discolored from use.

Field experience rather than systematic research is currently teaching about tolerance for injections and surgery-like procedures, knowledge that is now clearly needed. Implants seem better received in cultures where scarification is common (Sherris and Perkin, 1987), and injectables are popular in countries where shots are associated with the defeat of disease.

Overall, then, it is important to be aware of the variety of body image notions prevalent in each society. These notions may be undetected by program workers, particularly those from other nations, because they are intensely personal and, perhaps, even unconscious.

CONTRACEPTION AND PRESSURE FROM OTHERS

As noted above, general social approval of the idea of regulating births is an important precursor to birth-control use. However, at the individual level, approval from significant others is also important in contraceptive adoption and continued use.

Research on the adoption of vasectomy indicates that knowing other men who have had this procedure is an important predictor of acceptance, as is approval by family and friends (Clark and Swicegood, 1982; Miller, Shain, and Pasta 1985–1986; Philliber and Philliber, 1985). Studies among young people in the United States routinely show that those who perceive that their peers approve of sexual relations and of contraceptive use are more likely to consistently use birth control themselves (Herold and McNamee, 1982; Kastner, 1984; Lowe and Radius, 1987). Similarly, parental communication with young people about birth-control use and parental norms favorable to use seem usually (Herold and McNamee, 1982; Jorgensen and Sonstegard, 1984; Mosher and Bachrach, 1987), but not always (Herceg-Baron et al., 1986; Thompson and Spanier, 1978), related to contraceptive use.

In developing countries, the perception of general social support for one's decision to use contraception also appears to be related to use (Kar, 1978, 1981–1982; Kar and Cumberland, 1984). Moreover, a study in Nigeria found that perceptions of disapproval about contraceptive use appear to lead to discontinuation (Weiss, Udofia, and Madunagu, 1981). Certainly, these are not surprising findings.

Of all the social approval variables, however, none seems so ubiquitous and strong in its relationship to contraceptive use as approval by the partner or spouse. In one form or another, this variable frequently appears in research in both developed and developing countries.

In Nigeria (Weiss, Udofia and Madunagu, 1981), Senegal (Nichols et al., 1985), Kenya (Dow and Werner, 1983), Indonesia (Joesoef, Baughman, and Utoma, 1988; Setiadi, Psikologi, and Psikologi, 1977), Thailand (Satayapan, Kanchanasinith, and Varakamin, 1983), and many other countries of the world, husband approval has been found to be positively related to birth-control use. Laing (1985) reports that in the Philippines, a husband's perceived attitude toward contraceptive use is positively related to the continuation and effectiveness of use. In that same country, husband approval has been reported to be the most important variable predicting acceptance of family planning among minority groups (Cabriles, 1981). In Honduras, husband approval is related to sterilization followthrough among women inquiring about this procedure (Janowitz et al., 1985).

Because of the importance of partner approval, and because such approval may be withheld, some women search for contraceptive methods that are not detectable (Bruce, 1987). For these women, the method must not require any male cooperation, must be invisible, and must not be palpable.

Some of these studies on partner approval have also documented nuances of partner relationships that play a role in contraceptive use. For example, partner support and encouragement are related to regularity of contraceptive use and to continuation of natural family planning (Daly and Herold, 1983; Kastner, 1984). Those in more committed or stable relationships seem most likely to use contraception and to use more effective methods (Cvetkovich and Grote, 1981; Fisher et al., 1979; Herold and McNamee, 1982; Hofferth, 1987; Nettelbladt and Uddenberg, 1984), a finding which suggests the bothersome conclusion that those risking pregnancy are those in the least promising relationships.

Research in the United States also suggests that the relative importance of husband approval may vary with education. Among the well-educated, husbands apparently have less influence because of the wife's tendency to control contraceptive use (Beckman, 1984). Results of this research thus parallel those of the sex role attitude studies.

Overall, it would be difficult to overestimate the impact of partner approval on birth-control adoption, continuation, and effective use. Partner approval has often meant husband approval, and whether unfortunate or not, husbands are going to have to accept new contraceptive methods or, alternatively, be convinced that they must take a passive role in the birth-control decision. The more partner cooperation that is required by each method, the bigger this approval will loom as a factor in acceptance.

PERSONALITY VARIABLES

It is clearly recognized that of all the variables reviewed here, personality traits or characteristics have been the most neglected. In fact, in his 1983 review of the normative and psychic costs of contraception, Bogue asserted that such variables were assumed ". . . to be somewhat of a blind alley in research" (p. 154). Perhaps such a requiem is fair, perhaps it is premature, and perhaps more than anything, it reflects the hope of some that nothing so immovable as stable personality traits will turn out to be important predictors of contraceptive use.

Of the variables that might be studied under such a heading, perhaps the most frequently examined is locus of control. This variable attempts to differentiate respondents along a continuum from those with the most internal or personal sense of control from those who believe themselves to be controlled by luck, fate, or some other outside force. It is most common to find that those with more internal control are more likely to use contraception (Fox, 1977; Hendricks and Fullilove, 1983; McKinney, Sprecher, and DeLamater, 1981; Rosen and Ager, 1981; Strecher et al., 1986; Visher, 1987). Some research does not support this finding and suggests that even if locus of control plays a role, it is not a very important one (Blignault, 1977; Gold and Berger, 1983; Lieberman, 1981). Almost all of this research was performed in the United States.

Bogue (1983) and others have recognized that when religion forms the basis for outside control, contraceptive adoption may proceed slowly, since a major change in world view may be required. This is a somewhat different use of the variable than in developed countries, where locus of control is seen as a more enduring personality trait than as an indicator of societal development.

There are other personality characteristics that have been found, however infrequently, to be related to contraceptive use. These include level of striving, orientation toward future goals, positive value orientations, and social optimism, all of which were found to be positively related to adopting contraception before the occurrence of the first pregnancy (Kar, 1971). Possession of communication skills and assertiveness are positively related to the use of effective birth-control methods (Lowe and Radius, 1987). Having a positive self-concept, having coping skills, and planfulness have also been found to be related to birth-control use (Mindick and Oscamp, 1982). An attempt to increase cognitive skills through treatment also yielded more favorable attitudes toward contraception (Gilchrist and Schinke, 1983).

In this same tradition, women in Finland who have had repeat abortions have been found to have lower impulse control, poor emotional balance, poorer self-esteem, lower realism, and a lower capacity for relationships (Niemela et al., 1981). There are also studies which find that some of these variables are not related to contraceptive use (Hynes and Bruch, 1985; Kar and Gonzalez-Cerrutti, 1978).

Overall, the search for personality traits that might predict contraceptive use patterns has not been a vigorous one and is largely confined to the United States. There is little research evidence at the moment to suggest that even the most studied of these variables will explain substantial variance in contraceptive use behavior.

CHARACTERISTICS OF CONTRACEPTIVE METHODS

The variables discussed thus far are psychosocial characteristics of potential contraceptive users that may influence the adoption, continuation, and effectiveness of contraceptive method use. There are also, however, a variety of characteristics of methods themselves which, in interaction with the person-centered variables discussed above, influence these behavior patterns.

The characteristics of the method itself that are known to be important include its *perceived* effectiveness, mode of administration, convenience, reversibility, detectability, and side effects. The emphasis on perceived is important since the *true* measures of these variables count less than what potential acceptors believe to be the case.

Of course, the degree to which a method is perceived to actually work in preventing pregnancy is an important consideration in its adoption. In societies where abortion is not available as a backup in case of method failure, potential adopters are likely to be the most sensitive to this issue. As already noted, those who have all the children they want choose methods perceived as being more effective than do users who are spacing their children.

What users must do to actually get and use a method, or its mode of administration, is also important. Service delivery variables are important here, but there are other psychosocial aspects of method administration. For example, Bruce (1987) argues that a method controlled by the user has more appeal than one controlled by providers. This is apparently true, unless the method interferes with sexual activity, like a condom or diaphragm, which although controlled by the user, are less convenient than a yearly injection.

Regarding the reversibility dimension, the stage of the user's life cycle certainly becomes an important consideration. Reversibility on demand is also important to some users. Methods that cause a delay in the return of fecundity are less attractive.

Of all these characteristics of the methods themselves, however, probably the most important is their real, imagined, or anticipated side effects. The user perspective tradition of research has recognized that even the reporting of side effects can be subject to great objective error, but this ultimately matters little. A woman who perceives that she has gained weight, has had substantially increased bleeding, or is having increased menstrual cramping may be little interested in the actual data on these topics, if such information were even available to her.

In the United States, several studies have documented a correlation between increased fears about side effects and decreasing use of oral contraceptives and IUDs (Forrest and Henshaw, 1983; Hale and Char, 1982; Silverman, Torres, and Forrest, 1987). This anxiety has also been linked to media reports about various studies of these methods. Teenagers in the United States routinely report that they do not use contraceptives because of fear of side effects (Olson and Rollins, 1982; Zelnik and Kantner, 1979).

In developing countries as well, where contraceptive continuation rates are often low, perceived side effects have played a major role in the use of contraceptives (Iddhichiracharas et al., 1983; Mauldin, 1979; Nair and Smith, 1984; Narkavonnakit, Bennett, and Bala-krishnan, 1982). An eight-country study in developing countries found that over 40 percent of women felt that taking pills was more hazardous than childbearing, while very few knew of the protective effects pills can have (Grubb, 1987). When 55 percent of Kenyan women report that they believe that oral contraceptives are harmful and 50 percent cast an equal judgment on sterilization, these views must be acknowledged as important (Dow and Werner, 1983).

To some contraceptive users, side effects are so important that they prefer the abstinence and low effectiveness that accompany natural family planning over the risks perceived to be associated with other birth-control methods (Laing, 1984; Verzosa, Llamas, and Mahoney, 1984). Moreover, rumors and tales of negative experiences with contraceptives can spread quickly, since negative information about methods is more often remembered than positive information (Porter, 1984), especially when it comes from a personal friend.

The interpretation of information about side effects, the partic-ular side effects that can or cannot be tolerated, the beliefs that are circulated, and the overall weight of these variables show much varia-tion from nation to nation. For example, in Sri Lanka, the menstrual disruption associated with the use of Depo-Provera and implants was apparently more tolerable than the pregnancy-like symptoms accom-panying the use of oral contraceptives (Basnayake et al., 1984; Bas-nayake, Thapa, and Balogh, 1988). In Nepal, weakness and inability to work were believed to accompany contraceptive use, thus damp-ening their acceptance (Schuler, Goldstein, and Goldstein, 1986). In rural Peru, condoms were believed to create spots on a women's face, and rumors circulated that use of oral contraceptives led to giving birth to monsters (Tucker, 1986).

It seems clear, then, that side effects are worrisome worldwide. While some have argued that contraceptive use is less dangerous than pregnancy, this is a comparison that most men and women seem either unable or unwilling to accept. In any case, such calculations have proved to be no substitute for reassurance that side effects are not harmful.

MODELS OF PSYCHOSOCIAL IMPACTS ON CONTRACEPTIVE USE

It would seem useful to create and utilize a comprehensive theo-retical framework to organize these findings on psychosocial variables and to guide research on these topics. While there have been few attempts to do this, several partial theoretical frameworks have been used.

For example, socialization models focus on early childhood or adolescent learning experiences as predictive of contraceptive use. Studies on variables such as sex guilt sometimes cite early socialization as instilling these attitudes which, in turn, are related to contraceptive choices (e.g., Berger et al., 1985). A study of contraceptive use among teenagers found that when young people are socialized to moral absolutes, they are less likely to use contraceptives once they become sexually active than are teens exposed to more relativistic parental views (Thomson, 1982). This kind of work occurs mostly in developed-country settings.

Another frequent approach, again in developed nations, is the utilization of developmental theories. In this work, contraceptive use or nonuse is most commonly predicted from characteristics such as degree of reliance on parents and peers (e.g., Jorgensen, 1980; Thornburg, 1973) or stage of cognitive development (Gilchrist and Schinke, 1983). Perhaps such variables will become more popular in developing countries as attention to teen fertility increases.

Contraceptive adoption and discontinuation have also been studied by using a diffusion of innovation frameworks (e.g., Porter, 1984). Here adopters are characterized as innovators, and research concentrates on identifying the demographic and other characteristics of these societal leaders.

In addition to these theoretical approaches, numerous conceptual frameworks have been created to describe some of the psychosocial correlates of contraceptive use patterns (Ainsworth, 1985; Bogue, 1983; Bruce, 1987; Sherris and Perkin, 1987). Taken together, these frameworks and the literature reviewed here suggest that the search for important psychosocial predictors of contraceptive use should consider at least the variables included in Figure 1.

While this is a beginning list of variables to be considered in each setting and culture, repetitive two-by-two analyses of the relationships of each of these variables with some contraceptive use measure is far short of what is needed. Some research, in fact, has now moved beyond such analyses to test more specific, multivariate models from decision and attitude theory (Davidson and Morrison, 1983; Fishbein and Ajzen, 1975).

According to these models (often called Fishbein or the value-expectancy models), the likelihood that a person will adopt a given

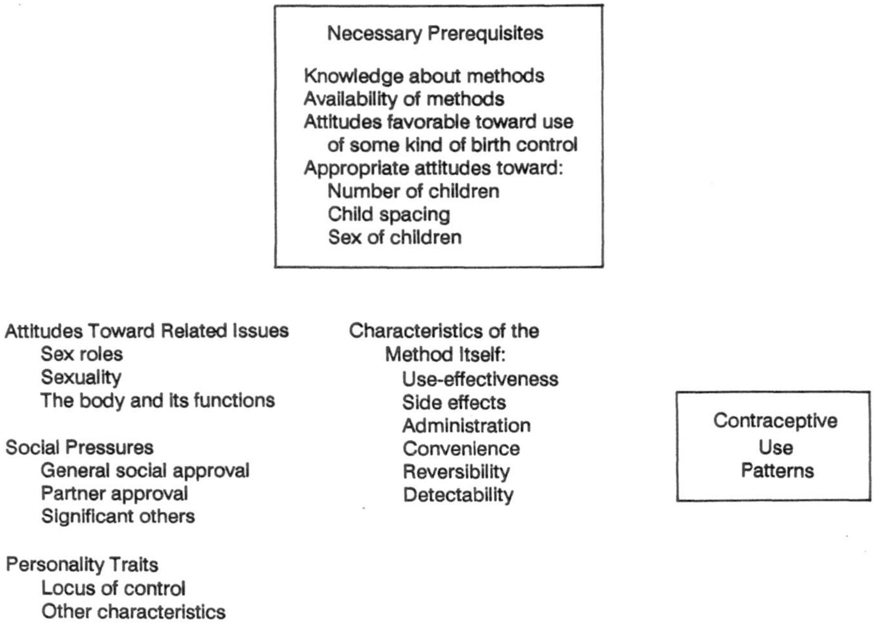

```
                    ┌─────────────────────────────────┐
                    │  Necessary Prerequisites        │
                    │                                 │
                    │  Knowledge about methods        │
                    │  Availability of methods        │
                    │  Attitudes favorable toward use │
                    │     of some kind of birth control│
                    │  Appropriate attitudes toward:  │
                    │     Number of children          │
                    │     Child spacing               │
                    │     Sex of children             │
                    └─────────────────────────────────┘
```

Attitudes Toward Related Issues   Characteristics of the
   Sex roles   Method Itself:
   Sexuality   Use-effectiveness
   The body and its functions   Side effects
                         Administration   Contraceptive

Social Pressures   Convenience   Use
   General social approval   Reversibility   Patterns
   Partner approval   Detectability
   Significant others

Personality Traits
   Locus of control
   Other characteristics

FIGURE 1   Psychosocial variables predicting contraceptive use patterns.

contraceptive (or continue its use or use it effectively), is a function of
(1) the perceived outcomes associated with each option, (2) the subjective evaluation of each anticipated outcome, and (3) the relative
intensities of these attitudes. The alternative to be chosen, including
the use of no contraception, is thus predicted to be that alternative
with the highest expected value.

Tests of expectancy value models have been rather common
in the United States, particularly among those trying to predict
contraceptive use among teenagers (e.g., Ewald and Roberts, 1985;
Jorgensen and Sonstegard, 1984; Kastner, 1984; McCarty, 1981;
Philliber et al., 1986). Such models have also been used in Venezuela,
the Philippines, and Kenya (Kar, 1978, 1983–1984; Kar and Cumberland, 1984).

Indeed, these models seem to offer an excellent payoff for family planners because they tend to identify the exact attitudes and

motivations associated with each contraceptive and their relative intensities. Ignoring the measurement of attitudes toward contraceptives in general, these theorists search for the engaged attitudes relevant to each specific method and in each particular setting. Several researchers have suggested that method-specific models of this sort may be necessary (Cohen, Severy, and Ahtola, 1978; Crawford, 1973).

For example, research that tries to predict the acceptance of female sterilization would not ask a general question about the acceptability of this method. Rather, each respondent might be asked whether she believed the procedure would cause an ugly scar, whether it would hurt, whether it would be doing something her sister approved of, whether it would cost a lot, and so on. Then, for each outcome anticipated, women would be asked how bad or good the anticipated outcome would be. Summed scales of expected utility would then form the predictive measure, revealing, in addition, the content of the engaged attitudes that predicted the choice.

A U.S. study illustrates how important this kind of specific attitude measurement can be. Tanfer and Rosenbaum (1986) found that oral contraceptives were thought to be the most unsafe of the methods they studied. In spite of that evaluation, however, oral contraceptives were the overall first choice among these women, owing to their superior ratings on such dimensions as convenience and interference.

Social marketing researchers and practitioners have been very sensitive to capturing the engaged attitudes that predict specific contraceptive actions (Harvey, 1984; Schellstede and Ciszewski, 1984). For example, an advertising campaign in Bangladesh touting family planning as beneficial to wives brought little response. However, when family planning was advertised as beneficial to family economic needs, such as food and shelter, the response was much greater (Harvey, 1984). Such findings illustrate the need for research to target more and more specific attitudes in order to improve the prediction of contraceptive adoption and use.

IMPLICATIONS FOR ADOPTION OF NEW CONTRACEPTIVES

This paper began with the reminder that adoption and effective, continuing use of contraceptives are more likely when several important conditions exist. These include knowledge about the possibility of fertility control; knowledge and availability of methods to bring about such control; generally favorable attitudes toward the use of contraceptives; and certain attitudes surrounding the number of children, the sex of those children, and the intervals between their births.

Beyond these, however, there are a variety of psychosocial variables that will influence the rate at which any new technology is adopted. It seems likely that groups with more egalitarian sex role attitudes will be more receptive to all of these technologies, especially the male methods. Personality variables, including a sense that fertility is controlled by oneself rather than by a deity, luck, or fate probably also play a role.

The important psychosocial variables, however, seem to be attitudes toward sexuality, pressure from others, attitudes toward one's body and its functions, and the perceptions users have about the characteristics of the birth-control methods themselves.

Relative to attitudes toward sexuality, societies with more open and accepting attitudes about sexual pleasure may adopt new contraceptives more quickly than more traditional, guilt-ridden groups. In addition, more open societies will be more likely to accept the genital manipulation that is required for the use of vaginal rings, male and female condoms, and disposable diaphragms. Methods that create menstrual changes, particularly increased bleeding and unpredictable bleeding, seem likely to be received less enthusiastically.

There is little systematic information on the likely reception that will be accorded to injections and implants, except what is now being gained in the field. The convenience of these methods suggests high acceptance rates, but their impacts on menses suggest the opposite. Groups that associate wellness with shots will be most receptive to injections, while those who practice scarification may be more likely to embrace implants.

For each of these new technologies, partner approval will be important. It is easy to lose sight of partners because women are often unaccompanied to family planning visits and may even conceal their use of birth control from their spouses. Still, visible implants and methods like condoms that require partner discussion or cooperation are likely to be less popular than an invisible injection.

DISCUSSION

The discussion in this paper has been artificially limited to psychosocial variables, omitting the demographic and service delivery characteristics that are strongly related to contraceptive behavior. Actually, each of the patterns described here will vary by demographic characteristics and will be affected by the particular service delivery mechanisms used to distribute new technologies.

Data are still lacking from many areas of the world on many of the variables discussed here. Some of this information is not going to be captured in focus group and ethnographic studies, nor even in user testimony. Some of it will be, however. In any case, there is a need for more multivariate analyses, guided by models to predict the adoption of each contraceptive from the specific expectancies and values attached to it. Similar equations are required to predict continuation and effective use.

Currently, the kinds of variables being studied in relationship to family planning use are quite different in developed and developing countries. Researchers in developed countries are studying personality traits and women's concerns over long-term health risks associated with contraceptive use, while those in developing countries are more likely to emphasize parity, distance to a service facility, and tolerance for menstrual changes. It is interesting to note that some variables are important in both settings. For example, attitudes and norms surrounding sexuality are important in traditional and permissive societies and in developed and developing nations.

This discussion has centered on psychosocial variables related to adoption, continuation, and correct use of contraception. Additional research could produce a country-by-country catalog of psychosocial variables and their impacts in order to more accurately predict the acceptance of new contraceptive methods.

REFERENCES

Ainsworth, M.
    1985   Family Planning Programs: The Clients' Perspective. World Bank Staff Working Papers no. 676. Population and Development Series No. 1. Washington, D.C.: The World Bank.
Basnayake, S., S. Thapa, and S. Balogh
    1988   Evaluation of safety, efficacy, and acceptability of NORPLANT® implants in Sri Lanka. *Studies in Family Planning* 19(1):39–47.
Basnayake, S., J. Higgins, P. Miller, S. Rogers, and S.E. Kelly
    1984   Early symptoms and discontinuation among users of oral contraceptives in Sri Lanka. *Studies in Family Planning* 15(6):285–290.

Basu, A.M.
    1984   Ignorance of family planning methods in India: An important con-
            straint on use. *Studies in Family Planning* 15(3):136–142.
Beckman, L.J.
    1984   Husbands' and wives' relative influence on fertility decisions and
            outcomes. *Population and Environment* 7(Fall):182–197.
Beckman, L.J., R. Azenberg, A. Forsythe, and T. Day
    1983   A theoretical analysis of antecedents of young couples' fertility deci-
            sions and outcomes. *Demography* 20(4):519–533.
Berger, C., J. Jacques, W. Brender, D. Gold, and D. Andres
    1985   Contraceptive knowledge and use of birth control as a function of sex
            guilt. *International Journal of Women's Studies* 8(1):72–79.
Blignault, I.
    1977   Locus of Control and Contraceptive Knowledge, Attitudes, and Prac-
            tice. B.Sc. Thesis, School of Psychology, University of New South
            Wales, New South Wales, Australia.
Bogue, D.J.
    1983   Normative and psychic costs of contraception. Pp. 151–192 in *Deter-
            minants of Fertility in Developing Countries*, vol. 2, Rodolph Bulatao
            and Ronald Lee, eds. New York: Academic Press.
Bruce, J.
    1987   Users' perspectives on contraceptive technology and delivery systems.
            Technology in Society 9:359–383.
Cabriles, D.C.
    1981   Factors Associated with the Acceptance and Nonacceptance of Family
            Planning Programs Among Cultural Minorities in Bukidnon, Philip-
            pines. SEAPRAP Research Report no. 79. Singapore.
Caldwell, J.C., and P. Caldwell
    1988   Is the Asian family planning program model suited to Africa? *Studies
            in Family Planning* 19(1):19–28.
Cassell, C.
    1984   *Swept Away: Why Women Fear Their Own Sexuality.* New York:
            Simon & Schuster.
Clark, M.P., and G. Swicegood
    1982   Husband or wife? A multivariate analysis of decision making for
            voluntary sterilization. *Journal of Family Issues* 3(9):341–360.
Clark, S.D., L. Zabin, and J. Hardy
    1984   Sex, contraception and parenthood: Experience and attitudes among
            urban black young men. *Family Planning Perspectives* 16(2):77–82.
Cleland, J., J. Verrall, and M. Vaessen
    1983   Preferences for the sex of children and their influence on reproductive
            behaviour. Comparative Studies, vol. 27. World Fertility Survey.
            London.
Cohen, J.B., L. Severy, and O.T. Ahtola
    1978   An extended expectancy-value approach to contraceptive alternatives.
            Journal of Population 1(1):22–41.
Crawford, T.J.
    1973   Beliefs about birth control: A consistency theory analysis. *Represen-
            tatvie Research in Social Psychology* 4(1):53–65.

Cvetkovich, G., and B. Grote
 1981 Psychosocial maturity and teenage contraceptive use: An investigation of decision making and communication skills. *Population and Environment* 4(4):211–226.
Daly, K.J., and E.S. Herold
 1983 Natural family planning: A comparison of continuers and discontinuers. Population and Environment 6(4):231–240.
Davidson, A.R., and D.M. Morrison
 1983 Predicting contraceptive behavior from attitudes: A comparison of within- versus across-subjects procedures. *Journal of Personality and Social Psychology* 45(5):997–1009.
Dow, T.E., and L.H. Werner
 1983 Perceptions of family planning among rural Kenyan women. *Studies in Family Planning* 4(2):35–43.
Ewald, B.M., and C.S. Roberts
 1985 Contraceptive behavior in college-age males related to Fishbein model. *Advances in Nursing Sciences* 7(3):63–69.
Fishbein, M., and I. Ajzen
 1975 *Belief, Attitude, Intention, and Behavior.* Reading, Mass.: Addison-Wesley.
Fisher, W.A.
 1984 Predicting contraceptive behavior among university men: The role of emotions and behavioral intentions. *Journal of Applied Social Psychology* 14(2):104–123.
Fisher, W.A., D. Byrne, M. Edwards, C. Miller, K. Kelley, and L. White
 1979 Psychological and situation-specific correlates of contraceptive behavior among university women. *Journal of Sex Research* 15(1):38–55.
Forrest, J.D., and S. Henshaw
 1983 What United States women think and do about contraception. *Family Planning Perspectives* 15(4):157–166.
Fox, G.L.
 1977 Sex-role attitudes as predictors of contraceptive use among unmarried university students. *Sex Roles* 3(3):265–283.
Gadalla, S., J. McCarthy, and O. Campbell
 1985 How the number of living sons influences contraceptive use in Menoufia Governorate, Egypt. *Studies in Family Planning* 16(3):164–169.
Gilchrist, L., and S.P. Schinke
 1983 Coping with contraception: Cognitive and behavioral methods with adolescents. *Cognitive Therapy and Research* 7(5):379–388.
Gold, D., and C. Berger
 1983 The influence of psychological and situational factors on the contraceptive behavior of single men: A review of the literature. *Population and Environment* 6(2):113–129.
Grady, W.R., M.B. Hirsch, N. Keen, and B. Vaughan
 1983 Contraceptive failure and continuation among married women in the United States, 1970–1975. *Studies in Family Planning* 14(1):9–19.
Grubb, G.S.
 1987 Women's perceptions of the safety of the pill: A survey in eight developing countries. *Journal of Biosocial Science* 19:313–321.

Hale, R.W., and D. Char
  1982   Sexual and contraceptive behavior on a college campus: A five year
          follow-up. *Contraception* 25(2):125–134.
Hardy, E.E., Q. Reyes, F. Gomez, R. Portes-Carrasco, and A. Faundes
  1983   User's perception of the contraceptive vaginal ring: A field study
          in Brazil and the Dominican Republic. *Studies in Family Planning*
          14(11):284–290.
Harvey, P.D.
  1984   Advertising family planning in the press: Direct response results from
          Bangladesh. *Studies in Family Planning* 15(1):40–42.
Hendricks, L.E., and Robert E. Fullilove
  1983   Locus of control and the use of contraception among unmarried black
          adolescent fathers and their controls: A preliminary report. *Journal
          of Youth and Adolescence* 12(3):225–233.
Herceg-Baron, R., F. Furstenburg, J. Shea, and K. Mullan Harris
  1986   Supporting teenagers' use of contraceptives: A comparison of clinic
          services. *Family Planning Perspectives* 18(2):61–66.
Herold, E.S., and M.S. Goodwin
  1981   Premarital sexual guilt and contraceptive attitudes and behavior.
          Family Relations 30:247–253.
Herold, E.S., and J. McNamee
  1982   An explanatory model of contraceptive use among young single
          women. *Journal of Sex Research* 18(4):289–304.
Hofferth, S.
  1987   Contraceptive decision-making among adolescents. Pp. 56–77 in *Risk-
          ing the Future*, Vol. II, S. Hofferth and C.D. Hayes, eds. Washington,
          D.C.: National Academy Press.
Hynes, M.J., and M. Bruch
  1985   Social skills and responses in simulated contraceptive problem situa-
          tions. *Journal of Sex Research* 21(4):422–436.
Iddhichiracharas, N., P. Chiowanich, S. Zankel, and J. Rogosch
  1983   The user perspective in Northern Thailand: A series of case studies.
          Studies in Family Planning 14(2):48–56.
Janowitz, B., J. Nunez, D. Covington, and C. Colven
  1985   Why women don't get sterilized: A follow-up of women in Honduras.
          Studies in Family Planning 16(2):107–112.
Joesoef, M., A. Baughman, and B. Utoma
  1988   Husband's approval of contraceptive use in metropolitan Indonesia:
          Program implications. *Studies in Family Planning* 19(3):162–168.
Jones, E.F., L. Paul, and C.F. Westoff
  1980   Contraceptive efficacy: The significance of method and motivation.
          Studies in Family Planning 11(2):39–50.
Jorgensen, S.R.
  1980   Contraceptive attitude-behavior consistency in adolescence. *Popula-
          tion and Environment* 3(2).
Jorgensen, S.R., and J. Sonstegard
  1984   Predicting adolescent sexual and contraceptive behavior: An appli-
          cation and test of the Fishbein model. *Journal of Marriage and the
          Family* 46(1):43–55.

Kar, S.
  1971   Individual aspirations as related to early and late acceptance of contraception. *Journal of Social Psychology* 83:235–245.
  1978   Consistency between fertility attitudes and behaviour: A conceptual model. *Population Studies* 32(1):173–185.
  1981-   Factors in consistency between attitudes and behavior: Implications
  1982   for policies and programs. *International Quarterly of Community Health Education* 2(1):3–22.
  1983-   Psychosocial environment: A health promotion model. *International*
  1984   *Quarterly of Community Health Education* 4(4):311–341.
Kar, S., and W. Cumberland
  1984   Impacts of behavioral intentions, social support, and accessibility on contraception: A cross-cultural study. *Population and Environment* 7(1):17–31.
Kar, S., and R. Gonzalez-Cerrutti
  1978   *Psychosocial Determinants of Fertility and Contraception in Venezuela.* Washington, D.C.: Pan American Health Organization.
Karki, Y.
  1988   Sex preferences and the value of sons and daughters in Nepal. *Studies in Family Planning* 19(3):169–178.
Kastner, L.S.
  1984   Ecological factors predicting adolescent contraceptive use: Implications for intervention. *Journal of Adolescent Health Care* 5:79–86.
Keller, J.F., and A. Sack
  1982   Sex guilt and the use of contraception among unmarried women. *Contraception* 25(4):387–393.
Kelley, K.
  1979   Socialization factors in contraceptive attitudes: Roles of affective responses, parental attitudes and sexual experience. *Journal of Sex Research* 15(1):6–20.
Khan, M.E., and C.V.S. Prasad
  1985   A comparison of 1970–1980 survey findings on family planning in India. *Studies in Family Planning* 16(6):312–320.
Kirk, D.
  1966   Factors affecting Moslem natality. Pp. 56–79 in *Family Planning and Population Programs*, B. Berelson, ed. Chicago: University of Chicago Press.
Kisker, E.E.
  1985   Teenagers talk about sex, pregnancy and contraception. *Family Planning Perspectives* 17(2):83–90.
Laing, J.E.
  1984   Natural family planning in the Philippines. *Studies in Family Planning* 15(2):49–61.
  1985   Continuation and effectiveness of contraceptive practice: A cross-sectional approach. *Studies in Family Planning* 16(3):138–153.
Levy, S., R. Taylor, I. Higgins, and D. Grafton-Wasserman
  1988   Fertility and contraception in the Marshall Islands. *Studies in Family Planning* 19(3):179–185.
Lieberman, J.J.
  1981   Locus of control as related to birth control knowledge, attitudes and practices. *Adolescence* XVI(61):1–10.

Lowe, C.S., and S. M. Radius
  1987   Young adults' contraceptive practices: An investigation of influences.
          Adolescence XXII(86):291–304.
MacCorquodale, P.
  1984   Gender roles and premarital contraception. *Journal of Marriage and
          the Family* 46(1):57–63.
Marsiglio, W.
  1985   Husbands' sex-role preferences and contraceptive intentions: The case
          of the male pill. *Sex Roles* 12(5/6):655–663.
Mauldin, W. P.
  1979   Experience with contraceptive methods in developing countries. In
          Contraception: Science, Technology, and Application. Washington,
          D.C.: National Academy of Sciences.
McCarty, D.
  1981   Changing contraceptive usage intentions: A test of the Fishbein model
          of intention. *Journal of Applied Social Psychology* 11(3):192–211.
McKinney, K., S. Sprecher, and J. DeLamater
  1981   The Self and Contraceptive Behavior. Center for Demography and
          Ecology Working Paper no. 81-37. University of Wisconsin, Madison.
Miller, W.B.
  1986   Why some women fail to use their contraceptive method: A psycho-
          logical investigation. *Family Planning Perspectives* 18(1):27–32.
Miller, W., R. Shain, and D. Pasta
  1985-   A model of the determinants in married women of sterilization method
  1986   choice. *Population and Environment* 8(Fall/Winter):223–239.
Mindick, B., and S. Oskamp
  1982   Individual differences among adolescent contraceptors: Some impli-
          cations for intervention. Pp. 140–176 in *Pregnancy in Adolescence*,
          I. Stuart and C. Wells, eds. New York: Van Nostrand Reinhold.
Morrison, D.M.
  1985   Adolescent contraceptive behavior: A review. *Psychological Bulletin*
          98(Nov.):538–568.
Mosher, D.L., and S.G. Vonderheide
  1985   Contributions of sex guilt and masturbation guilt to women's contra-
          ceptive attitudes and use. *Journal of Sex Research* 21(1):24–39.
Mosher, W.D., and C.A. Bachrach
  1987   First premarital contraceptive use: United States, 1960–1982. *Studies
          in Family Planning* 18(2):83–95.
Nair, N.K., and L. Smith
  1984   Reasons for not using contraceptives: An international comparison.
          Studies in Family Planning 15(2):84–92.
Narkavonnakit, T., T. Bennett, and T.R. Balakrishnan
  1982   Continuation of injectable contraceptives in Thailand. *Studies in
          Family Planning* 13(4):99–105.
Nettelbladt, D., and N. Uddenberg
  1984   Contraceptive behavior in Swedish women—a follow-up study. *Jour-
          nal of Psychosomatic Obstetrics and Gynecology* 3:205–214.
Nichols, D., S. Ndiaye, N. Burton, B. Janowitz, L. Gueye, and M. Gueye
  1985   Vanguard family planning acceptors in Senegal. *Studies in Family
          Planning* 16(5):271–278.

Niemela, P., P. Lehtinen, L. Rauramo, R. Hermansson, R. Karjalainen, H. Maki, and C. Stora
  1981   The first abortion—and the last? A study of the personality factors underlying repeated failure of contraception. *International Journal of Gynecology and Obstetrics* 19:193–200.
Olson, L., and J. Rollins
  1982   Psychological barriers to contraceptive use among adolescent women. Pp. 177–193 in *Pregnancy in Adolescence*, I. Stuart and C. Wells, eds. New York: Van Nostrand Reinhold Co.
Philliber, S.G., and W.W. Philliber
  1985   Social and psychological perspectives on voluntary sterilization: A review. *Studies in Family Planning* 16(1):1–29.
Philliber, S., P. Brickner Namerow, J. Williams Kaye, and C. Hammer Kunkes
  1986   Pregnancy risk-taking among adolescents. *Journal of Adolescent Research* 1(4):463–481.
Porter, E.G.
  1984   Birth control discontinuance as a diffusion process. *Studies in Family Planning* 15(1):20–29.
Rosen, R.H., and J. Ager
  1981   Self concept and contraception: Pre-conception decision making. *Population and Environment* 4(1):11–23.
Satayapan, S., K. Kanchanasinith, and S. Varakamin
  1983   Perceptions and acceptability of NORPLANT® implants in Thailand. *Studies in Family Planning* 14(6/7):170–176.
Schellstede, W., and R.L. Ciszewski
  1984   Social marketing of contraceptives in Bangladesh. *Studies in Family Planning* 15(1):31–39.
Schuler, S., R. Goldstein, and M.C. Goldstein
  1986   Family planning in Nepal from the user's and nonuser's perspectives. *Studies in Family Planning* 17(2):67–77.
Setiadi, B., L.R. Psikologi, and F. Psikologi
  1977   Relationship Between Several Socio-Psychological Variables and the Decision to Follow the Family Planning Program. SEAPRAP Research Report No. 18. Singapore.
Shaaban, M., M. Salah, A. Zarzour, and S. Abdullah
  1983   A prospective study of NORPLANT® implants and the TCu 380Ag IUD in Assiut, Egypt. *Studies in Family Planning* 14(6/7):163–169.
Sherris, J.D., and G. Perkin
  1987   Cultural perspectives on contraceptive technology. *Technology in Society* 9:323–337.
Silverman, J., A. Torres, and J.D. Forrest
  1987   Barriers to contraceptive services. *Family Planning Perspectives* 19(3):94–102.
Strecher, V.J., B. McEvoy DeVellis, M. Becker, and I. Rosenstock
  1986   The role of self-efficacy in achieving health behavior change. *Health Education Quarterly* 13(1):73–92.
Tanfer, K., and E. Rosenbaum
  1986   Contraceptive perceptions and method choice among young single women in the United States. *Studies in Family Planning* 17(6):269–277.

Thompson, L., and G. Spanier
   1978   Influences of parents, peers and partners on the contraceptive use
           of college men and women. *Journal of Marriage and the Family*
           40(3):481–492.
Thomson, E.
   1982   Socialization for sexual and contraceptive behavior. *Youth and Society*
           14(1):103–128.
Thornburg, H.D.
   1973   Behavior and values: Consistency or inconsistency? *Adolescence*
           8:513–520.
Tucker, G.M.
   1986   Barriers to modern contraceptive use in rural Peru. *Studies in Family
           Planning* 17(6):308–316.
Vaessen, M.
   1980   Knowledge of Contraceptive Methods. Comparative Studies no. 8.
           World Fertility Survey. London.
Verzosa, C., N. Llamas, and R. Mahoney
   1984   Attitudes toward the rhythm method in the Philippines. *Studies in
           Family Planning* 15(2):75–78.
Visher, S.
   1987   The relationship of locus of control and contraception use in the
           adolescent population. *Journal of Adolescent Health Care* 7:183–186.
Weiss, E., G. Udofia, and B. Madunagu
   1981   The Use of Modern Family Planning in Rural Nigeria. Paper
           presented at annual meeting, American Public Health Association,
           November, Los Angeles, Calif.
World Health Organization, Task Force on Psychosocial Research in Family
Planning
   1981   A cross cultural study of menstruation. *Studies in Family Planning*
           12(1):3–16.
Zelnik, M., and J. Kantner
   1979   Reasons for nonuse of contraception by sexually active women aged
           15–19. *Family Planning Perspectives* 11(5):289–296.
Zetina-Lozano, G.
   1983   Menstrual bleeding expectations and short-term contraceptive discon-
           tinuation in Mexico. *Studies in Family Planning* 14(5):127–133.

Part III
Consequences for Health

New Contraceptive Methods and Reproductive Health

MAHMOUD F. FATHALLA

A DEFINITION OF REPRODUCTIVE HEALTH

Health is defined in the World Health Organization (WHO) Constitution as a "state of complete physical, mental and social well-being and not merely the absence of disease or infirmity." In the context of this positive definition, reproductive health should not mean the absence of diseases or disorders of the reproductive process. It should mean that the reproductive process is accomplished in a state of complete physical, mental, and social well-being. Reproductive health in this definition would have a number of basic elements, involving ability, success, and safety in reproduction (Fathalla, 1988). Reproductive health would mean that people have the ability to reproduce, the ability to regulate their fertility, and the ability to practice and enjoy sexual relationships. It would mean that reproduction is carried to a successful outcome through infant and child survival, growth, and healthy development. It would mean that women can go safely through pregnancy and childbirth, that fertility regulation can be achieved without health hazards, and that people are safe in having sex.

According to this definition, the ability to regulate and control fertility effectively and safely is an integral element of reproductive health. A woman who is unable to regulate and control her fertility effectively and safely cannot be condsidered in a state of complete physical, mental, and social well-being. Besides being an integral element of reproductive health, fertility regulation and contraceptive use have a potential impact on all the other basic elements. They have implications for infertility, sexuality, child survival, safe motherhood, and sexually transmitted diseases, all of which will be dealt with in separate sections of this paper.

RATIONALES FOR CONTRACEPTIVE USE

The potential impact of contraceptive methods on reproductive health depends on the rationale for their use and the objective accomplished under this rationale. In other words, it is not the contraceptive use, in itself, but what is accomplished through contraceptive use that will have an impact on reproductive health.

There are three major rationales for contraceptive use and for the organized family planning movement; the demographic rationale, the health rationale, and the human rights rationale (Fathalla, 1987a). The three rationales have evolved separately, at different points in time, and for different objectives. Although most people are willing to embrace the three rationales, they do not necessarily coincide, and in fact, they can sometimes conflict with each other.

The Human Rights Rationale

In historical terms, this was the first basis around which organized efforts for contraceptive use were built. The evolution of that right followed in sequence the time when women began to claim their rights as equals and as partners. When that happened, it was not long before women realized that without the ability to control their fertility, they would not be able to control and shape their lives. Without family planning, women's rights are just words. A woman who has no control over her fertility cannot complete her education, cannot maintain gainful employment, cannot make independent marital decisions, and has very few real choices open to her.

Contraceptive use within the human rights rationale has a potential impact on reproductive health, through raising the status of women. A well-nourished and educated woman will enjoy a safer motherhood. Her infants and children will have a better chance of survival. Moreover, she will also have better access to fertility regulation and other health care services.

The Demographic Rationale

The demographic rationale for family planning came after the human rights rationale, as a response to the concern about the unprecedented phase of population growth in human history and its impediment to efforts for socioeconomic development. The objective of this rationale is to provide for a decrease in birthrates, to allow ongoing efforts of socioeconomic development to bear fruits to the individuals and to the society.

Contraceptive use within the demographic rationale has its impact on reproductive health. Socioeconomic development is the ultimate goal of the demographic rationale, and socioeconomic development is a powerful determinant of health, including reproductive health. When socioeconomic development is poor, it is the vulnerable groups in the society who suffer most. Women and children are in the forefront of these vulnerable groups.

There is another way in which the demographic rationale can influence reproductive health, and that is through its potential impact on the health care system. In a passive way, it can have an impact by simply relieving an already overloaded health care system by reducing the number of pregnancies, thereby improving its efficiency. More important, in an active way reproductive health care interventions can be built upon and integrated with an already existing family planning infrastructure initially developed to promote demographic objectives.

The Health Rationale

In the health rationale, contraceptive use is advocated to prevent high-risk and unwanted pregnancies. It differs from the demographic rationale in that it is a selective approach. Pursuing the demographic objective will not necessarily reduce first the number of high-risk births. The health rationale may also not have a large and immediate impact on the total number of births. The health rationale is concerned more with when rather than with how many.

Contraceptive use to prevent high-risk and unwanted pregnancies will have the most direct impact on reproductive health.

In summary, the discussion of the potential impact of contraceptive methods on reproductive health would really be examining the potential impact of what can be accomplished with the help of contraceptive use within the three above-mentioned rationales, in terms of advancement of the status of women, checking of excessive population growth, and modification of reproductive behavior to prevent high-risk and unwanted pregnancies. There is no question that contraceptive use is only one determinant, though an important and necessary one, in the achievement of these objectives. It is, however, beyond the scope of this paper, if not beyond the scope of the present state of knowledge, to try to disentangle the contribution of contraceptive methods from other contributions.

NONCONTRACEPTIVE HEALTH IMPACT OF CONTRACEPTIVE METHODS

Apart from the contraceptive effect, specific contraceptive methods may have noncontraceptive effects. These could be health benefits or adverse effects. They must be taken into consideration when the impact of contraceptive use on reproductive health is considered.

Noncontraceptive health benefits include the prevention of sexually transmitted diseases through the use of barrier methods, the health benefits to the infant through breastfeeding, and the beneficial side effects of hormonal contraception. Adverse side effects can be encountered with almost any contraceptive method. An example of an adverse effect that has an impact on reproductive health is the risk of pelvic inflammatory disease associated with use of an intrauterine device (IUD).

CONTRIBUTION OF NEW METHODS TO THE IMPACT OF CONTRACEPTIVE USE

New methods would contribute to the impact of contraceptive use on reproductive health through two mechanisms. The first mechanism is general and applies to all new methods: broadening contraceptive choice. The second mechanism is specific to the method under consideration and is based on what advantages the method can offer in terms of contraceptive performance (effectiveness, safety, acceptability, and continuation) and availability, together with any noncontraceptive health benefits the method may have.

Broadening the Choice of Contraceptives

The range of currently available contraceptive methods is very limited. This becomes more apparent if we consider the large numbers of users and potential users all over the world. These include women and men living in a large diversity of socioeconomic conditions, health service settings, and cultural situations. They include women at different phases of their reproductive lives that extend over a period of about 30 years and in which each phase has different contraceptive requirements. To meet the needs of different users and those of the same users at different periods, a wide array of methods is needed.

The range of choice is further limited by the lack of availability of certain methods to family planning programs for cultural, religious, or political reasons or within family planning programs because of lack of a required health care service infrastructure (Fathalla, 1983).

The addition of a new method of contraception that satisfies generally accepted criteria for effectiveness and safety will broaden the choices available for contraceptive users. This, in turn, can be expected to have an impact on reproductive health in the following ways (Berelson, 1976):

• Adding a new layer of acceptors from nonusers who will find the new method attractive, and who will thus have access to the reproductive health benefits of contraceptive use.

• Adding to contraceptive continuation by offering an alternative to users who are dissatisfied with and discontinue other methods. Continuation of contraceptive use will ensure the continuation of the reproductive health benefits.

• Improving contraceptive safety. The availability of a wider choice of methods will ensure that more users will have access to methods that match their safety requirements, and thus will carry less or no health hazards to them.

• Extending contraceptive availability. New methods can stimulate the extension of the delivery system itself. Program managers feeling that they have something that they can sell will be encouraged to increase their service outlets.

It could be argued that a large contraceptive use prevalence is possible with a very limited range of contraceptive methods. The demographic transition in developed contries was achieved without any of the modern contraceptives. This argument holds the view that contraceptive use is a yes or no matter, that people who want to use a contraceptive will use one, however unattractive or inconvenient it may be, and that people who do not want to use a contraceptive will not use one, however attractive or convenient it may be. It is true that there will always be a yes group of highly motivated couples and a no group of couples, for example, those who are ideologically opposed to the concept of contraceptive use. There is also a group in between, however, for whom attractive and convenient methods can tip the balance for contraceptive use. The size of this group will be relatively large when the motivation for contraceptive use is not high. Such is the situation in most developing countries.

All new methods of contraception will broaden the choice of contraceptives. The magnitude of the impact will, however, be influenced by the users' perception of the method as being new. A user would probably perceive a new contraceptive approach in a way that is different from a technological improvement within an existing approach. Examples of new contraceptive approaches in the pipeline include implants, hormone-releasing vaginal rings, female condoms, antiprogestin-prostaglandin combinations, vaccines for fertility regulation, and a systemic method for male fertility regulation.

Method Advantages

The introduction of a new contraceptive method will result in the shifting of certain users of other methods to the new method. The new method will have an impact if it offers an improvement in terms of effectiveness, safety and freedom from side effects, or both, resulting in higher continuation rates.

A new contraceptive method will have an impact on reproductive health if it can reach couples and individuals who do not use current methods. Several of the new methods in the pipeline have less service delivery requirements and would thus lend themselves to a potentially wider availability.

A new contraceptive method will make an additional impact on reproductive health if it confers noncontraceptive health benefits, beyond what is already available through existing methods.

FERTILITY CONTROL

The ability to regulate and control fertility is an essential element of reproductive health. It is an essential element, on its own, irrespective of its interrelationship to other elements of reproductive health. The reproductive health right of fertility regulation and control cannot be implemented without the availability of effective, safe, and acceptable contraceptive methods.

According to a recent report (Population Crisis Committee, 1987), of the 2.8 billion people in the developing world outside China, about 660 million are women aged 15 to 49. Around 460 million of these women are sexually active, but the number needing contraceptives at any one time is reduced to about 370 million because of women who are infertile or who are in the process of having another child. Only 124 million women use an effective method of contraception. That leaves about 250 million women in developing countries who need effective contraception to prevent unwanted pregnancies. These women either lack the motivation, do not have access to the services, or are not satisfied with existing contraceptive methods. The introduction of new contraceptive methods could have a potential impact on all three of these factors. As rightly stated by Berelson (1976), in the developed countries the quality and availability of services and the level of motivation are probably high enough to take care of deficiencies in technology; in the developing world, improved and wider options of contraceptive technology can take care of some of the deficiencies in the services and in the motivation.

Motivation for contraceptive use is not an absolute yes or no. Data from the World Fertility Survey and from Contraceptive Prevalence Surveys indicate that there is a wide gap between the desire for contraception and the use of contraceptives, resulting in a significant proportion of unwanted births (Population Reports, 1985). Except in Africa, couples in surveyed countries had an average of about two unwanted births. Differences between the total fertility rate (TFR) and the wanted total fertility rate (WTFR) averaged 1.7 in Asia, 1.9 in Latin America, and 2.0 in the Middle East. Differences between TFR and WTFR were smallest in Africa—0.6 on average—since women reported that most births were wanted. Still, WTFRs in Africa were lower than actual fertility rates in every country analyzed except Mauritania.

More direct evidence that the availability of new contraceptive methods will increase contraceptive use has been seen in the early experience of family planning programs in developing countries, where the addition of a new method has been shown to attract a new layer of acceptors (Freedman and Berelson, 1976).

More recent experience with the introduction of new methods also supports this evidence. In a study of NORPLANT® introduction in Indonesia involving 8,681 subjects, 46.7 percent of the acceptors were not using another contraceptive method (Affandi, 1987).

Access to birth control is inadequate in most developing countries. A recent study has reported that family planning services were inadequate in 80 out of the 95 developing countries studied (Population Crisis Committee, 1987). These 80 countries contain 58 percent of the population in the developing world. If China's 1 billion people are excluded, men and women in countries with 80 percent of the population in the developing world have inadequate access to birth control.

There are two mechanisms through which new contraceptives may extend the availability of contraception. Several of the new methods under development will have less service delivery requirements and can thus be made more widely available. Also, the introduction of new methods has a stimulatory effect on the delivery system, encouraging more expansion. This observation is supported by the experience in early family planning programs (Berelson, 1976).

Discontinuation is an indicator of method dissatisfaction. Reported discontinuation rates for the reversible effective methods are high, ranging from 30 to 80 percent for the birth-control pill and 15 to 60 percent for the IUD after 1 year of use (Kreager, 1977). From a reproductive health point of view, it is not method continuation that is important but contraceptive practice continuation. The availability of a broader choice will increase practice continuation by offering more alternatives.

Another observation that points in the direction of method dissatisfaction is the number of induced abortions. Approximately 3.3 million legal abortions are performed in the world; adding the estimated number of illegal abortions to the number would increase the world total to between 40 million and 60 million abortions per year (Henshaw, 1987).

Fertility control, as a positive element of reproductive health and as a human right, must give full consideration to the user perspective. It implies more demand for methods that are user controlled. New methods under development would, to a certain extent, address this requirement. The levonorgestrel-releasing vaginal ring will be the first long-acting contraceptive method that is completely user controlled. (The ring under development with WHO support confers protection for 3 months.) It does not require any fitting and is simply inserted by the user. It also does not require any help in removal, and its action is immediately reversible after removal. The development of a female condom would also give the woman more control in protecting herself from pregnancy and from sexually transmitted diseases.

INFERTILITY

The ability to reproduce is a basic element of reproductive health. Infertility, in itself, may not threaten physical health, but it can certainly have a serious impact on mental and social health. The WHO estimates that there are 60 million to 80 million infertile couples worldwide. From a public health point of view, one should distinguish between core infertility and acquired infertility. There would probably always be a certain percentage of couples who would be infertile, because of reasons we cannot prevent, we cannot treat, or we do not know. This is what is referred to as *core infertility*. The percentage of core infertility is probably not less than 3 and not more than 5. A prevalence of infertility higher than that is considered as *acquired infertility*, which generally indicates that there are causes in the community for adding a new layer of infertile couples. In certain parts of sub-Saharan Africa, the prevalence of infertility may be as high as 30 percent or more (Frank, 1983; Meheus, Reniers, and Colletet, 1986). The most common and most important cause of acquired infertility is pelvic infection as a result of sexually transmitted diseases, unsafe abortion, or puerperal infection.

The potential impact of contraceptive methods on infertility is either general or specific to the use of certain methods. In general, an expansion in contraceptive use, promoted by the introduction of new methods, will reduce the incidence of unsafe abortion and its complications. Pelvic infection is one of these complications and can result in occlusion of the fallopian tubes, with subsequent permanent infertility. In addition, family planning clinics can also, and often do, provide infertility-related services such as counseling, early detection and diagnosis of sexually transmitted diseases, certain infertility tests, and referrals.

Specific contraceptive methods have their own impact. Since sexually transmitted diseases (STDs) are an important cause of infertility, the impact of barrier methods on STDs will be particularly relevant. There is evidence that a high proportion of the public health problem of infertility in sub-Saharan Africa is attributable to STDs (Meheus, Reniers, and Colletet, 1986). Providing barrier contraceptive methods will help men and women to protect themselves and their partners from STDs and from the complication of infertility. The development of new barrier methods such as antiviral medicated condoms, female condoms, and disposable diaphragms could expand the utilization of barrier methods.

TABLE 1 Estimates of Maternal Mortality

Region	Live Births (millions)	Maternal Mortality Ratio (per 100,000 live births)	Maternal Deaths (thousands)
Developing countries	110.1	450	494
Developed countries	18.2	30	6
Worldwide	128.3	390	500

SOURCE: World Health Organization (1986a). 1983 estimates.

Curative treatment of infertility due to pelvic infections caused by STDs or septic abortion is difficult, time-consuming, expensive, and not widely available and is successful in only a small proportion of cases; hence, preventive measures are important. This includes the availability of effective contraceptive methods and the expansion of barrier method use.

Although the return of fertility may be delayed in some women after hormonal contraceptive use, there is no evidence of any permanent impairment (Vessey, 1986). The same will probably hold true for the hormonal methods under development. IUDs increase the risk of pelvic inflammatory disease (PID) in women exposed to STDs (World Health Organization, 1987b). The availability of a broader range of contraceptive choices will allow women to utilize methods more suited to their safety requirements.

Oral contraceptives, on the other hand, can decrease the risk of PID (Senanayake and Kramer, 1980). This protective effect, however, may not apply to chlamydial infections (Washington et al., 1985). It is highly likely that the new hormonal methods will offer the same health benefits.

SAFE MOTHERHOOD

The World Health Organization estimates that about 500,000 women die every year because of complications of pregnancy and childbirth. Ninety-nine percent of these deaths take place in developing countries (Table 1).

In many parts of the world, maternal mortality has been reduced to levels as low as 6 or 7 per 100,000 live births. In other parts of the world, rates of over 1,000 are still encountered.

It should be noted that the number of pregnancies and deliveries that the woman goes through determines her lifetime risk of maternal death. In some parts of rural Africa, this risk can be as high as 1 in 20. In Europe, it is as low as one in several thousand. This must be noted in any discussion on the impact of contraceptive use on safe motherhood.

Maternal mortality, moreover, should be looked upon as just the tip of the iceberg of maternal morbidity, ill health, and human suffering.

An increase in the prevalence and effectiveness of contraceptive use, through the introduction of new methods, can have a potential impact on safe motherhood through a number of mechanisms. A direct impact can be achieved through the prevention of unwanted and high-risk pregnancies. An indirect impact can operate through improvement in the efficiency of health care services, advancement of the status of women, and enhancement of socioeconomic development as a result of checking population growth.

Prevention of Unwanted Pregnancy

Prevention of unwanted pregnancy will decrease the incidence of unsafe abortion. It will also avoid the needless risk of maternal morbidity and mortality for a pregnancy that is not wanted and that is often of higher risk than a wanted pregnancy (Fathalla, 1989).

In a series of studies reported by WHO (1986b) illegal induced abortion accounted for 7 to 50 percent of maternal deaths, with a median of 15 percent. The impact of contraception on decreasing the incidence of illegal abortion has been documented in the experience of Chile. In the early 1960s, contraceptive use among women of reproductive age in Chile was only about 3 percent; the birthrate was about 37 per 1,000 population; abortion complications accounted for about one of every five admissions to obstetric services and abortion mortality was 11.8 deaths per 10,000 live births. By 1978–1979, after contraceptive services were made available, contraceptive use increased to 23 percent, birthrates declined to 22 per 1,000, obstetric admissions for abortion fell to one in eight, and abortion mortality was down to 2.4 deaths per 10,000 live births (Population Reports, 1980).

Using World Fertility Survey data, Maine et al. (1987) estimated the proportion of maternal deaths that would be prevented if all women who stated that they wanted no more children and who were not currently using effective contraception were able to prevent all these unwanted pregnancies. For 26 developing countries, the median proportion of deaths averted was 29 percent, with a range from 5 percent in Ivory Coast to 62 percent in Bangladesh. The median reductions were 17 percent for 8 African countries, 35 percent for 10 Asian countries, and 33 percent for 8 Latin American countries. Taking into consideration the prevailing high levels of maternal mortality in these countries, the number of lives saved could be enormous.

Prevention of High-Risk Pregnancy

The availability of effective and acceptable contraceptive choices will enable women to modify their reproductive behavior pattern and to avoid having pregnancies that are too early, too close, too many, or too late. A decrease in these unfavorable patterns of childbearing, particularly pregnancies that are too early or too many, will have an impact on safe motherhood.

A recent study estimated that in rural Bangladesh, the maternal mortality rate would decline by one-third if births were confined to women between the ages of 20 and 39 who were having their first through fifth births (Trussell and Pebley, 1984).

A methodological limitation is to be recognized in mathematical models that attempt to measure the effect of childbearing patterns on maternal mortality. Since family planning prevents deaths through preventing births, the use of mortality rates that relate the number of deaths to the number of births tends to grossly underestimate the number of deaths averted (Fortney, 1987; Winnikoff and Sullivan, 1987).

Improving the Efficiency of Maternal and Child Health Care Services

Contraceptive use can reduce the load on the overburdened and overstretched maternal and child health care services in developing countries through reduction of the total number of pregnancies, births, and children who may require the service, with the improvement of childbearing patterns resulting in a reduction of high-risk pregnancies and a decrease in the incidence of illegal abortion and the load it imposes, through its complications, on the health ser-

TABLE 2 Infant and Child Mortality

Region	Mortality Rate (per 1,000 births)		Deaths (in millions)	
	Infants	Children Under 5	Infants	Children Under 5
Developed countries	15	18	0.27	0.05
Developing countries	84	127	9.3	4.8
Worldwide	74	112	9.6	4.8

SOURCE: U.N. Population Division and U.N. Statistical Office (1985). Estimates from 1985.

vice. A health service relieved of an unnecessarily heavy load will be expected to function with more efficiency.

Nortman, Halvas, and Rabago (1986) made a sophisticated analysis of the benefit of family planning services in terms of the savings that accrued from a reduction in the load on its maternal and infant health care services. They concluded that for every 1 peso spent on family planning services, a savings was made by the Mexican Social Security System of 9 pesos in maternal and child health care services that were not utilized. These savings can be utilized to improve the services.

CHILD SURVIVAL

Table 2 shows the world death toll of infants and children in numbers and rates. It also demonstrates the gross inequity in health between developed and developing countries.

These mortality figures are an indication of much higher figures of morbidity and ill health in surviving children.

New contraceptive methods can have a potential impact on child survival. The mechanisms are somewhat similar to those discussed above for safe motherhood. Modifying childbearing patterns to increase child spacing and to decrease births to adolescents will have a direct impact on child survival. An indirect impact will be achieved through improvement of the efficiency of health services, advancement of the status of women, and checking rates of population growth to facilitate efforts for socioeconomic development.

Childbearing Patterns

Data from the World Fertility Survey provided a rich source of information on the impact of childbearing patterns on the survival of infants and children. A badly spaced prior birth raises the average chances of dying in infancy by about 60 to 70 percent and the chances of dying before the age of 5 by about 50 percent (Hobcraft et al., 1987). An infant born to a teenager mother is 24 percent more likely to die in the first month of life than is an infant born to a mother aged 25 to 34; the excess mortality is 37 percent for the remainder of the first year of life and 33 percent in early childhood (Hobcraft, 1987).

There are methodological limitations in attempting to measure the effects of contraceptive use and childbearing patterns on health (Population Reports, 1983). Contraception is a choice. Any sample of contraceptive users will, in a sense, be a self-selected sample. The factors underlying the choice of contraception in general or of a contraceptive method in particular could well be, in fact, in the majority of cases probably are, significant determinants of reproductive health as well.

It should be noted that a favorable childbearing pattern does not necessarily always follow a prevalent contraceptive use advocated for demographic objectives. An example in which the demographic and health impacts may not coincide has been pointed out in a study by Bongaarts (1987) in which it was shown that the family building pattern, in the presence of prevalent contraceptive use, may be associated with short birth intervals, and hence, may not reflect the desired impact of a lower infant mortality rate.

Socioeconomic Development

An example of an important parameter determined by socioeconomic development and with a strong influence on child survival is environmental sanitation. Of 149 countries providing information to WHO in 1987, only 62 reported that 80 percent or more of their populations have access to safe drinking water (World Health Organization, 1986c). Within countries there was also a marked disparity between urban and rural areas. The situation with regard to facilities for waste disposal are much worse, particularly for rural populations, for which some countries reported as little as 1 percent coverage in 1987. The WHO estimates that if the improvement in water supply and sanitation is to make a full impact, over 1 billion more people must be provided with adequate and safe drinking water (over 80 percent of those in the rural areas of the world's developing countries), while over 1.5 billion must be provided with adequate sanitation. Without putting the brakes on population growth rates, it is difficult to see how the socioeconomic development in developing countries can meet this enormous demand.

Specific Methods

Breastfeeding is the outstanding contraceptive method with demonstrable health benefits to the infant in terms of nutrition, protection from infection, and psychological bonding. Breastfeeding, with our better understanding on how it works, is a renewed contraceptive method with a major potential impact on infant and child health.

The development of the progesterone-releasing vaginal ring as a new method of contraception is directed to maintaining the health benefits of continued lactation while protecting the mother (and also the infant) from the effect of an unwanted pregnancy. At the same time, it safeguards the infant from any possible remote hazard caused by the transmission of the hormone in the mother's breast milk.

SEXUALITY

Human sexuality has always been a taboo subject. It was only recently that attention has been focused on this important aspect of human behavior.

In general, it can be postulated that a wider availability of effective contraceptive choices will help couples to enjoy better a rewarding relationship without the fear of unwanted pregnancy.

The influence that specific hormonal contraceptives, existing or new, may have on sexuality is not yet fully understood, but it is probably not great. The frequency of sexual activity appears to be higher in oral contraceptive users than in women who use nonsteroidal contraception (Westoff, Bumpass, and Ryden, 1969). This, however, may reflect differences in the sexual attitudes of oral contraceptive users. It has also been suggested that sexual effects could well be correlated with the mood changes that occur with the use of hormonal methods (Bancroft et al., 1987).

SEXUALLY TRANSMITTED DISEASES

One of the most disappointing aspects of medicine during the past 25 years has been the great increase in the incidence of infections caused by sexually transmissible agents. STDs are now the most common group of notifiable infectious diseases in most countries (World Health Organization, 1986c).

General Contraceptive Use

An increased prevalence of contraceptive use as a result of the introduction of new methods can influence the spread of STDs.

It can be postulated that the availability of contraception may encourage casual sexual relations. Although the postulate has never been proved, it explains the restrictive attitudes in some societies toward contraceptive availability to adolescents and unmarried individuals.

It can also be postulated that the availability of the more convenient systemic methods of contraception may have decreased reliance on the coitus-related barrier methods that offer protection against STDs. This could contribute to the spread of STDs.

On the other hand, demographic factors can have significant consequences for STDs. The increase in the number and proportion of the young population as a result of excessive population growth, disorderly urbanization, and the explosion of poverty are known factors underlying the spread of STDs (World Health Organization, 1986c).

The availability of family planning services can provide opportunities for sex and health education, screening and diagnostic facilities, treatment, or referral services, as well as making available barrier methods. This should contribute to a decrease in the spread of STDs.

In developed countries, there was an apparent time coincidence among the sexual revolution, the contraceptive revolution, and the explosive epidemic of STDs. This may have been a reason for postulating a link. In developing countries, on the other hand, there is no such correlation. African countries with large incidences of STDs have the lowest prevalence of contraceptive use. A country such as the People's Republic of China, which has the highest prevalence of contraceptive use, does not seem to have the public health problem of STDs.

Several of the agents of STDs can be passed to the fetus from the infected mother, resulting in congenital lesions of varying severity and seriousness, and they can be potentially fatal. An increasing prevalence of effective contraceptive use can decrease the perinatal spread of STDs.

Specific Methods

Specific methods of contraception can have an impact on STDs, both on the spread and the course of the disease.

Barrier methods can have an impact on controlling the spread of STDs. Condoms can protect the wearer from diseases acquired through penile exposure to infected cervical, vaginal, or rectal secretions and can protect the partner from diseases acquired through semen, urethral secretions, and penile lesions. The diaphragm provides a mechanical barrier to the cervix, and in addition, is nearly always used with a spermicide, which itself has a protective effect. Several spermicidal agents provide some protection against certain sexually transmitted diseases (Rosenberg and Feldblum, 1986). The contraceptive sponge (which contains about 1 gram of the spermicide nonoxynol-9) probably protects against the same STDs as spermicides alone (Rosenberg et al., 1987).

The introduction of new barrier methods such as an antiviral medicated condom, a female condom, and a disposable diaphragm would broaden the choices available for users and would expand their use.

The course of STDs is also modified by specific contraceptive methods, particularly in relation to PID. The role of IUDs and hormonal contraceptives has already been mentioned above in the discussion of infertility.

Impact on Human Immunodeficiency Virus (HIV) Infection

The observations noted above on the relation of general contraceptive use to STDs would also apply to the heterosexual transmission of acquired immune deficiency syndrome (AIDS). They also highlight the importance of the expanded availability of effective contraception in preventing the perinatal spread of the disease.

Barrier methods, in particular, the condom, remain the best prophylaxis (Feldblum and Fortney, 1987; Rietemijer et al., 1988).

There is much uncertainty and several wide gaps in our knowledge about the mechanisms of heterosexual transmission of the disease, whether from male to female or male to female. This does not allow more than speculation about the relationship of specific methods of contraception to the spread of the disease. Any possible modifying effect of hormonal contraception (including the new methods) on susceptibility to the disease or on the course of the disease remains to be seen. If the virus enters the male reproductive tract via the epididymis, then men who are positive for HIV and who have a vasectomy might be protecting their partners. In that case, the development of a percutaneous method of vas occlusion could have a significant health impact.

New contraceptive methods involving skin or tissue piercing procedures, such as implants, injectables, and vaccines, will need to conform to the standard medical precautions to prevent the spread of AIDS.

CONTRACEPTIVE SAFETY

Contraceptive safety is not a simple concept. Evaluation of the comparative safety of different contraceptive methods must take into consideration three important attributes of the method: effectiveness, noncontraceptive health benefits, and the health hazards associated with its use (Fathalla, 1987b). Different methods of contraception rank differently in these attributes. The weight attached to each of these attributes, however, differs among populations, for different individuals, and even for the same individual at different periods of life. A method's safety is therefore relative and is a feature of the method's use in a particular population, a particular social setting, by particular users, at a particular time.

The importance attached to effectiveness, for example, as a safety criterion depends on the level of health risk associated with the pregnancy it is meant to avert. Generally, this will vary in relation to two main factors: the prevalent level of the maternal mortality ratio and the availability of safe services for pregnancy termination. Specifically, it will also vary from one user to another. When a particular pregnancy carries a more than average health risk (physical, mental, or social), then contraceptive effectiveness becomes more important as a safety criterion.

The significance of noncontraceptive health benefits in the assessment of contraceptive safety will also vary in different situations.

The prevention of STDs as a noncontraceptive health benefit could mean nothing for a couple in a stable mutually faithful sexual partnership. For others, it could mean protection from serious morbidity, permanent infertility, and even death.

The health hazards associated with the use of contraceptive methods will also vary in different users. For example, an IUD user with multiple sexual partners could incur a much higher risk of developing PID, whereas a woman in a monogamous relationship will not have such a risk. For a young woman who is a nonsmoker, the cardiovascular hazards of oral contraceptive use are almost nil. For a heavy smoker aged 35 years or over, the health hazards of oral contraceptive use outweigh all contraceptive and noncontraceptive health benefits.

Impact of Broadening Contraceptive Choice

The introduction of new contraceptive methods will broaden the available contraceptive choices. Since different methods of contraception carry different risks to different users, a limited choice of contraceptives can result in more people using methods that are not optimal for their safety requirements. Making a wide range of methods available, on the other hand, will help to ensure that methods and users are better matched to improve safety.

Specific Methods

Specific new contraceptive methods can provide an improvement in the safety profile over existing methods.

New long-acting steroidal contraceptives, such as implants and the levonorgestrel-releasing vaginal ring, have three features that should contribute to improved safety. They are free of estrogen, and thus avoid all the health hazards associated with estrogen use. They release very small amounts of the hormone, much smaller than those released with oral preparations or injectables. In addition, they maintain a more or less constant rate of release, thus avoiding the high initial levels associated with other modes of administration.

The levonorgestrel-releasing IUD overcomes one major safety concern associated with IUD use, namely, increased menstrual blood loss. This is of particular importance in populations with a high prevalence of iron deficiency anemia.

One safety concern in the use of hormonal contraceptives during lactation is a possible remote effect on the child, particularly on hypothalamic maturation. The development of the progesterone-releasing vaginal ring addresses this concern. It releases the natural hormone. The hormone will also not be bioavailable to the infant when ingested in breast milk.

An antifertility vaccine based on chorionic gonadotropin represents a unique approach in terms of safety. It is targeted against a substance that is present only when conception occurs. It should not affect other body systems, if its development meets expectations.

Need for Further Research

Contraceptive methods are subjected to extensive testing before they can be allowed for general use. This includes both extensive animal experimentation and phased, controlled trials in humans (World Health Organization, 1987a). In spite of all these requirements, the potential noncontraceptive health benefits and risks of a contraceptive method will not be completely known before it is put into wide use. No amount of animal experimentation or clinical trials will enable us to predict absolutely the absence of any long-term or remote effects.

This need must be addressed for all new methods. Postmarketing drug surveillance is a well-developed research system with a number of well-defined strategies and methodologies aimed at detecting rare or late side effects (Petitti and Shapiro, 1987). A coordinated international research effort for postmarketing surveillance of new contraceptive methods will be critical for ensuring contraceptive safety.

SUMMARY

Reproductive health is a positive state of physical, mental, and social well-being and includes a number of basic elements concerned with ability (fertility, fertility control, and sexuality), success (infant and child survival, growth, and development), and safety (safe motherhood, contraceptive safety, and protection from sexually transmitted diseases) in human reproduction. Although contraceptive methods are primarily concerned with the elements of fertility control and contraceptive safety, they have an impact on all the other elements.

The potential impact of contraceptive use on reproductive health depends on the rationale for contraceptive use and the objectives achieved through its use. The human rights, demographic, and health rationales all have an impact on reproductive health, through advancement of the status of women, checking of excessive population growth, improvement of the efficiency of maternal and child health care services, and above all, modifying reproductive behavior to prevent high-risk and unwanted pregnancies.

Apart from the impact through the contraceptive effect, specific methods can have a noncontraceptive impact on reproductive health as well.

New contraceptive methods introduced into health and family planning services would contribute to the impact of contraceptive use on reproductive health through the broadening of contraceptive choice, resulting in more users, more practice continuation, improved safety, and extended availability. In addition, the specific advantages of the method can result in improving contraceptive performance, expanding the availability of contraception, as well as conferring noncontraceptive health benefits.

REFERENCES

Affandi, B.
    1987   Clinical, Pharmacological and Epidemiological Studies on a Levonorgestrel Implant Contraceptive. Unpublished Ph.D. dissertation. University of Indonesia, Jakarta.
Bancroft, J., D. Sanders, P. Warner, and N. Loudon
    1987   The effects of oral contraceptives on mood and sexuality: A comparison of triphasic and combined preparations. *Psychosomatic Obstetrics and Gynaecology* 7:1.
Berelson, B.
    1976   The impact of new technology. *Proceedings of the Royal Society of London Series B* 195:25.
Bongaarts, J.
    1987   Does family planning reduce infant mortality rates. *Population and Development Review* 13:323.
Fathalla, M.F.
    1983   A synthesis of the various experiences and problems encountered with available methods of fertility regulation in developing countries. P. 76 in E. Diczfalusy and A. Diczfalusy, eds., *Research on the Regulation of Human Fertility*, vol. 2. Copenhagen, Denmark: Scriptor.
    1987a   Health and family planning issues: A global perspective. P. 11 in *Better Health for Women and Children through Family Planning: Report of an International Conference*, Nairobi, Kenya, October 5–9, 1987. New York: The Population Council.
    1987b   Contraceptive Technology and Safety. Background paper to International Conference on Better Health for Women and Children through Family Planning, Nairobi, Kenya, October 5–9, 1987. The Population Council, New York.

1988   Promotion of research in human reproduction: Global needs and perspectives. *Human Reproduction* 3:7.

1989   Unwanted pregnancy. The future: Meeting the unmet need: A reproductive health approach. *People*. In press.

Feldblum, P.J., and J.A. Fortney

1987   Condoms, spermicides and the transmission of human immunodeficiency virus: A review of the literature. *American Journal of Public Health* 78:52.

Fortney, J.A.

1987   The importance of family planning in reducing maternal mortality. *Studies in Family Planning* 18:109.

Frank, O.

1983   Infertility in Sub-Saharan Africa: estimates and implications. *Population and Development Review* 9:137.

Freedman, R., and B. Berelson

1976   The record of family planning programmes. *Studies in Family Planning* 7:1.

Henshaw, S.K.

1987   Induced abortion: A worldwide perspective. *International Family Planning Perspectives* 13:12.

Hobcraft, J.

1987   Does Family Planning Save Children's Lives? Background paper to International Conference on Better Health for Women and Children through Family Planning, Nairobi, Kenya, October 5–9, 1987. The Population Council, New York.

Kreager, P.

1977   *Family Planning Drop-outs Reconsidered: A Critical Review of Research and Research Findings.* London: International Planned Parenthood Federation.

Maine, D., A. Rosenfield, M. Wallace, A.M. Kimball, B. Kwast, E. Papiernik, and S. White

1987   Prevention of Maternal Mortality in Developing Countries. Background paper to Safe Motherhood International Conference, Nairobi, Kenya, February 1987. World Bank, Washington, D.C.

Meheus, A., J. Reniers, and M. Colletet

1986   Determinants of infertility in Africa. *African Journal of STD* 2:31.

Nortman, D., J. Halvas, and A. Rabago

1986   A cost-benefit analysis of the Mexican Social Security Administration's family planning programme. *Studies in Family Planning* 17:1.

Petitti, D.B., and S. Shapiro

1987   Strategies for post-registration surveillance of contraceptive steroids. In Proceedings of a WHO Symposium on Improving the Safety Requirements for Contraceptive Steroids. Geneva: World Health Organization.

Population Crisis Committee

1987   Access to Birth Control: A World Assessment. Population Briefing Paper no. 19. Washington, D.C.: Population Crisis Committee.

Population Reports

1980   Complications of abortion in developing countries. *Population Reports* Series F, no. 7.

1983   Infertility and sexually transmitted diseases: A public health challenge. *Population Reports* Series L, no. 4.
1985   Fertility and family planning surveys: An update. *Population Reports* Series M, no. 8.
Rietemijer, C.A.M., J.W. Krebs, P.M. Feorino, and F.N. Judson
1988   Condoms as physical and chemical barriers against human immunodeficiency virus. *Journal of the American Medical Association* 259:1851.
Rosenberg, M.J., and P.J. Feldblum
1986   Do spermicides protect against sexually transmitted diseases? *African Journal of STD* 2:42.
Rosenberg, M.J., W. Rajanapithayakorn, P.J. Feldblum, and J.E. Higgins
1987   Effect of the contraceptive sponge on chlamydial infection, gonorrhoea and candidiasis. A comparative clinical trial. *Journal of the American Medical Association* 257:2308.
Senanayake, P., and D.G. Kramer
1980   Contraception and the etiology of pelvic inflammatory disease: New perspectives. *American Journal of Obstetrics and Gynecology* 138:852.
Trussel, J., and A.R. Pebley
1984   The potential impact of changes in fertility on infant, child and maternal mortality. *Studies in Family Planning* 15:267.
U.N. Population Division and U.N. Statistical Office.
1985   *World Demographic Estimates 1985.* New York: United Nations.
Vessey, M.P.
1986   Benefits and risks of contraception. P. 121 in C.R. Austin and R.V. Short, eds., *Reproduction in Mammals*, 2d ed. *Book 5: Manipulating Reproduction.* Cambridge, England: Cambridge University Press.
Washington, A.E., S. Gove, J. Sachacter, and R.L. Sweet
1985   Oral contraceptives, Chlamydia trachomatis infection, and pelvic inflammatory disease. *Journal of the American Medical Association* 253:2246.
Westoff, C.F., L. Bumpass, and N.B. Ryden
1969   Oral contraception, coital frequency and the time required to conceive. *Social Biology* 16:1.
Winnikoff, B., and M. Sullivan
1987   Assessing the role of family planning in reducing maternal mortality. *Studies in Family Planning* 18:128.
World Health Organization
1986a   *Maternal Mortality Rates. A Tabulation of Available Information.* FHE/86.3. Geneva: World Health Organization.
1986b   Maternal mortality: Helping women off the road to death. *WHO Chronicle* 40:175.
1986c   Expert Committee on Venereal Diseases and Treponematoses. Sixth Report of the Expert Committee on Venereal Diseases and Treponematoses. Technical Report Series 736. Geneva: World Health Organization.
1987a   WHO Special Programme of Research, Development and Research Training in Human Reproduction. *Guidelines for the Toxicological and Clinical Assessment and Post-registration Surveillance of Steroidal Contraceptive Drugs.* Geneva: World Health Organization.
1987b   *Mechanism of Action, Safety and Efficacy of Intrauterine Devices.* Technical Report Series 753. Geneva: World Health Organization.

Effects of New Contraceptive Methods on Abortion Utilization

JACQUELINE DARROCH FORREST AND STANLEY K. HENSHAW

For two reasons, the effect of new contraceptives on abortion is a relevant topic for discussion considering the demographic impact of new contraceptive methods: the level of abortion is an indicator of the efficiency with which fertility is being controlled through control of pregnancy and, in times and places where it is not available in safe, legal settings, abortion is an important contributor to infertility and to mortality of women of reproductive age.

LEVELS OF ABORTION

Table 1 shows the most recently published data on abortion rates for 35 countries. Not all countries tally data on the level of abortions, and the data available are not always complete and accurate. The range in abortion rates is wide, from 0.2 to 181 per 1,000 women aged 15 to 44. In 14 of these 35 countries, the data are of unknown accuracy or are thought to be inaccurate by at least 20 percent. These include such large countries as China, India, and the USSR and such diverse countries as Bangladesh and France. Among the countries with quite accurate abortion statistics, the abortion rate ranges from 5.6 per 1,000 women aged 15 to 44 in The Netherlands to 70.5 in Yugoslavia. The 35 countries for which abortion data are shown in Table 1 represent 64 percent of the world's population. It is clear from reports made by a wide variety of professionals that abortion is also common in most other countries of the world. It has been estimated that in addition to the 33 million abortions occurring each year in these 35 countries, some 10 million to 20 million abortions

177

TABLE 1 Number of Legal Abortions, Abortion Rate, Abortion Ratio, and Total Abortion Rate, Selected Countries

Country (Year)	Number of Abortions	Abortion Rate	Abortion Ratio	Total Abortion Rate
Australia (1984)	54,600	15.2	18.5	U
Bangladesh (1984-1985)[a,b]	68,600	3.4	1.5	U
Bulgaria (1984)	113,500	61.9	48.1	U
Canada (1984)[c]	62,300	10.2	14.2	288
(1982)[d]	77,500	13.0	17.2	U
China (1983)[a]	14,371,800	61.5	43.1	U
Cuba (1984)	139,600	58.6	45.9	U
Czechoslovakia (1984)	113,800	34.5	33.8	1,005
Denmark (1984)	20,700	18.4	28.6	554 (1983)
England and Wales (1984)[c]	136,400	12.8	17.3	367
Finland (1983)	13,400	12.1	16.8	362
France (1984)[a,e]	177,000	14.9	18.9	U
German Democratic Republic (1984)[f]	96,200	26.6	29.7	708 (1976)
German Federal Republic (1984)[a,g]	97,900	7.3	14.4	U
Greenland (1983)	580	44.7	37.1	U
Hong Kong (1964)	14,500	11.3	15.8	U
Hungary (1984)	82,200	37.1	40.9	1,044 (1983)
Iceland (1983)	690	12.9	14.0	U
India (1983-1984)[a]	518,600	3.3	2.1	U
Israel (1984)	18,900	21.9	16.1	U
Italy (1984)[a]	227,400	19.0	28.0	U
Japan (1983)[a,h]	567,500	21.5	27.2	U
(1975)	2,250,000	84.2	54.7	U
The Netherlands (1984)[c]	18,700	5.6	9.7	161
New Zealand (1984)	7,300	9.7	12.4	272 (1983)
Norway (1984)	14,100	15.9	21.9	465
Poland (1984)[a,i]	133,000	16.5	16.0	U
Romania (1983)[a,j]	421,400	90.9	56.7	U
Scotland (1984)[k]	9,900	8.9	13.2	236 (1983)
Singapore (1983)[a]	19,100	28.1	32.0	792
South Africa (1982)[a,k]	1,000	0.2	0.1	U

occur elsewhere in the world, for an average abortion rate in those lands of about the same as in those for which data are available (Henshaw, 1987).

Projection of the impact of new contraceptive methods on the use of abortion is severely hampered by the lack of accurate data on abortion for many countries of the world. Levels of reported abortion reflect not only the level of undesired pregnancies but also access to abortion and the accuracy of reporting on abortions. High

Sweden (1984)	30,800	17.7	24.7	534
Tunisia (1985)	21,300	13.6	8.9	617 (1977)
USSR (1982)[e,i]	11,000,000	181.0	68.0	U
United States (1983)	1,575,000	28.5	30.4	790
Vietnam (1980)[a]	170,600	14.6	8.1	U
Yugoslavia (1984)	358,300	70.5	48.8	U

NOTE: Abortion rate is number of abortions per 1,000 women aged 15-44. Abortion ratio is number of abortions per 100 known pregnancies (abortions plus births that occurred six months later). Total abortion rate is number of abortions that would be experienced by 1,000 women during their reproductive lifetimes, given present age-specific abortion rates. U = Unknown.

[a]Data are believed to be at least 20 percent inaccurate or are of unknown accuracy.
[b]Menstrual regulations only.
[c]Residents only.
[d]Includes Canadian women who obtained abortions in the United States and at private clinics in Quebec.
[e]Provisional.
[f]Includes East Berlin.
[g]Includes West Berlin; also includes West German women who obtained abortions in England and in The Netherlands.
[h]Data for 1983 are most recent official government statistics; 1975 data are estimates made to account for suspected abortion underreporting.
[i]Excludes abortions performed in physicians' offices.
[j]Includes illegal and spontaneous abortions treated by health care providers.
[k]Incudes women who obtained abortions in England.
[l]All data came from survey-derived abortion ratios (abortions per live births).

SOURCE: Henshaw (1987:14).

reported abortion rates undoubtedly indicate high levels of undesired pregnancy. Low reported abortion rates may reflect few unplanned pregnancies, women's inability to obtain abortions, or lack of data on the number of women who do have abortions. The first situation indicates that there is potential room for improved contraceptive use, but both unmet need and the effect of better contraceptive use on abortion are obscured for women who have difficulty obtaining abortion services and for whom abortions are underreported.

RELATIONSHIP BETWEEN
CONTRACEPTION AND ABORTION

Contraception and abortion are both ways to prevent births. Contraceptives do so by preventing pregnancies, and abortions prevent births by terminating pregnancies that have occurred. (Although, as discussed below, some new technologies and differences in definitions blur the distinction between action before or after a pregnancy has occurred.) Christopher Tietze (1983) noted that the relationship between these two means of preventing births varies over time and across countries. While levels of both contraceptive and abortion use will be low when there is little interest in limiting the number of births, the levels of the two may be either inversely or directly related when people are trying to limit the number of births. The levels of contraceptive use and of abortion can both be moderately high when access to contraceptives is limited and couples desire small families. Both contraceptive use and abortion rates may rise when the desire for limiting family size is increasing and contraceptives are being introduced into an area. The levels of both contraceptive use and abortion can also be high if the contraceptive methods available or chosen have high failure rates and women must frequently turn to abortion as a backup for contraceptive failure.

The more generally expected relationship between contraceptive use and abortion is an inverse one, in which the abortion rate is lower when contraceptive use is higher and abortion rates decline when contraceptive use increases. This is usually the case in developed countries where the desired family size is low. While in some countries a great deal of attention has been focused on attaining a low abortion level through high contraceptive use and prevention of unplanned pregnancies, it must be recognized that this is not necessarily a universal goal. In the United States, and many other countries as well, there is a general consensus that abortion is less desirable than averting a birth through contraceptive practice. In some other countries, or at other times, there may not be a moral or ethical imperative seeking to limit abortion or it may be overridden by other considerations. For instance, abortion practitioners may have little interest in making effective contraceptives available because of concern that they would gain less financially from providing the contraceptives than they would lose through the abortions that would be averted. A de facto choice of abortion over contraception is also made when countries cannot afford to spend their hard currency to import contraceptives or when countries limit contraceptive availability to encourage a high birthrate.

While recognizing that peoples of the world hold differing judgments regarding the moral and ethical dimensions of contraception and abortion, there is little disagreement that contraception is almost always a more efficient and safer way to limit births than is abortion. If no contraception is used, 31.2 abortions could be expected by a sexually active woman, using no method of fertility control other than abortion for women between the ages of 17 and 44, while only 0.3 abortions would be expected for the termination of the unintended pregnancies that would occur if she used an effective method such as the pill continually over that time period (Ory, Forrest, and Lincoln, 1983:31–32). Even in the United States, where mortality from both abortion and childbirth are low, the strategy entailing the lowest mortality risk is the use of barrier contraceptives backed up by abortion for those unintended pregnancies that might occur (Ory, Forrest, and Lincoln, 1983). In the United States, mortality risk from legal abortion is so low that it is slightly exceeded by the risk entailed in using some contraceptives unless they are backed up by abortion, but where abortion is not available from legal, safe providers, mortality from abortion is probably much higher than from the use of any contraceptive.

The level of abortion in a country or group of women reflects five factors:

1. The proportion of women who are sexually active and physically able to become pregnant who do not want a birth at the time, that is, the proportion of women at risk.
2. The distribution of contraceptive methods (including nonuse) employed by women at risk.
3. The rates of pregnancy associated with each method and with nonuse, that is, failure rates.
4. The proportion of unplanned pregnancies that are terminated by induced abortions.
5. The level of intended pregnancies terminated by abortions.

The following discussion presents information on factors 2 to 4 from a recent study of contraceptive use and pregnancy in Western countries (Jones et al., 1987). Unfortunately, this information is limited to Western, industrialized countries which all fall within the Judeo-Christian religious background and which all have abortion services quite readily accessible, in fact, if not also by law. Although it is recognized that the availability of a new contraceptive method may affect the first factor, for instance, by contributing to increased sexual activity or to a desire for smaller families (Scrimshaw, 1981), the following discussion assumes that the proportion of women at risk remains stable, both because changes in the level are apt to be of a more long- than short-term nature and because it is questionable that a specific contraceptive technology can have sizable effects in and of itself. Some abortions also occur to women who had planned pregnancies but decided to have abortions (factor 5) because of something that occurred during their pregnancy, such as health problems, diagnosis of fetal abnormalities, or changes in a woman's personal life (Torres and Forrest, 1988). Most of them would not be prevented by new contraceptive methods or improved use, but they are not considered further here because such cases probably represent a small proportion of abortions.

The level of abortion in a country, or among a group of women, reflects the level of unintended pregnancy to the extent that women choose and are able to terminate unintended pregnancies by abortion. Table 2 and Figure 1 show the relationship between rates of unplanned pregnancy and abortion for several Western, industrialized countries for which data on both measures are available. There is a clear pattern of higher abortion rates when rates of unintended pregnancy are higher, but the proportion of unintended pregnancies resulting in abortion is well below unity for all of these countries. There is little apparent relationship in these countries between the level of contraceptive use among women aged 15 to 44 and the rate of unplanned pregnancy, as shown in Figure 2. However, when only use of the most effective methods of contraception (sterilization, pill, or the intrauterine device [IUD]) is considered, a strong pattern emerges, as shown in Figure 3. The rates of unplanned pregnancy are lower in the three countries with relatively high levels of use of effective contraceptives than in any of those with lower levels of use.

Given the above relationships, that unplanned pregnancy is lower when use of effective contraceptive methods is higher and that abortion is lower when unplanned pregnancy rates are lower, the relationships between contraceptive use and abortion rates are not surprising. Figure 4 presents information on the proportions of women aged 15 to 44 who use any contraceptive method and the abortion rate for 12 Western, industrialized countries. Although the lowest abortion rates are seen in five of the seven countries with high contraceptive

TABLE 2 Level of Use of Any Method of Contraception and of Effective Methods of Contraception[a], Total Unplanned Pregnancy Rate[b], and Total Abortion Rate[c], Selected Countries

Country Code	Country Name	Level of Contraceptive Use		Total Unplanned Pregnancy Rate	Total Abortion Rate
		Any Method	Effective Methods		
BEL	Belgium	H	H	0.83	0.29
CAN	Canada	H	H	0.79	0.36
DEN	Denmark	M	M	1.18	0.58
FIN	Finland	H	M	1.06	0.38
FRA	France	H	M	1.35	0.63
GB	Great Britain	H	H	0.63	0.34
GRE	Greece	H	L	--	2.24
ITA	Italy	M	L	--	0.80
NTH	Netherlands	H	H	0.28	0.18
NOR	Norway	M	M	--	0.46
SWE	Sweden	M	M	0.80	0.54
USA	United States	L	M	1.31	0.76

NOTE: -- = Not available; H = high; M = medium; L = low.

[a]Sterilization, pill, and IUD.
[b]Sum of the total unplanned fertility rate and the total abortion rate.
[c]Sum of 5-year age-specific abortion rates for women aged 15-19 through 40-44.

SOURCE: Jones et al. (1987). Adapted with permission.

use, the country in this group with the highest abortion rate, Greece, also has relatively high contraceptive use. This high abortion rate for Greece, even though contraceptive use is widespread, is because the primary method used there is the condom. Figure 5 shows a clear trend toward lower abortion rates when more women use effective contraceptives.

The potential effects of a new contraceptive method on the level of abortion can be calculated from the following equation, in which the number of abortions (ABS) is expressed as the result of multiplying the number of women of reproductive age (WOM) by the proportion who are at risk of unintended pregnancy (WAR/WOM) and by the sum of the proportions of women at risk using each specific method of contraception, including no method $(METHa/WAR \ldots METHz/WAR)$, times the expected pregnancy rates for each specific method $(PRa \ldots PRz)$ and times the proportion of unintended

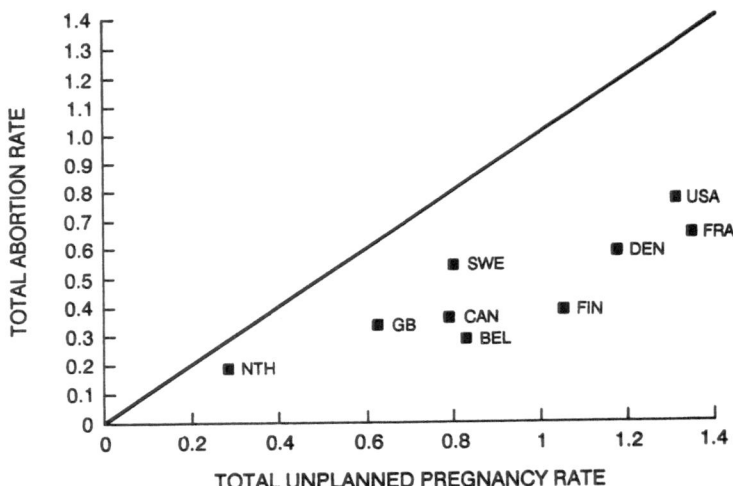

FIGURE 1   Total abortion rate by total unplanned pregnancy rate. See Table 2 for country codes. Source: Jones et al. (1987).

pregnancies that are terminated by abortion ($TERMa \dots TERMz$).[1] Thus,

$$ABS = (WOM) * (WAR/WOM) * [(METHa/WAR) * (PRa)*$$
$$(TERMa) + (METHb/WAR) * (PRb) * (TERMb)$$
$$+ \dots + (METHz/WAR) * (PRz) * (TERMz)]. \qquad (1)$$

---

[1]Intended pregnancies terminated by abortion are assumed to equal zero. Although they do occur, the level is probably very low compared with those from unintended pregnancies, as discussed above. The proportion of all abortions would increase, however, as those resulting from unintended pregnancies decrease, and they provide an indication that even complete control of unintended pregnancy would not eliminate the need for abortion services.

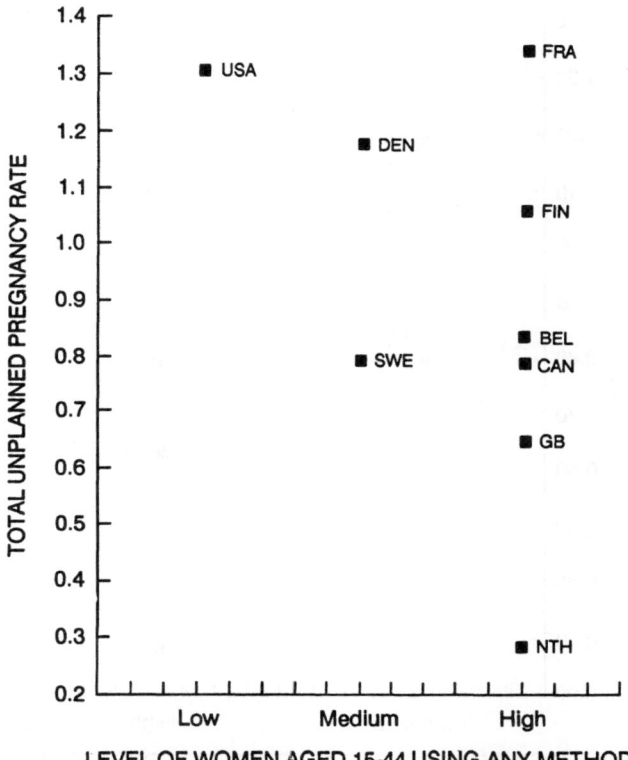

FIGURE 2   Unplanned pregnancy rate by level of women aged 15 to 44 using any contraceptive method. See Table 2 for country codes. Source: Jones et al. (1987).

This also equals the sum of the number of women who use each specific method times the expected pregnancy rates for each specific method multiplied by the proportion of unintended pregnancies terminated by abortion,

$$ABS = [(METHa) * (PRa) * (TERMa) + (METHb) * (PRb) * \\ (TERMb) + \ldots + (METHz) * (PRz) * (TERMz)]. \quad (2)$$

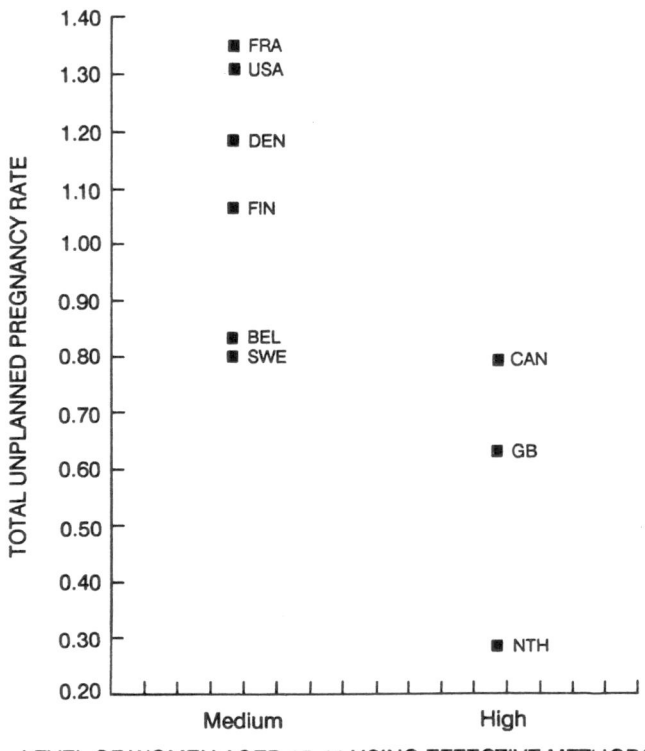

FIGURE 3   Unplanned pregnancy rate by level of women aged 15 to 44 using effective contraceptive methods. See Table 2 for country codes. Source: Jones et al. (1987).

If it is assumed that the proportion of unintended pregnancies that end in abortion is not related to the method that had been used to try to prevent the pregnancy, it can be expressed more simply as,

$$ABS = [(METHa) * (PRa) + (METHb) * (PRb)$$
$$+ \ldots + (METHz) * (PRz)] * (TERM). \tag{3}$$

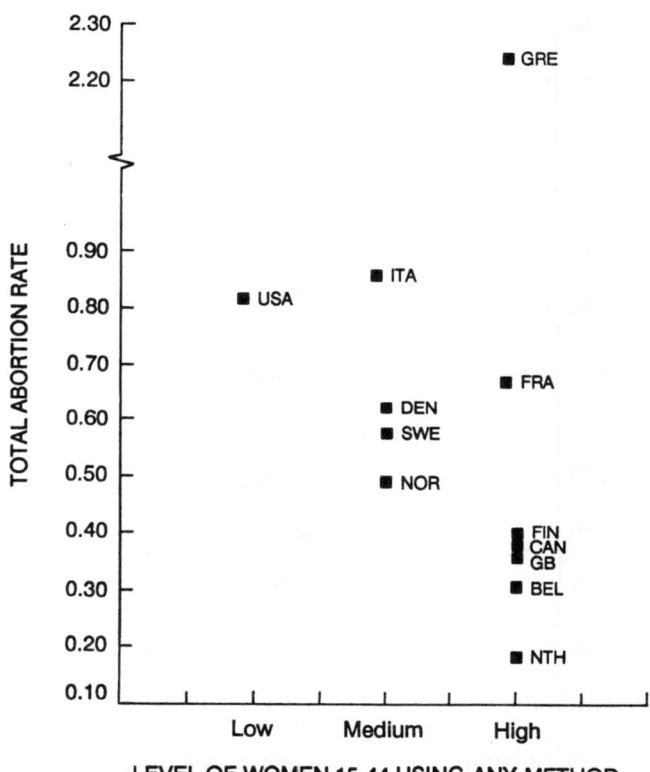

FIGURE 4 Total abortion rate by level of women aged 15 to 44 using any contraceptive method. See Table 2 for country codes. Source: Jones et al. (1987).

In this form, it can be seen that the effect of new contraceptive methods on abortion levels is a clear and simple one: If the net effect of their introduction is to move nonusers to contraceptive use or to move users to a more effective method than they are currently using, there will be fewer unintended pregnancies and fewer abortions. Any change among method users that results in less effective use will contribute toward increasing the level of abortions, and changes that

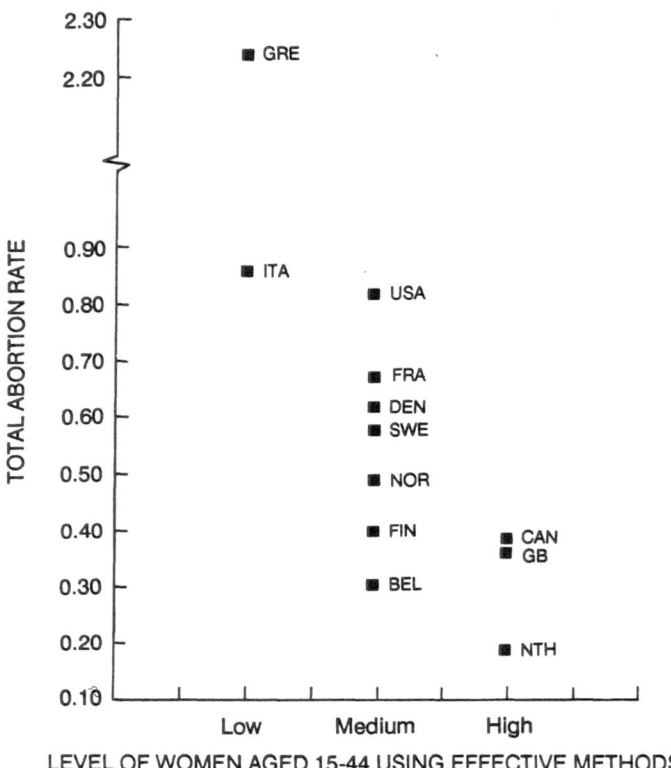

FIGURE 5   Total abortion rate by level of women aged 15 to 44 using effective contraceptive methods. See Table 2 for country codes. Source: Jones et al. (1987).

do not produce any change in the level of unintended pregnancy will have no impact on the level of abortion.

While this model can be used to indicate the direction and effect of introducing a new method, it should be noted that the actual results are seldom so clear or so simple. A new method may, for example, cause couples to reassess their satisfaction with current methods and their level of concern about unintended pregnancy in ways that might affect the failure rates of those methods. Such possible effects are not only more difficult to predict but also may differ across times and countries when new methods are introduced. The introduction of a new method may change the characteristics of those who use existing methods in ways that will alter the average failure rates of those methods. One can imagine, for instance, that a method that promises to have a very high effectiveness will cause those who are most concerned with avoiding an unintended pregnancy to adopt it, leaving in the pool of those still using the originally available methods women and men who are not so highly motivated and who are likely to have higher failure rates with those methods.

There is some indication from the United States that women who were using more effective methods are more likely to have abortions if they become pregnant, probably because their choice of a more effective method reflects their greater desire to avoid unplanned pregnancy (Westoff et al., 1981). The proportion of pregnancies ending in abortion also varies by age and marital status. Since younger, unmarried women, who are more likely than others to choose abortion, are also less likely to choose any contraceptive method or to choose certain other methods such as the IUD or diaphragm, these factors may also result in differences across methods in the proportion of pregnancies ending in abortion (Westoff, Hammerslough, and Paul, 1987). It is assumed here that the introduction of a new method would not affect the proportion of unintended pregnancies that end in abortion, that is, that the likelihood of choosing to have an abortion if an unintended pregnancy occurs is a function of the woman's characteristics, regardless of what method she chooses or whether she uses any method at all. Changes might occur, however, if, for instance, changes in the types of providers from which contraceptive methods are obtained affect women's access to abortion services. The proportion of all unintended pregnancies ending in abortion might also be affected by changes in method use, even with no change in an individual's likelihood of having an abortion once they become unintentionally pregnant. This could occur, for example, if women with a high likelihood of choosing abortion moved to a much more effective method and would therefore represent a smaller proportion of all unintended pregnancies. Further information about the specific circumstances in each country is needed to estimate the extent of change in the proportion of pregnancies ending in abortion, but it is likely to be less susceptible to changes in available methods than is the level of unintended pregnancy.

EXAMPLES OF EFFECTS OF NEW METHODS

Westoff (1988) has calculated the contraceptive use status of women exposed to the risk of unintended pregnancy at any time during the 24-month period ending 9 months prior to the U.S. National Survey of Family Growth (NSFG) in 1982 and the average annual conception rates for each method including nonuse. As Table 3 shows, 100 women exposed to the risk of unintended pregnancy and who use contraceptive methods for the entire year in the same proportion and with the annual conception rates found in the NSFG would have 9.6 unintended pregnancies. (Since an estimated 47 percent of unintended pregnancies in the United States end in abortion, there would be 4.8 abortions per 100 women at risk of unintended pregnancy.) In 1982, women at risk represented 61.8 percent of all women aged 15 to 44. An abortion rate of 4.8 per 100 among those who are at risk implies a rate of 3.0 for every 100 women aged 15 to 44, consistent with the actual U.S. rate of 2.9 per 100 in the years 1979 through 1982 (Henshaw, Forrest, and Van Vort, 1987). The United States is used as a model in this discussion because of the availability of data. Women in the United States tend to have lower levels of contraceptive use than those in many other Western, industrialized countries and may have lower contraceptive effectiveness rates as well (Jones et al., 1987). The use levels tend, however, to be higher than those in most non-Western and developing countries (Ross et al., 1988).

Table 3 shows the expected number of pregnancies per 100 women at risk of unintended pregnancy that result from multiplying the number of women using each method ($METHa \ldots z$) by the average annual conception rate ($PRa \ldots z$). Method failure rates range from 0.002 per year for those relying on sterilization to 0.297 per year for those using no method of contraception. Of the total 9.64 pregnancies per 100 women at risk, 6.36, or 67 percent, are to nonusers. Any movement to more effective methods would decrease the overall pregnancy rate and, by implication, the abortion rate as well. For example, the 52.1 percent of women using a reversible method have an average failure rate of 0.062. If all of them adopted the implant or another method that would actually have a use failure rate of 0.01 or less per year, the unintended pregnancy rate would change by 52.1 * (0.010 − 0.062), or −2.71 to 6.93, a decrease of 28 percent. Movement to less effective methods would increase the number of pregnancies. If, for example, those who would have chosen sterilization would decide instead to use implants, a new method of

TABLE 3 Estimated Woman-Years of Exposure to Unintended Pregnancy Among 100 Women at Risk of Unintended Pregnancy for 1 Year by Method of Contraception, Average Annual Conception Rates, and the Expected Number and Percentage Distribution of Unintended Pregnancies by Method Used, United States

Method	Women-Years of Exposure	Average Annual Conception Rates	Estimated Number of Pregnancies	Percent Distribution of Unintended Pregnancies
Sterilization	26.5	0.002	0.05	0.4
Pill	21.0	0.042	0.88	8.5
IUD	6.4	0.021	0.13	1.4
Condom	10.0	0.043	0.43	4.5
Periodic abstinence, withdrawal	5.2	0.131	0.68	6.2
Other methods	9.5	0.117	1.11	12.3
Nonusers	21.4	0.297	6.36	66.6
Total	100.0	0.096	9.64	100.0

SOURCE: Westoff (1988:5). Adapted with permission.

more reversible sterilization, or some other method with a 1 percent failure rate, the eventual unintended pregnancy rate would change by 26.5 ∗ (0.010 − 0.002), or by +0.212 to 9.85, a 2 percent increase.[2] The size of the effect on the pregnancy rate depends on the number of women whose use category will be changed ($METHa \ldots z$) and on the difference between the pregnancy rates (PR) of the current and new methods. The pregnancy rate among women at risk during periods they are using no contraceptive is much higher than among those using any method. In fact, it is probably even much higher relative to contraceptive users in populations in which method use is lower, and there is less selection of possibly less fecund women into the nonuse category. The greatest potential impact in terms of changing the failure rates, therefore, comes from decreasing this pregnancy rate, that is, moving women from nonuse to any method. If all nonusers in the sample population used here were attracted to a method such as the levonorgestrel-releasing vaginal ring with an

---

[2]Another effect might be a small increase in the number of desired births, since in the United States as many as one-quarter of sterilized couples would like to have more children (Henshaw and Singh, 1986).

average pregnancy rate of 0.035, the overall pregnancy rate would drop by $21.4 * (0.035 - 0.297)$, or -5.61 to 4.03. Assuming no change in the proportion of unintended pregnancies terminated by abortions, the abortion rate would drop by 58 percent.

These examples illustrate the types of outcomes implied in movement between contraceptive methods with different failure rates or between nonuse and contraceptive use. While the patterns of probable method use are difficult to predict, it is clear that the biggest potential decrease in the level of abortions comes from moving a large proportion of women at risk of unintended pregnancy from the highest pregnancy rate category (usually the nonuse category) to a method with a much lower pregnancy rate.

EFFECTS OF A NEW METHOD OF ABORTION

The typical division of types of methods of birth limitation among sexually active couples has been between contraception and abortion, with contraception variously defined as acting before ovulation, fertilization, or implantation and abortion as acting after a pregnancy occurs. Some methods on the horizon would act in part or totally after ovulation, but at a time when a woman would not be aware of any possible fertilization or implantation. Although one method under development (mifepristone with or without prostaglandin) may eventually be used in a once-a-month regimen that would be similar to what are commonly termed contraceptives, research is also being done on its use as an early abortifacient that would induce menses if used during the first 8 weeks of pregnancy in 95 percent of cases. One form, RU-486, has been approved as a method of early abortion in China and France. While the replacement of surgical or other current means of abortion by such a method would undoubtedly entail changes in the way abortion services are delivered and perhaps lower the risks of morbidity and mortality from abortion, its impact on abortion levels is difficult to predict.

The argument asserted by some in opposition to RU-486 that numbers of abortions would increase if a safe, easily available nonsurgical method of abortion existed (Kolata, 1988) rests on two major assumptions: that many women who now have unintended pregnancies carry them to term rather than have abortions because of inaccessibility or unattractiveness of current abortion services and that some women and men who now prefer to try to avert unplanned births through contraceptive use would instead rely on abortion if it were available through a method such as this.

It is clear that many women live where abortion services are not readily accessible to them. Even in the United States, where abortion is provided legally throughout the country, there are few providers in nonmetropolitan areas, where 25 percent of women of reproductive age live. Indeed, only 2 percent of all abortions occur in nonmetropolitan areas, and an estimated total of 39 percent of women obtaining abortions travel outside of their home county for services (Henshaw, Forrest, and Van Vort, 1987, and tabulations from 1987 Alan Guttmacher Institute Abortion Patient Survey). In many countries of the world, legal, safe abortion services are virtually unavailable to most women, yet many women obtain them from nonmedical sources. Oral and/or vaginal administration of a nonsurgical method of abortion would offer the potential for obtaining an abortion outside the current abortion service delivery systems or with fewer barriers to those systems than currently exist. How many more women would use it than currently have abortions would depend on how many women who want abortions are unable to obtain them under the current levels of access to abortion services, how many would recognize their pregnancy and decide to terminate it early enough in pregnancy to be eligible for this technology, and on how widely a new, nonsurgical method would be made available. Its impact on abortion levels would be greatest in those areas where abortion services are now quite inaccessible, but where a new method would become readily accessible to women in terms of their knowledge of it, its availability, the ease and cost of procuring it, and judgments about the risk of side effects involved in using it. However, concerns about the need for medical treatment of those women with incomplete abortions have caused its current and planned future use to be restricted to provision in medical settings with surgical backup available. At least for the near future, it appears more likely that the availability of a nonsurgical abortion method will alter the techniques used for abortion than have much of an effect on the number of women who have abortions.

As discussed earlier, the projections of potential decreases in the levels of unintended pregnancy and abortion from introduction of new contraceptive methods rested on the assumption that women and men would be interested in more effective means to prevent births through preventing unplanned pregnancies. This assumption appears to be an accurate one for many times and places, but is not necessarily universal. The preference between contraception and abortion for preventing births reflects not only moral and ethical views but also other factors such as the financial costs and health risks entailed in each choice and other method-related factors such as time involved in obtaining each method, effectiveness in preventing births, and the "hassles" involved in their use. Nonsurgical methods of early abortion appear to offer advantages over later abortions, but it is not clear that they would be preferred to preventing the unintended pregnancy through contraceptive use.

It is unlikely that the availability of a nonsurgical method of abortion would greatly alter the choices of women and men where safe surgical abortion services are now readily available. Since the current estimate is that 1 in 20 women who use this method of abortion will have an incomplete abortion, the availability and accessibility of backup surgical abortion care for these women will also affect its use. Any speculations are highly tentative, however. The characteristics of mifepristone with prostaglandin or other such methods are becoming clearer through research. The extent to which such technologies will change current patterns of abortion will depend primarily on how these new methods and the necessary care for incomplete abortions will be provided.

SUMMARY

Potential methods of contraception offer the hope of reducing rates of unintended pregnancy, and thereby the levels of abortion, because many of them offer lower failure rates than methods currently being used and because they might be used by couples who are currently using no method. The extent to which they will do so will depend on the comparison between pregnancy rates from current methods, including nonuse, and those that will be attained from the new methods. The greatest potential reduction in pregnancy rates will come from changing women at risk of unintended pregnancy from nonuse to use of contraceptives with low failure rates. Since many factors determine preferences for method use, however, it cannot be assumed that all movement to new methods will result in lower pregnancy and abortion rates. Some choices, such as substitution of new reversible methods over current surgical sterilization techniques, would usually represent an increase in the likelihood of unintended pregnancy and abortion.

While the availability of methods of contraception currently on the horizon would most probably decrease levels of abortion in the United States and in the rest of the world, the potential impact of a new, nonsurgical method of early abortion on the numbers of abortions is less easy to predict. Its availability will undoubtedly affect how abortion services are provided. Its effect on the level of abortion, however, will depend on how many women who currently have unintended pregnancies and want abortions are not able to obtain them but would be able to do so using the new method, and on the extent to which women and men who now prefer to prevent unplanned births through contraceptive use would change their preference toward preventing them through a nonsurgical method of abortion.

REFERENCES

Henshaw, S.K.
   1987   Induced abortion: A worldwide perspective. *International Family Planning Perspectives* 13:12.
Henshaw, S.K., J.D. Forrest, and J. Van Vort
   1987   Abortion services in the United States, 1984 and 1985. *Family Planning Perspectives* 19:63.
Henshaw, S.K., and S. Singh
   1986   Sterilization regret among U.S. couples. *Family Planning Perspectives* 18:238.
Jones, E.F., J.D. Forrest, S.K. Henshaw, J. Silverman, and A. Torres
   1987   *A Study of Family Planning in Developed Countries.* Final report submitted to Office of Population Affairs, U.S. Department of Health and Human Services. FPR-000046-02-0. New York: The Alan Guttmacher Institute.
Kolata, G.
   1988   France and China allow sale of a drug for early abortion. *New York Times* Sept. 24.
Ory, H.W., J.D. Forrest, and R. Lincoln
   1983   *Making Choices: Evaluating the Health Risks and Benefits of Birth Control Methods.* New York: The Alan Guttmacher Institute.
Ross, J.A., M. Rich, J.P. Molzan, and M. Pensak
   1988   *Family Planning and Child Survival, 100 Developing Countries.* New York: Center for Population and Family Health, Columbia University.
Scrimshaw, S.C.M.
   1981   Women and the pill: From panacea to catalyst. *Family Planning Perspectives* 13:254.
Tietze, C.
   1983   *Induced Abortion: A World Review, 1983,* 5th ed. New York: The Population Council.
Torres, A., and J.D. Forrest
   1988   Why do women have abortions? *Family Planning Perspectives* 21:169.

Westoff, C.F.
   1988   Contraceptive paths toward the reduction of unintended pregnancy
           and abortion. *Family Planning Perspectives* 20:4.
Westoff, C.F., J.S. DeLung, N. Goldman, and J.D. Forrest
   1981   Abortions preventable by contraceptive practice. *Family Planning
           Perspectives* 13:218.
Westoff, C.F., C.R. Hammerslough, and L. Paul
   1987   The potential impact of improvements in contraception on fertility
           and abortion in Western countries. *European Journal of Population*
           3:7.

Part IV
Introduction of
New Contraceptive Methods

NORPLANT® Introduction:
A Management Perspective

JOANNE SPICEHANDLER

INTRODUCTION

In 1983, the Population Council initiated an effort that had never before been undertaken by a public sector organization: the systematic introduction of NORPLANT® implants, a contraceptive developed through its own research and development program. This decision has continued to have an overall impact on the approach taken by other public sector institutions in this field.

It has now been over 5 years since the Population Council established the Contraceptive Introduction Program as one of its institutional priorities. Over $6 million and major investments of staff time of the Council and several international agencies, including Family Health International, the Program for Appropriate Technology in Health, and the Association for Voluntary Surgical Contraception, have contributed to the introduction of NORPLANT®. Among the most critical collaborators, however, have been the clinical researchers, service providers, social scientists, and NORPLANT® users in over 35 countries who have contributed significantly to our knowledge about the method and who have expanded our understanding of its diverse informational, training, counseling, cultural, and logistical requirements.

The purpose of this paper is to review the strategy for the introduction of NORPLANT® and the lessons learned from this experience, and to draw conclusions about the applicability of this approach to other public sector introduction efforts.

The paper focuses on NORPLANT® introduction as a management process requiring the careful coordination of a variety of activities and a broad collaboration with a number of institutions and agencies to achieve a common goal. The programmatic implications and responsibilities of this clinic-based, provider-dependent contraceptive are presented here from the Council's perspective, based on firsthand experience or on interactions with staff of the agencies and institutions that have shared in this experience. More systematic approaches to evaluating the service delivery experience with NORPLANT® are being developed in several countries. Available findings from those projects and their implications for the introduction process, will also be discussed.

RATIONALE FOR THE INTRODUCTION POLICY

The Council's decision to take an active role in the introduction process was guided by three overriding concerns. The first and foremost related to serious shortcomings of earlier efforts to introduce the intrauterine device (IUD) into family planning programs around the world. Problems experienced with the IUD's entry into the family planning program in India, for example, are among the most frequently cited and bear relevance to the introduction of any new method, particularly one that requires skilled health professionals for its insertion and removal. The Lippes loop, in the mid-1960s, was viewed as a revolution in the contraceptive field. A single IUD insertion provided years of contraceptive protection at a high rate of efficacy in comparison to other reversible methods available at the time. It was:

> enthusiastically introduced as the vital missing link in the [Indian] programme. Within two years of its introduction 1.7 million IUDs were inserted. But the success and optimism were short-lived as inadequate pre-insertion checks, poor follow-up genuine side effects and grossly exaggerated rumours led to high termination rates and a 7-year slump in annual insertions. The programme had, quite simply, been rushed through without organisational preparedness to cope with the known side effects (Soni, 1984).

This situation led Population Council President Bernard Berelson to comment in his annual address at the end of 1966:

> In the first flush of enthusiasm about a method that was both new and loaded with promise, too much attention was given

to speeding the work and too little attention paid to inform-
ing women about difficulties they might expect in the first two
months of wearing an IUD . . . where initial service has been
inadequate, dissatisfied women have spread adverse gossip and
encouraged others to discontinue. . . . The quality of service is of
critical importance when a new and unfamiliar method is being
introduced. In short, important as it is to have a satisfactory
method, it is equally important that women be given an adequate
understanding of what they can expect (Berelson, 1966).

The second concern was the Council's increasing awareness of
the importance of recognizing the needs of potential acceptors of
contraception and understanding how the family planning service
delivery system could best address those needs. In the mid-1970s,
the Council, under the leadership of Judith Bruce, senior associate,
began to articulate an agenda for placing primary emphasis on the
user's perspective in the design of family planning programs. This has
become a guiding force in the design of the Council's contraceptive
introduction strategy. As stated by Judith Bruce (1987):

> Most simply put, users are consumers, and no product—especially
> one to be employed by healthy people—will be accepted if its
> intrinsic properties (the hardware) or its service delivery mecha-
> nisms (the software) are inimicable to the user's personal, phys-
> ical and cultural needs.

The third concern was that misinformation about contraceptives
generates controversy which, all too frequently results in limiting
contraceptive choice. A recent example is the impact of the U.S.
litigation climate on the availability of an important contraceptive
option, the copper IUD. In 1986, the company marketing the copper
IUD in the United States discontinued the product because the cost
of successfully defending it in litigation outweighed the profitability
of the small IUD market. The copper IUD was still Food and Drug
Administration (FDA) approved, but access to the method was cur-
tailed because the manufacturer would no longer distribute it. As
a result, American women were deprived of the only long-acting,
reversible method available to them.

Equally detrimental was the misunderstanding that this business
decision created. The American public, having received significant
negative publicity about a faulty product, the Dalkon Shield, made
an erroneous association between that IUD and all others. Rumors
spread that all IUDs were harmful, and no distinction was drawn
between the model that presented an increased health risk and other
IUDs that were still viewed as safe by FDA standards. The impact

of this misunderstanding spread beyond U.S. borders and generated concern throughout the world. Governments of developing countries questioned why a product no longer available to U.S. women was allowed to be used overseas. Since then, a great deal of effort was invested inside and outside the United States to correct these misconceptions. Return of the copper IUD to the U.S. market in 1988 has done much to restore confidence in intrauterine contraception.

BUILDING AN INTRODUCTION STRATEGY

In the late 1970s, it became clear that two of the products developed through the Population Council's International Committee for Contraception Research (ICCR), NORPLANT® contraceptive subdermal implants and the copper T-380 IUD, would soon be ready for worldwide introduction. The clinical research findings on safety and efficacy were promising. The Council recognized its responsibility to ensure both wide-scale availability of the methods and an awareness of the above concerns. The challenge was for an institution like the Council, with no prior experience or public sector model to follow, to design and implement a comprehensive management plan and develop an infrastructure for introduction.

An introduction strategy must take into consideration the overall objectives of the institution, the characteristics and requirements of the contraceptive method itself, and the service delivery environments into which it will be introduced.

The Council's Agenda

Experience has shown that no one method is the best contraceptive option for the majority of women. Each method has its tradeoffs—its advantages and disadvantages. These tradeoffs are often subjective choices based on such factors as: different fertility goals, perceptions by individuals (and across cultures) of what constitutes a tolerable side effect, male/female attitudes toward contraception in general or toward specific methods, preferences regarding ease of use, and potential obstacles with access to services. The Council, in recognizing that no one method could meet the different fertility goals, preferences, and requirements of each couple, has embraced a user-oriented rather than a method-specific approach to family planning.

In addition to recognizing the diverse needs of couples, the Council stresses the broader objective of ensuring better use of family planning services rather than promoting any specific method. This required a nonpromotional approach to NORPLANT® introduction. The council has encouraged programs to present NORPLANT® in a balanced way, discussing its advantages and disadvantages in the context of the other available methods. Jain (1989) summarizes this point of view: ". . . from a demographic as well as an individual perspective, it is less important to focus on the continuation of any particular method than on the total contraceptive behavior of couples, which takes into account the need for and practice of switching between methods."

Reviewing several studies, he notes inadequacy of the one-method program and the positive effect of multiple method use and method switching on continuation of use and contraceptive prevalence. One-method programs cannot possibly recognize the diverse fertility goals of individual couples, ranging from birth spacing to termination of fertility. It is infeasible, for example, to expect young couples to consider a permanent-method program and, at the other extreme, unfair to ask couples who have achieved desired family size to bear with less effective, inconvenient methods rather than long-term options (Jain, 1989).

There is a strong case to be made for the impact that a multiple-method and method-switch approach can have on the individual's continued use of family planning services as well as on contraceptive prevalence in general. In Matlab, Bangladesh, where service providers actively promoted method switching when clients were dissatisfied with the method they were using, it was found that while method-specific continuation rates were low, overall prevalence remained high because other methods were offered (Phillips et al., 1987).

From this frame of reference, the Council's objectives for introduction of contraceptives were defined as:

• to expand the number of safe and effective contraceptive options available for couples to achieve their desired family size and meet their birth spacing needs;

• to ensure women's rights to reproductive choice by providing clear and accurate information on the risks and benefits of all available methods, enabling potential users to make an informed decision;

- to ensure, through proper training, that providers have the requisite skills to administer the methods offered, allow access to method reversibility (for methods like the IUD and implants), and to counsel users; and
- to further user satisfaction with family planning services by promoting integrated services that address their needs (i.e., follow-up services including counseling, medical advice, and access to method switching or method termination).

Method Characteristics and Strategy Design

Any contraceptive introduction plan depends on the characteristics of the contraceptive product and the service delivery requirements dictated by that product profile. The intrinsic features of the method, or *product hardware* (its efficacy, duration, side effects, reversibility, and mode of administration) must be balanced by the appropriate *management software* in order for it to achieve any degree of success in satisfying users' needs. This management software is particularly important for a provider-dependent, clinic-based method like NORPLANT®. Service delivery systems must be prepared with trained staff, appropriate facilities and supplies, information for counseling, recordkeeping procedures and clinic hours to make the contraceptive easily available and to manage any problems that users might experience.

The method profile became evident in the earliest phases of research and development, which for NORPLANT® began in 1966. The advantages were a low-dose, progestin-only, five-year duration, highly effective, reversible method. In addition, the method contained two well-known, well-used ingredients, with both the Silastic and the levonorgestrel already approved by the FDA for use in other forms. (Silastic is used in a wide variety of prosthetic devices including cardiac pacemakers and hydrocephalic shunts, and levonorgestrel is used in the oral contraceptive).

The NORPLANT® method places specific responsibilities on family planning service delivery systems. It induces disruptive menstrual bleeding patterns that might cause the user great inconvenience. It requires trained clinic staff for counseling, insertion, removal, and clinical management. From the outset of the introduction program, it became clear that NORPLANT® would be both a training-intensive and service-intensive method. Its ability to fill a niche in the family planning "cafeteria" of methods would therefore

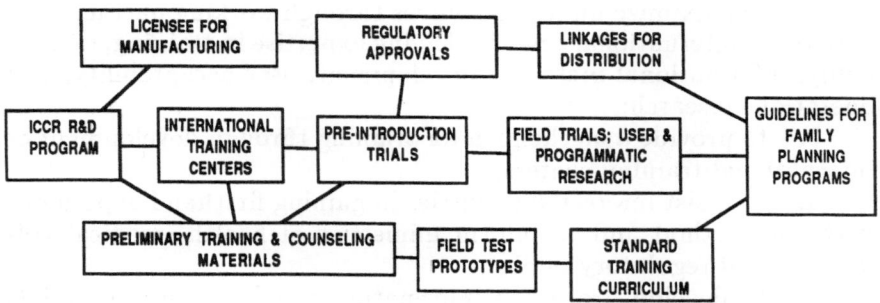

FIGURE 1   Council's introduction plan.

depend heavily on the ability of service delivery systems to adapt to its requirements.

In 1982, the Council devised a long-term strategy to ready family planning programs for the introduction of NORPLANT®. Forrest Greenslade, who has pharmaceutical industry experience, was employed to help design the strategic plan. The plan became the blueprint for a large-scale endeavor that would require a more extensive management orientation than past Council programs. The multifaceted program that was implemented is now managed by a core team of three professionals in the Council's New York office, as well as three full-time medical professionals stationed in regional offices in Latin America, Southeast Asia, and sub-Saharan Africa. Two multidisciplinary advisory bodies have been organized to provide critical inputs to the program's development. One advises on overall policy and on issues of a biomedical and regulatory nature; the second on addressing users' needs and understanding the service dynamics through which access to the NORPLANT® technology is attained. Greenslade's consulting service, INTERCARE, advises the Council on implementation of the plan.

The Council's introduction strategy envisioned a phased-in approach (shown in Figure 1), that built on each existing step of experience in order to proceed to the next. It entailed the following specific objectives:

1.   to facilitate the widespread availability of NORPLANT® at the lowest possible price to the public sector;

2. to maximize limited resources through working partnerships with other international agencies having expertise in training, clinical study, informational materials development, user acceptability, and operations research;

3. to provide a mechanism for training through development of international training centers;

4. to assist interested countries in gaining firsthand experience with the method and to inform ministries of health, medical colleagues, and regulatory bodies;

5. to develop prototype informational and training materials for decision makers, clinicians, counseling staff, users, and their families;

6. to conduct user-oriented research in order to learn, from the user's perspective, those factors about NORPLANT® and service delivery systems that would contribute to increasing user satisfaction with this method.

EXECUTING THE INTRODUCTION PROGRAM

The first step in ensuring product availability was to identify a company to manufacture, register, and distribute NORPLANT® implants. Leiras, an experienced and established international pharmaceutical firm based in Turku, Finland, collaborated with the Council during the last stages of research and development of the product. The Council and Leiras worked out a licensing agreement for worldwide distribution of NORPLANT®, which included a lower price to public sector family planning programs. NORPLANT® was approved for commercial distribution in the country of manufacture, Finland, in 1983. In accordance with international conventions, this approval allowed Leiras to begin registration and distribution of the NORPLANT® in countries around the world.

Emphasis on Training

Physicians from the international centers established for NORPLANT® training emphasize that, while the insertion and removal procedures are easy to learn, it is important to provide hands-on practice in order to understand the delicacy of the technique. Those who have not had an opportunity to observe a demonstration and perform the procedure under supervision themselves may have more difficulty, for example, in understanding correct manipulation of the trocar (the long hollow needle used to insert the capsules), to ensure that implants are not placed too deeply or pushed too far from the implant incision site. Although these problems may not present immediate complications for the user, they will make it more difficult to locate the implants when she returns to the clinic for their removal. Training physician advisers advocate the importance of training for removal in the context of insertion because the quality of the insertion will affect the ease of removal (personal interviews, 1985; Population Council, 1989).

The Council, in recognizing the importance of training as a component in the introduction process, identified three centers that had a long experience with the ICCR clinical trials to serve as international NORPLANT® training centers. These were PROFAMILIA in Santo Domingo, the Dominican Republic; the Instituto Chileno de Medicina Reproductiva in Santiago, Chile; and Raden Saleh Clinic, in Jakarta, Indonesia. These centers provided a large caseload of both insertions and removals, and experienced staff familiar with the counseling requirements of the method.

NORPLANT® is not a method that requires any special surgical background. It is a rather simple, straightforward technique that nurse-midwives can handle as easily as physicians. Experience in Indonesia exemplifies this point. The Indonesian National Family Planning Coordinating Board (BKKBN), although well-organized with broad outreach of services to all the provinces, was faced with an important logistical problem for expansion of NORPLANT® availability on a large scale: a tremendous shortage of physicians. There are only 17,000 physicians in Indonesia in comparison with 11,000 midwives and 150,000 nurses. If NORPLANT® were to be made widely available, it would depend on the ability of nurse-midwives to master the insertion and removal techniques.

A study was conducted at Raden Saleh Clinic in Jakarta to compare the skills of 105 physicians and 72 nurses and midwives who participated in a training program held between September 1982 and August 1984. A total of 828 insertions were performed during the period; 285 by physicians and 543 by nurses or midwives. The results showed no significant differences in the mean time required to perform insertions (Table 1), or in complications detected at the insertion site (Table 2). Figures on performance of removal also show no significant differences in time required by either group (Table 3) or in complications at time of removal (Affandi et al., 1987).

TABLE 1 Time of Full Insertion Procedure for NORPLANT®, by
Type of Health/Medical Personnel, Raden Saleh Clinic, Jakarta, 1985

Time	Number of Insertions		
(minutes)	Physician	Nurse/Midwife	Total
≤4	38	65	103
5-9	204	427	631
10-14	40	45	85
15 +	3	6	9
Total	285	543	828
Mean time	7.64	7.43	7.50
Standard deviation	2.81	2.48	2.60

NOTE: $p > .1$.

SOURCE: Affandi et al. (1987).

TABLE 2 Comparison of Complications that Resulted from
NORPLANT®Insertions, by Type of Personnel Performing
Insertion, Raden Saleh Clinic, Jakarta, 1985

	Number of Cases	
Complication	Physician	Nurse/Midwife
Hematoma	5	9
Wound infection	4	6
Abscess	2	0
No complications	274	528
Total	285	543

NOTE: $p > .20$.

SOURCE: Affandi et al. (1987).

The researchers concluded that nonphysicians performed the insertion and removal with skills equivalent to that of physicians. As a result, the BKKBN extended the use of NORPLANT® with the confidence that nonphysicians as well as physicians could provide the method.

PREINTRODUCTION TRIALS AS LEARNING EXPERIENCE

During the extensive research and development program, NOR-PLANT® had been confined to more experienced clinical research institutions in order to determine whether the safety and efficacy data continued to reflect the initial findings as the use of the method

TABLE 3 Time It Took Physicians and Nurse/Midwives to Remove NORPLANT® Contraceptive Subdermal Implants, Raden Saleh Clinic, Jakarta, 1985

Time (minutes)	Number of Cases		
	Physician	Nurse/Midwife	Total
≤9	4	6	10
10–19	9	19	28
20–29	27	48	75
30 +	3	6	9
Total	43	79	122
Mean time	21.74	21.83	21.8
Standard deviation	7.38	7.21	7.27

NOTE: p > .9.

SOURCE: Affandi et al. (1987).

expanded to larger numbers and more culturally diverse settings. These research institutions, however, provide a level of treatment to their clients that is not typical of the general service setting in most developing countries. Users who enroll in clinical studies are generally accorded a special status by the clinical investigator and the research team. Such treatment facilitates return by users to the clinic for the frequent follow-up visits required (up to four times a year), and the inconveniences imposed by the need to take blood samples or conduct other examinations that may be required by the study protocol. Research-oriented clinics frequently have lower-volume caseloads than the average clinic, allowing more time for interaction with the user. Often the user is given some special identification indicating that she is participating in a study. Special status often allows the woman to move to the front of the line when she comes for her follow-up. Home visits may be made if she has missed a follow-up visit. Often the clinic pays more attention to the user than she is accustomed to in the course of her routine dealings with health care services in general.

Clinical research settings could therefore not be considered the laboratory for understanding the service delivery needs for the method in the average clinic. Accordingly, the Council assisted interested family planning programs in gaining experience with the method in settings more closely reflecting the realities of clinical visits in different countries. Preintroduction evaluations were conducted to examine factors affecting the method under the conditions in the routine clinical setting. The Council collaborated with institutions in several developing countries to conduct preintroduction trials that would serve as a learning experience for both the Council and its collaborators. For the collaborating institution, the trial provided the opportunity to understand the niche that NORPLANT® might serve in the program and the demands it would place on the clinic. For the Council, it provided the opportunity to understand the broader programmatic implications of the contraceptive information not available from earlier phases of research. It also provided data that allowed monitoring of the clinical experience with NORPLANT® from a few thousand users in the first 10 years of research and development to over 40,000 by the end of 1987.

Preintroduction trials were designed to achieve several objectives:

    1.   to provide leading clinicians in developing countries with a firsthand experience with the insertion and removal techniques and an understanding of side effects, particularly the bleeding pattern disruptions;

    2.   to inform government officials, and the medical community about the method and to facilitate local regulatory approval;

    3.   to develop training capabilities for future expansion of the method to clinics throughout the country; and

    4.   to serve as the basis for further study of service delivery implications and user needs.

During the past 5 years studies, which were coordinated by the Council, Family Health International, and Leiras, were conducted by institutions in Latin America, Asia, Africa, and the Middle East. Clinics representing a broad range of service settings—including public hospitals, university teaching centers, IPPF affiliates, and Ministry of Health clinics—have been involved in the program.

In each participating country the preintroduction evaluation involved a carefully coordinated collaboration among generally 2 to 10 centers. In those studies conducted in conjunction with the Population Council, one institution was generally identified as the study coordinating center and organized activities with the other in-country clinics. In general two staff members, a physician medical adviser and a nurse midwife, were responsible for ensuring that all activities, including data collection, medical and clinical procedures, and counseling were handled according to a general protocol. These staff members were key to the project's in-country supervision; they were trouble-shooters responsible for identifying and addressing problems experienced by any clinic.

In one Latin American country, for example, data indicated a higher than average rate of infection and expulsion at the site of implant placement. As a result, a medical adviser selected by the coordinating center worked with the study staff to identify potential problems with insertion and removal techniques and aseptic procedures. In another country, a site visit by project supervisors indicated that social workers in one clinic had not received adequate information on the method and had, therefore, assumed that the side effects of NORPLANT® were identical to those of combined oral contraceptives. On-site refresher training placed emphasis on the bleeding pattern disruptions of progestin-only contraceptives and the potential advantages of a method that could be used by women who were contraindicated for estrogen. A similar experience occurred in Colombia:

> "In the beginning," [the counselor] said, " we only told [potential users] that implants had the same contraindications as the pill, but when we perceived other side effects on the implants users, we told the new acceptors about the possibility of them having amenorrhea, heavy bleeding, etc., as a result of the implant" (Vollmer, 1985:35).

These experiences highlight the problems that can arise when insufficient informational materials are available at the service provision level. Although several pieces of scientific literature describing the method were available at the clinic, they were above the level of comprehension of the social worker who played a critical role in communicating with users.

It is impressive to talk to informed NORPLANT® users, for example those in the waiting rooms of any of the four participating Dominican clinics, and hear them describe the bleeding patterns they had been informed they might experience if they chose to use this method. This, of course, is not an indication of the extent to which women were able to tolerate the irregular bleeding, despite the prior information. It does, however, contribute to more satisfied use in that women are less afraid that something is wrong, in the event that they experience irregular bleeding. In a survey conducted of 309 current and former users of NORPLANT® in the Dominican Republic, 98 percent responded that they had been informed to expect changes in their menstrual pattern. More than two-thirds of the sample indicated that they had received a sufficient explanation of the method and had no additional questions (Hardy et al., 1988:6).

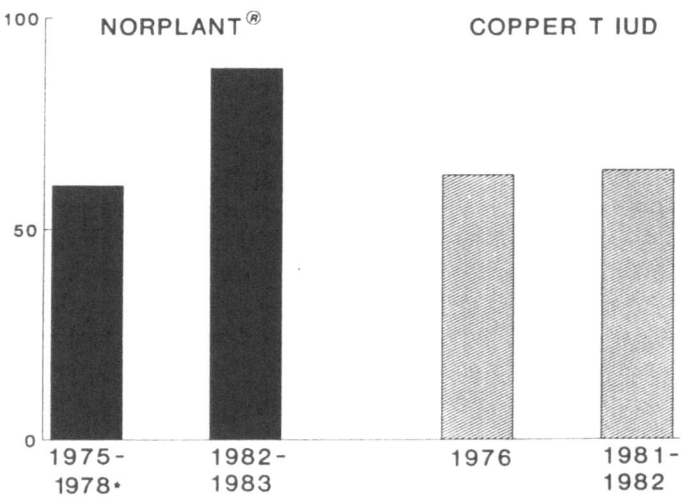

FIGURE 2 Net cumulative continuation rates after 13 months of use of NORPLANT® implants and copper T IUDs in two cohorts.

This experience is confirmed by a retrospective study conducted by the staff at the Centro de Investigaciones y Servicios en Reproduccion Humana y Anticoncepcion (CINSERHA), PROFAMILIA, the Dominican Republic. This clinic had been involved in conducting clinical research with NORPLANT® since participating in the first international multicenter trial begun in 1975. Net cumulative termination and continuation rates were reviewed for two cohorts of NORPLANT® users: 200 who had enrolled in the period from 1975 to 1978, when NORPLANT® was first introduced into clinical trial, and 212 users who enrolled from March 1982 to December 1983, after the staff had already acquired 5 years of experience. Staff noted a significant difference in overall continuation rates between the earlier and later cohorts (60.5 in the first cohort versus 88.1 in the later cohort at the end of the first year of use). (Figure 2) (Alvarez et al., 1988).

Statistically significant differences were observed in discontinuations primarily for medical reasons; the most important single reason for termination was irregular bleeding. Staff compared these data with data on the IUD, another provider-dependent but well-known method at the clinic. They noted no statistically significant differences between the earlier and later cohorts in overall continuation rates or in reasons for discontinuation. What factors might produce these significant differences between the two NORPLANT® cohorts?

The investigators hypothesized two sets of factors: one clinic-related, the second related to the population served by the clinic. They postulated that, first, the staff's increased understanding of the method through their own experience allowed them to gain confidence in answering users' questions and concerns about the main side effects. Second, the users themselves played a signficant role in sharing information with their friends and neighbors. CINSERHA has reported that a good number of the women entering the clinic requesting NORPLANT® have learned about it from current or former users and often are already familiar with the method's advantages and disadvantages.

In addition to conveying information about their experience with the method, past and current users who have had a satisfactory experience themselves with the contraceptive, help to inspire trust in the method with potential new acceptors. If the satisfied user of a new method inspires trust thereby stimulating demand, so, too, can the dissatisfied user serve equally to detract from the method. This will not only have a serious negative impact on the broader use of the method, but can also create a distrust of the family planning service as a whole.

The preintroduction trials taught the clinicians themselves several important lessons. The local coordinating centers were encouraged to organize investigators' meetings for the clinicians and social work staff. These meetings became the forum for sharing questions and concerns about the new method and discussing problems that were encountered.

There is, of course, no substitute for the direct learning experience. Council staff had cautioned the participating investigators many times that enthusiasm with a new product can generate over-promotion of the method by clinic staff. Occasionally, in the past, this had taken the form of understating the menstrual bleeding disruptions in the hope of encouraging users to enroll in the project. In several of the preintroduction trials, this caused high initial enrollment followed by early discontinuation (several removals requested after only the first few months of use). At one investigators' meeting at the end of the first 12 months of experience in the Dominican preintroduction trial, a clinician reported that her early efforts to enroll new users simply caused a high demand for removal at the outset. She informed the group that, as a result, she counseled very carefully about the bleeding and even invited women to bring their husbands to the clinic for information. Although enrollment proceeded more slowly, she had fewer complaints from users about the method. In Colombia, a physician complained that a hectic clinic schedule made it impossible to devote proper attention to performing removals if he did them whenever the user appeared with the request. Colleagues suggested that a specific day for removals be scheduled and posted in the clinic so that users seeking removals were aware of the scheduled weekly dates. This approach diminished the burden on him while addressing the user's right to prompt removal.

Both the training and preintroduction trial experience have given us insights into the importance of the supervisory infrastructure to the introduction of a provider-dependent technology. Supervision affects both access to the method and to its reversibility. In settings in which only one physician in a clinic is trained, services are often limited. When that physician is on leave or traveling, users may find themselves without access to service, causing inconvenience and possibly great frustration. Users experiencing problems may have to travel long distances at great personal expense in order to return to the clinic. A lack of transition between staff members leaving and new staff entering a program has occasionally created a void in service delivery until appropriate training could be arranged. In Colombia, for example, after participating in a clinical study conducted in 1982-1984, a physician transferred from one clinic in Bogota to another, leaving word with the nurse to have users directed to the new address for services. With time, however, and possibly a change in staff, the rumor spread that that physician had retired, and the nurse was left to handle follow-up visits (Vollmer, 1985). Although there were no reports of any unattended requests for removal due to this situation, it was a problem for routine follow-up visits.

An equally critical issue is supervision of training. Most countries using NORPLANT® are still working on a relatively small scale, continuing to provide implants to the already experienced clinics that participated in the preintroduction trials. Those currently planning to scale-up the introduction process must now ensure that a larger number of care givers have demonstrated skill in the insertion and removal techniques. A caseload of users for the practice of insertions is rarely a problem in countries that have already conducted preintroduction trials. A caseload of users for the practice of removals is, however, a problem. NORPLANT® has exhibited very high continuation rates. In 13 countries where ICCR studies and several of the preintroduction trials were conducted, the cumulative continuation rates per 100 users at the end of 1 year of use ranged from 80 to 99, declining by the end of 5 years to between 25 and 78 in the countries that have continued through the 5-year follow-up period (Sivin, 1988). This provides very few cases of removal in a training program in a country where the initial study enrolled no more than 300 to 500 women. Each country will have to consider alternative strategies for training in removal. It may be necessary to send project supervisors to trainees' clinics when the first cases of removal are scheduled. In countries that have already experienced 5 years of use and have many users ready for removal, it may be possible to organize large-scale removal training or refresher training. Unfortunately, there are currently no data evaluating removal training in the interim period or measuring the impact of sparse training in removal on the availability of removals to women seeking them.

User Feedback to the Management Process

Preintroduction trials tend to focus on the clinic's experience with NORPLANT® rather than on that of the user. The data collected measures continuation rates, reasons for discontinuation, and pregnancy rates. With a provider-dependent method, continuation rates may not necessarily reflect satisfaction with the method. In some instances high continuation rates may reflect lack of access to a provider trained in removal or difficulties the woman might have had in gaining access to the clinic. High continuation rates might indicate the user's perception of the provider's resistance to performing a removal. For example, what the provider interprets as "encouraging" the user to try the method a little longer may be seen as a refusal to remove the implants by the woman who is reluctant to question an authority figure. It is also possible that the woman has actually been turned away.

Research on the perceptions of women using NORPLANT® is a critical element in the Council's introduction process. From a management perspective, the feedback provided by users generates information needed to ensure that NORPLANT® is introduced with adequate attention to user satisfaction. This information is incorporated into materials and techniques for counseling users, and in clinic management practices.

As stated earlier, there are many dimensions to be evaluated in introducing a new clinic-based method. The clinic setting, including the number of trained staff available, facilities provided, and the information available for counseling is one dimension. Another critical dynamic in the process is the user-provider interaction, and it must be given equal attention. Are users and service providers communicating adequately? Are service providers responding to users' concerns? Do providers have enough information and experience with the method to feel comfortable with their responses?

Loraine Vollmer, a Colombian anthropologist who conducted focus group discussions with current users and discontinuers of NORPLANT® , has illustrated some of these issues. Vollmer interviewed women who enrolled in a clinical study at two centers in Colombia conducted during 1982 to 1984. This was the first clinical experience with NORPLANT® in Colombia; therefore some of the observations provide important insights into the user's and provider's experience with an unfamiliar method. Users who said they did not feel they received enough information on NORPLANT® were asked why they did not request a fuller explanation.

> When we asked our informants why they did not request more complete information, many of them said they felt embarrassed to do so. . . . They feel doctors don't like to be questioned. In general, they are used to receiving medical treatment without asking questions. "The doctor was in a hurry" was another frequent comment. . . . (Vollmer, 1985)

On the other hand, counseling staff confessed that they lacked information about the side effects and felt "insecure" and concerned when confronted with bleeding complaints raised by users (Vollmer, 1985:42).

To provide critical feedback on user experiences with NORPLANT®, the Council and its collaborators launched a comprehensive program of research on the determinants of user satisfaction with the method and the service delivery system through which it is offered.

This work focuses on:

1.   the reasons why women continue with the method despite the menstrual bleeding side effects and the factors that they determine outweigh the method's disadvantages;

2.   problems with or perceived obstacles to access to removal on demand;

3.   adequacy of information about NORPLANT® and other available contraceptives for informed decision making;

4.   adequacy of counseling and support when choosing NORPLANT® during use, and when removal is sought; and

5.   the impact of bleeding pattern disruptions on daily life, as well as on religious and cultural activities.

A variety of research techniques have been employed to learn about user experiences with NORPLANT®. Surveys have been conducted in Brazil, the Dominican Republic, and Thailand and are ongoing in Indonesia and Mexico. Focus group discussions have been held with users and discontinuers in Colombia. In 1986, PATH collaborated with institutions in Thailand, Indonesia, the Dominican Republic, and Egypt to conduct focus groups with NORPLANT® users, discontinuers, and service providers.

The research has already identified some problems with delivery of this method in the existing service infrastructure. However, these studies also indicate that most users have had a positive experience with NORPLANT® .

In Brazil, for example, a comparative study of NORPLANT® users and IUD users indicated that 86 percent of the NORPLANT® users rated their experience with the method as good or very good. This figure was similar to the rating given by IUD users about that method, indicating a similar degree of satisfaction in comparison to an already known provider-dependent method (Hardy et al., 1986). In a survey of NORPLANT® users in three different cities in Brazil, 80.6 percent indicated that they would recommend the implants to a friend (Hardy et al., 1986). In focus groups in Colombia, several of the women who terminated use of NORPLANT® indicated that they would still recommend the method to friends or relatives: ". . . they felt that the method was very convenient and effective; that if it didn't adapt to their bodies, it doesn't mean it wouldn't adapt to others" (Vollmer, 1985:70).

The characteristics of the method that most users cited as advantages were its efficacy and ease of use. The satisfied users who participated in focus groups indicated that these advantages outweighed the disadvantages—the most predominant of which was the irregular bleeding (Program for Appropriate Technology in Health, 1987).

Most of the studies, however, indicated some degree of difficulty with access to removal. For example, in a survey of users and discontinuers in three clinics in the Dominican Republic, the users were asked whether they had ever desired removal. Half of the women who were still using NORPLANT® at the time of the interview had at one time or another considered removal, mostly due to menstrual problems. Several of the women changed their mind about removal and therefore did not return to the clinic. Of the 68 women who returned to the clinic, however, but who did not have the implants removed, 25 percent cited clinic or personnel problems among the obstacles, and 25 percent indicated they were advised against removal. Some of the more specific responses given within these categories included:

- no one was available at the clinic to perform the removal;
- no one was available with whom to consult;
- sterile instruments were not available;
- there was an electrical blackout in the clinic.

Some women mentioned having been told by a nurse that the implants were too expensive or had been used for too short a time to be removed (Hardy et al., 1988). Similar problems and findings were reported in focus group discussions.

An interesting cultural issue in Indonesia came to light through the focus group discussions. NORPLANT® implants have been coined as *susuk KB* or *family planning susuk* in reference to the traditional practice of implanting a precious metal in the skin to impart beauty or strength. The word *susuk* has been widely used in printed materials and has generally been regarded as having a positive connotation. It was later realized that *susuk* is forbidden by Islam and is sometimes associated with imparting beauty to entice someone, often seen as a reference to prostitution. This created a negative association among the very religious community. Attempts are being made to choose a suitable alternative name, and printed materials using *susuk* are not distributed in certain districts (Program for Appropriate Technology in Health, 1987).

The results of these studies have so far been useful in sensitizing the agencies involved in the introduction effort and clinicians participating in the program to the informational, counseling, and access to service needs of users. They have also been helpful in highlighting the need for strengthening the counseling skills of clinic staff as well as designing strategies to facilitate access to removal.

The process coordinated by PATH to provide feedback from focus group discussions to service providers was as interesting as the results themselves. A workshop was organized where the focus group discussion leaders in each country presented their findings to service providers of the respective clinics whose clients were interviewed. The dialogue elicited certain differences in user and provider perceptions. For example, women in all four countries expressed concern that they were not clearly informed about the removal procedure and imagined it to be far more difficult and painful. In one country women thought the removal would require major surgery. The workshop participants concluded that counseling must include discussion of the removal procedure and the Council has also begun to advocate this in its program. Users in two countries indicated an interest in having more information about bleeding irregularities prior to insertion. Service providers had, in contrast, expressed the concern that too much information on changes in bleeding would frighten women.

It became clear that unanswered questions can create doubts about the method as well as lead users to think that routine side effects are potentially hazardous to health (Program for Appropriate Technology in Health, 1987).

COMMUNICATION IS CRITICAL

A critical and frequently overlooked element of the introduction process is good communication. Access to contraceptives has often suffered as a result of misinformation and rumors that circulate among the general public and the medical community. Even when the furor surrounding a particular controversy dies down, it is the negative publicity generated that the public tends to remember.

Investment in interactions that avoid the generation of negative publicity far outweighs the consequences of combatting an already existing campaign launched against a method or program. The damage caused has the potential for destroying faith in the new product, thereby affecting the introduction process itself.

The Council's introduction program has stressed communication about NORPLANT® and its service delivery requirements to a variety of audiences.

Governmental Officials

It is essential to initiate communication with health ministries and regulatory bodies in each country in order to obtain approval to conduct preintroduction trials. The process involves regular written reports as well as briefings throughout the course of the project, since regulatory approval will depend on the ministry's assessment of the data. Project investigators should be alerted to changes in ministries, particularly prior to registration. New administrations have been known to question decisions of their predecessors and may present their own reservations about a product with which they are unfamiliar. Lack of information may leave a contraceptive open to political controversy.

In one Latin American country, enrollment in a large-scale pre-introduction trial of NORPLANT® was suspended due to misunderstandings about the method and the clinical study criteria. The study had been approved by the regulatory body under one regime, but the changeover in governments resulted in a complete change of staff. The new agency staff stopped enrollment in the project prior to engaging in any scientific consultatation with the expert clinicians participating in the study. This was the subject of much media attention. As would be expected, the media generated enormous concern among users, many of whom returned for removal within the month following the announcement. The vast majority of users decided to continue use of the method, however, because of the responsiveness of service providers to the counseling needs that they realized would arise following the media campaign.

In another Latin American country the new minister of health, based on her awareness of the preceding situation, indicated that project approval would depend on a consultative meeting with expert clinicians as well as feminist leaders. This was a very successful example of constructive communication bringing service providers together with women's health care advocates. A variety of viewpoints were aired and questions addressed. The exchange resulted in project approval.

Women's Groups

In October 1986, the International Women's Health Coalition and the Population Council took the first steps toward initiating an open dialogue between the scientists and service providers involved in contraceptive development, introduction, and international family planning and representatives of the international women's health movement. The meeting acknowledged the need for greater information sharing between these groups on scientific and service delivery related aspects of contraceptives at an earlier rather than a later stage. It further acknowledged the important role of women's groups, with their knowledge of women's roles, health care needs, and interaction with the service system to inform the population field (International Women's Health Coalition and the Population Council, 1986). The contacts that these groups have with women in both developed and developing countries have allowed them to play an important role in advising women about contraceptives and reproductive health care services in general.

The meeting resulted in more open communication about issues to be addressed in the contraceptive development and introduction process and also helped broaden the channels of accurate information dissemination on contraceptive risks and benefits. Collaboration with women's groups in family planning could help serve as a conduit for focusing on user needs and rights when service delivery approaches are designed.

This meeting has helped the Council to recognize the importance of this kind of interaction in country-level introduction. Similar efforts have since been organized in different countries and regions.

Medical Community

Another often overlooked audience in the introduction process is the broader medical community—those who are not involved in family planning. Particularly during the introduction process, when the product is still relatively new or unknown there is the increased likelihood that other physicians will express skepticism about the method and its benefits to their patients. Some voice concern and opposition to continuation of use. Usually these have resulted from a medical consultation for some other medical condition, where information on the patient's medical history reveals that she was using NORPLANT®. This can also place the user in the awkward position of weighing the trust she places in one physician against the trust she has in the family planning service.

One solution is to inform the user to have other physicians contact the family planning service provider when questions about the method arise. Another is to seek appropriate vehicles for communication such as the media or participation in professional meetings.

At the initiation of the preintroduction trial the Council has generally emphasized that clinicians hold a briefing meeting for all clinic staff—including nurses, social workers, and receptionists as well as physicians. Clinic staff serve as referral sources to potential users in a variety of ways. Even those who are not involved in the provision of technical services (insertion, removal, advice on side effects), will be responsible for providing information on how to gain access to the method (who is qualified to perform the procedure, where to go, and when the service is provided). In addition, all levels of staff assist in inspiring confidence in the specific methods offered and in the family planning service as a whole.

Counselors and Users

Feedback from users has aided in improving the quality of information offered by the clinic. PATH has conducted focus groups in order to develop prototype illustrated materials for women of limited literacy. These focus groups with service providers, as well as with users, have also shown the gaps in knowledge that need to be addressed. The information gained has been incorporated into the development of a guide for counselors that addresses, in an easy-to-read format, answers to questions about the method and its advantages and disadvantages.

Satisfied users have been one of the most important sources of information to new users, particularly during the early phases of introduction.

APPLICATION OF THE NORPLANT® INTRODUCTION MODEL TO OTHER CONTRACEPTIVES

The principal elements of the Council's strategy—training, counseling, informational materials development, local experience, and information dissemination—are indispensable elements in the introduction of any contraceptive. However, the emphasis placed on each of these elements will vary depending on the nature of the contraceptive.

NORPLANT® is a training- and service-intensive method because it is provider dependent and requires access to clinic services and facilities. The techniques for insertion and removal must be learned and practiced beforehand, and the bleeding pattern side effects must be clearly understood in order to assist users in coping with them. The introduction of another method, the levonorgestrel vaginal ring for example, will require less technical skill (primarily understanding of how to instruct the woman to insert and remove it herself), but will have similar counseling requirements because of the progestin-induced bleeding pattern disruption.

Perhaps one of the principal accomplishments of the NOR-PLANT® introduction effort has has been the understanding of the impact of good counseling on the selection of the appropriate method for the user. The lessons learned from the NORPLANT® experience with counseling are now being applied to the introduction of the copper T-380A IUD in the United States and overseas.

The value of collaborative ventures and effective communication cannot be overstressed. A successful effort can turn adversaries into effective collaborators through mutual understanding and working toward common goals.

A public sector organization contemplating the introduction of a new contraceptive modality should consider the following:

1.   The introduction plan for a method should be directed to improving or adding to currently available family planning methods and services;

2.   The research and development team must coordinate smoothly with the introduction team to ensure that the registration of the product is timed to coincide with the demand for availability created by introduction efforts;

3.   The design of the strategy must consider the method profile and the service delivery requirements dictated by that profile;

4.   Each method fills a different niche in the program. Introduction efforts should emphasize contraceptive choice. Promotional tactics more frequently tend to push specific methods that may not be suited to the individual and are more likely to inspire early discontinuation;

5.   Training and service-intensive methods like NORPLANT® should plan to scale up slowly. It is more important to build a competent and skilled team of providers then to rush the method to the public before staff are adequately trained.

REFERENCES

Affandi, Biran, Joedo Prihartono, Firman Lubis, et al.
    1987   Insertion and removal of NORPLANT® contraceptive implants by physicians and nonphysicians in an Indonesian clinic. *Studies in Family Planning* 18(5):302–306.

Alvarez-Sanchez, Frank, Vivian Brache, and Anibal Faundes
  1988   The clinical performance of NORPLANT® implants over time: A
          comparison of two cohorts. *Studies in Family Planning* 19(2):118–121.
Berelson, Bernard
  1966   *The Population Council Annual Report, 1966. Report of the Presi-
          dent.* New York: The Population Council.
Bruce, Judith
  1987   User's perspectives on contraceptive technology and delivery systems:
          Highlighting some feminist issues. *Technology in Society* 9:359–383.
Hardy, Ellen, Clara Baez, Telma Rodrigues, et al.
  1988   User's Attitudes About NORPLANT® Contraceptive Subdermal Im-
          plants and Changes that Occur with Use of the Method. A two-part
          report of a study conducted in the Dominican Republic.
Hardy, Ellen, Maria das G. Coutinho, Patricia Goodson, et al.
  1986   Study of the Response of Acceptors to the Attributes of NORPLANT®
          Contraceptive Subdermal Implants and to Changes that Occur with
          Use of the Method. A four-part report of a study conducted in Brazil.
International Women's Health Coalition and The Population Council
  1986   The Contraceptive Development Process and Quality of Care in
          Reproductive Health Services. Report of a meeting held in New York
          City, October 8–9.
Jain, Anrudh K.
  1989   Fertility reduction and the quality of family planning services. *Studies
          in Family Planning* 20(1):1–16.
Phillips, James, Ruth Simmons, Michael Koenig, and J. Chakraborty
  1987   Determinants of Reproductive Change in a Traditional Society: Ev-
          idence from Matlab, Bangladesh. A Working Paper no. 135 from
          the Population Council's Center for Policy Studies. The Population
          Council, New York.
The Population Council
  1987   Contraceptive Introduction Program: Status: December 1987. A
          report prepared for the U.S. Agency for International Development,
          Washington, D.C.
  1989   The Research, Development, and Introduction of NORPLANT®
          Implants. Forthcoming.
Program for Appropriate Technology in Health
  1987   Use of Focus Group Discussion Research: Looking at the Acceptability
          of NORPLANT® Implants in Four Countries to Improve Product
          Introduction Efforts. Unpublished report. Program for Appropriate
          Technology in Health.
Sivin, Irving
  1988   International experience with NORPLANT® and NORPLANT® -2
          contraceptives. *Studies in Family Planning* 19(2):81–94.
Soni, Veena
  1984   The development and current organisation of the family planning pro-
          gramme. In Tim Dyson and Nigel Crook, eds., *India's Demography:
          Essays on the Contemporary Population.* New Delhi: South Asian
          Publishers Pvt. Ltd.

Spicehandler, Joanne, and Forrest Greenslade
    1986   Training, Counseling and Informational Needs for Introducing a New
            Contraceptive Technology: NORPLANT® Implants. Paper pre-
            sented at the 12th World Congress on Fertility and Sterility, Singa-
            pore, October 26–31, 1986.
Vollmer, Loraine
    1985   Women's Perspectives on the NORPLANT® Contraceptive Implants
            in Colombia. A report submitted to the Population Council, August
            1985. New York: The Population Council.
Zeidenstein, George
    1980   The User Perspective: An Evolutionary Step in Contraceptive Service
            Programs. *Studies in Family Planning* 11(1):24–29.

A Case Study of Contraceptive Introduction: Domiciliary Depot-Medroxy Progesterone Acetate Services in Rural Bangladesh

JAMES F. PHILLIPS, MIAN BAZLE HOSSAIN,
A. A. ZAHIDUL HUQUE, AND JALALUDDIN AKBAR

INTRODUCTION

The question of how to deliver contraceptive services effectively under difficult social economic and ecological conditions represents a critical issue in Bangladesh. Social support for contraceptive practice is fragile, and development has languished, hampering efforts to organize rural health and family planning services. This paper examines the role of new contraceptive technology in this setting and presents a synopsis of the experience of providing the injectable contraceptive depot-medroxy progesterone acetate (DMPA) as a domiciliary service. The experiences of two rural studies are compared, each of which provides contrasting operational contexts for contraceptive introduction.

The first study, a much documented project in operation since 1977, is located in the Matlab research station of the International Centre for Diarrhoeal Disease Research, Bangladesh (ICDDR,B). The Matlab Project was originally designed to test the hypothesis that a package of health and family planning services, if carefully delivered, and tailored to village needs, could increase prevalence of contraceptive use, reduce fertility, and sustain demographic change over time. When evidence from Matlab showed that such services could have demographic effects, a new project was launched to address the question of whether Matlab strategies could be effectively transferred into the public sector program. This second study, known as the Maternal and Child Health Family Planning (MCH-FP) Extension Project, was launched in 1983. Unlike Matlab, it is a collaborative project of the ICDDR,B and the government of Bangladesh Ministry of Health and Family Planning (MOHFP). It is located in two rural districts that are geographically remote from Matlab and remote from one another. Taken together, these projects permit a review of the lessons that have been learned from introducing new systems of contraceptive service delivery in rural Bangladesh (Bhatia et al., 1980; Phillips et al., 1984).[1]

Neither the Matlab nor the Extension Project was designed to examine questions concerning the introduction of new contraceptive modalities, complicating analysis of the role of DMPA in these studies. In both projects, treatment area services include provision of oral contraceptive pills, condoms, vaginal foam, injectables, the copper T intrauterine device (IUD), and sterilization services. Although DMPA is provided, the role of this modality is embedded in a system of care that is essentially invariant within treatment areas. Moreover, Matlab represents a trial of a package of services rather than a study of contraceptive introduction. The Extension Project differs from the Matlab Project in that research data are available on the intensity of care in treatment and comparison areas. Using longitudinal data on contraceptive use, it is possible to model the dynamics of DMPA use as a function of alternative strategies for understanding operational change in the program. We aim to test the hypothesis that domiciliary DMPA service strategies developed in Matlab can be transferred to the public sector program, and to review the operational context in which domiciliary DMPA services succeed or fail in rural Bangladesh.

THE MATLAB PROJECT

Matlab is an isolated rural and riverine area located near the deltaic confluence of the Megna and Jamuna rivers. Despite its proximity to Dhaka, seasonal flooding and other ecological features of the area have prevented the development of large towns, the construction of roads, or other modern amenities. Originally chosen as an area for researching vaccines against cholera, Matlab has since become a population laboratory known internationally for its unusually accurate and complete demographic surveillance system.

---

[1]The design of the Matlab Project is discussed in Bhatia et al. (1980). The MCH-FP Extension Project design is presented in Phillips et al. (1984).

Design of the Matlab Project

In the mid-1970s, controversies regarding the demographic significance of contraceptive services in traditional societies led to international interest in field trials of family planning programs. Matlab was uniquely suited to the need for field research on this issue. Treatment areas could be matched with neighboring comparison areas, study populations could be large, and societal conditions were sufficiently unfavorable to family planning so that the effects of the program would address basic questions about the demographic role of programs under unfavorable societal conditions.

The Matlab Project design was informed by the experience of an earlier project known as the Contraceptive Distribution Project (CDP). The CDP spanned 2 years of effort and tested the hypothesis that household distribution of oral contraceptives and condoms could initiate demographic change. Results, although initially promising, soon demonstrated that the provision of modern contraceptive technology alone cannot succeed in such a setting. The CDP staff composition, field strategy, and supervisory system were ill-suited to the social setting, and the limited range of methods offered—often without adequate counseling or paramedical backup, failed to address client needs. Lessons from the CDP experience indicated that intensive service outreach was required and that a large staff of young married women would therefore have to be recruited, trained, and equipped to provide domiciliary services if family planning was to succeed. Rigorous domiciliary services, in turn, would require a strong supervisory system, a well-developed paramedical backup system, and ancillary health services for mothers and children.

In 1977 a redesigned project was launched that continues now, over a decade later. Young married women were hired, trained, and assigned the task of visiting households in their villages to promote contraceptive practice and offer services. DMPA, oral contraceptive pills, and condoms were made available to women in their homes. As the project progressed, the health service role of these village workers has been expanded to include immunization and other child health care services. Community clinics were established in clusters of 20 villages, each of which was staffed by a resident paramedic and equipped to provide basic primary health care services. In the subdistrict headquarters, Matlab Bazaar, an MCH referral clinic, was established and staffed with a female medical officer.

Work routines were designed to support the community service delivery system. Fortnightly, staff meetings in project clinics review progress and set aims for the coming cycle of work. On meeting days, project physicians conduct a medical review of operations and an MCH clinic. Work routines for paramedics specify 2 hours of clinical work and village outreach. The aim of this system is to maximize support for village workers, enhance their prestige and credibility as health care providers, and minimize organizational and social obstacles to their success (Phillips et al., 1988).[2]

The demographic impact of the Matlab Project was immediate and pronounced: Contraceptive use prevalence increased dramatically in the first 6 months of the project, from 5 to over 20 percent, and subsequently to 32 percent within 2 years (Phillips et al., 1982). The fertility rate in treatment areas declined by 25 percent relative to those in comparison areas, a level of impact that has been sustained with time.

The Role of DMPA in Matlab

Trends in contraceptive prevalence suggest that strategies for improving the provision of DMPA may have contributed to the impact of the Matlab Project. This is illustrated by the treatment area prevalence trend for the period from 1977 to 1985, which is diagrammed in Figure 1. While it could be argued that other methods could have substituted for the DMPA component of overall use, over 40 percent of all use in Matlab is attributable to use of the DMPA, and even minor lapses in the supply of DMPA vials to workers or distractions that interrupted work routines have produced discernible declines in overall contraceptive practice. Other methods were also important, nonetheless. With the opening of a Matlab tubectomy clinic in 1978, over 800 operations were performed in that year. Oral contraceptive pill use, although somewhat less important than other methods, accounts for a continuing 45 percent of all contraceptive use over most of the past decade, corresponding to use by approximately one-fifth of all married women. In 1980 copper T IUD services were shifted from clinic services to domiciliary insertions. Thus, by the end of 1980, all methods shown in Figure 1, except tubectomy, were provided to women in their homes. Each improvement in the availability of methods and the expansion of choice has been associated with corresponding increases in overall contraceptive prevalence.

Survey research has shown that neighboring comparison area prevalence trends fall far short of the achievements in the Matlab

---

[2]The role of the sociology of supply is discussed in Phillips et al. (1988).

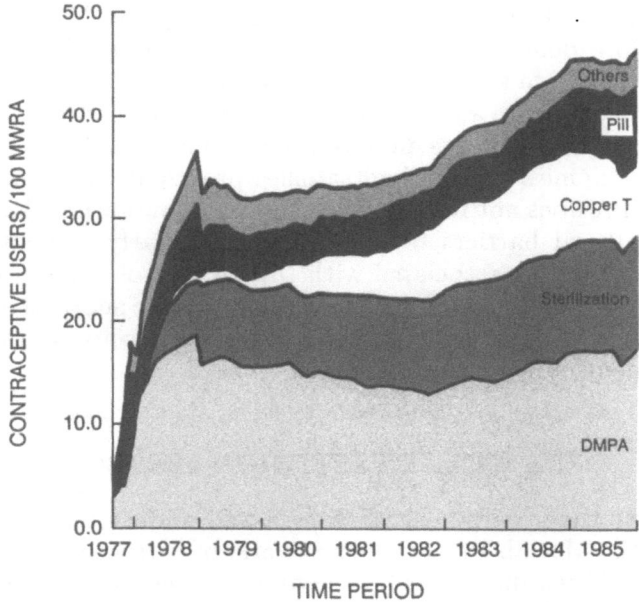

FIGURE 1   Contraceptive use prevalence among currently married women in Matlab, Bangladesh, 1977–1985. Source: Phillips (1988).

Project areas. Overall comparison area prevalence in 1984 was 17 percent, over one-third of which was tubectomy, much of which was provided in the Matlab clinic. Much of the remainder was the practice of traditional methods. Use of DMPA, in the absence of the domiciliary service system, was negligible.

Although aspects of DMPA render this method especially suited to rural Bangladesh, the Matlab services system is particularly suited to the efficient provision of DMPA. Elements of the operational design ensure that the quality and intensity of family planning care create a context in which limitations of DMPA can be greatly mitigated (Akbar, Koenig, and Phillips, 1988).[3] The Matlab Project has therefore demonstrated that the limitations of DMPA do not necessarily provide a barrier to the introduction of the method, and should not constitute a rationale for restricting access to the method. If well-trained workers are deployed to provide DMPA in the privacy of women's homes, the method satisfies prevalent client needs. The use of DMPA does not require client intervention for its effective use, nor are cultural barriers to injections particularly evident. Minor menstrual disorders associated with DMPA are tolerated if users are advised to anticipate such problems before they adopt the method and if they have convenient access to paramedics who can assist with the treatment of problems that arise.

THE MCH-FP EXTENSION PROJECT

In 1981 the government of Bangladesh undertook a systematic review of the Matlab Project with the aim of extracting lessons from its success. Much discussion and debate focused on the relevance of Matlab Project findings to national policy, since it was obvious that resources, staffing, supervision, logistics, and other aspects of the Matlab model differed fundamentally from the government service system. Adopting the Matlab Project service model in the national system was not politically, economically, or administratively feasible (Phillips et al., 1988).[4] Rather than reject the Matlab model as irrelevant, however, a decision was made to establish a new project in areas geographically remote from Matlab that would formally investigate the replicability of elements of the Matlab system in the public sector and diagnose barriers to organization development in the process.

---

[3] Akbar, Koenig, and Phillips (1988) have shown that first-method discontinuation rates are explained largely by complaints about side effects. Surprisingly few complaints relate to menstrual disorders, and high rates of switching sustain contraceptive practice. Thus, all method continuation rates are high, despite high rates of DMPA discontinuation. This pattern of low segment rates but sustained overall practices is generally characteristic of contraceptive practice in Matlab, irrespective of the method first adopted.

[4] As a test of the hypothesis that family planning could succeed, the Matlab Project was not intended to address what would work in the national bureaucracy, but rather to identify what would work in the village (see Phillips et al., 1988).

Key operational distinctions that were discussed in the course of this review are presented in Table 1. The provision of basic services in Matlab depends heavily on the role of female workers who deliver both health care and family planning services. In the government system, male workers, by tradition, are the primary health care workers, and family planning services are provided by a separate cadre of female workers known as family welfare assistants (FWA). In contrast to Matlab, where the high density of female workers permits a fortnightly visitation cycle for family planning, household visits from government family planning workers occur in cycles of 3 months or more. Paramedic staff strength in Matlab and government areas are comparable, but government paramedics are typically not resident in their clinics owing to the absence of security guards. Administrative links between the clinical system and field services have not been developed, in part because management information systems do not foster such links and in part because staff meetings at clinics are not an established routine.

Seemingly minor differences between the staffing composition of the Matlab and government programs can have major effects on the intensity of outreach and the climate of care. Matlab, while viewed as a relatively intensive service system, has a more efficient allocation of staff resources: more female staff, fewer male workers, and stronger administrative and supervisory systems that emphasize support for primary workers to perform a wide range of duties rather than targets for particular modalities. Health and family planning services are delivered by female village workers in Matlab, a strategy viewed by workers as crucial to their success. In the government system, village health services are provided by male workers, who rarely discuss family planning with villagers or coordinate their efforts with female family planning workers. The absence of a package of services that is sought by rural women and available from FWA dilutes the efficacy of client exchanges in government areas (Simmons et al., 1988).

Quite apart from the administrative climate, the intensity of care in Matlab generates a system that provides program support for contraceptive practice that, in other social settings, might naturally arise from indigenous social institutions. When social support is lacking, village workers must be much more than purveyors of supplies. They must know their clients, their families, and their needs so that concerns more general than contraception can be addressed in the course of outreach encounters. Studies of the Matlab system

TABLE 1 A Comparison of Service Systems of the Matlab Project and the Government of Bangladesh Ministry of Health and Family Planning

System Characteristics	Matlab	Government
Staffing pattern		
Primary service providers[a]		
Female village workers	1/1,200 population	1/6,800 population
Male health workers	0	1/5,000-1/10,000
Union level staff[a,b]		
Female paramedic	1/union	1/union
Male paramedic	0	1/union
Clinic guard	1	0
Subdistrict staff[a]		
Physician	1/subdistrict	1/subdistrict
Subdistrict supervisor	1 (female)	1 (male)
Work cycle		
Household visitation[a]	Fortnightly, routine	Quarterly, variable
Staff meetings[c]	Fortnightly	Monthly or irregular
Service content		
Health services[c]	Integrated (health and family planning provided by same personnel)	Parallel or partially integrated (separated into vertical wings)
Injectables[c]	DMPA only	NET-En+DMPA
Ancillary supplies[a]	Disposable syringes	Reusable
Medical backup[a]	Fortnightly field rounds	No field rounds
System support		
Primary worker training[c]	6 weeks (field oriented)	6 weeks (classroom)
Management information[c]	Task-oriented field registers	Unsystematic
Logistics[a]	Decentralized, demand pull	Centralized, "supply push"
Targets[a]	None	Copper T, sterilization

[a]Denotes operational policies that could not be modified.
[b]The union is a unit of government with 20 to 30 villages and populations ranging between 25,000 and 35,000.
[c]Denotes operational policies that were changed in the course of the Extension Project.

strongly suggest that DMPA, while representing an important and useful technology, succeeds mainly because the sociology of supply lends support to fertility regulation that is otherwise absent when couples weigh options for family planning.

As a joint ICDDR,B-MOHFP endeavor, the Extension Project represents a collaborative trial of changes in the government of Bangladesh field operation. In this trial the operational contrasts presented in Table 1 were preserved when rules, structures, and re-sources prevented change. When flexibility was possible, however, efforts were undertaken to fashion a new operational design on the Matlab model. A system of committees was devised to jointly review proposed changes. Whenever necessary, formal orders were issued by the secretary of the MOHFP. The provision of DMPA by FWA, for example, required a special order. On the whole, however, orders concerned procedural matters but left unchanged the structure of the government program, its staffing, and its resource base (Phillips, 1988).[5]

The introduction of operational change was undertaken through a system of staff training and collaborative introduction of the Mat-lab model in two rural subdistricts. The selection of two areas, with a combined population of over 1.2 million, was deliberately intended to dilute the special character of the project and preserve its public sector identity. Although the entire work system was the subject of-investigation, special attention was addressed to the role of fe-male village workers, since their role in Matlab is so crucial to the success of that project (Simmons, Koblinsky, and Phillips, 1986). ICDDR,B workers were instructed to function as "change agents" and were temporarily removed from their Matlab posts and assigned to work in Extension Project areas as counterparts to their gov-ernment colleagues for a 90-day period. The ICDDR,B staff was charged with the task of introducing change but was given no for-mal authority over their government counterparts. The government workers, in turn, were instructed, by official order, to collaborate in developing a new system and to function as its implementors. They were requested to cooperate with the ICDDR,B staff, but existing government orders were to remain in effect. Implementation of the Matlab model was thus to be an adaptive process, and formal orders were free of specifics on what was to be done. It was recognized by all who were involved in this process that the system developed in

---

[5] A discussion of the strategy for introducing change appears in Phillips (1988).

the Extension Project would differ very substantially from that in the Matlab Project, and would differ from the existing government system, but at the onset of the project, no one knew what would be possible given the constraints imposed on its operational design. It was an aim, nonetheless, to review the Matlab Project success from the perspective of government field staff, to attempt change consistent with that model, and to learn from the process of change in ways that could inform national policy deliberations on how to improve the program.

Two Extension Project treatments were designated, each of which defined a means of introducing change: a *training only* cell, in which participants in a training course were to be instructed in the Matlab work system, and a *counterpart cell*, in which trainees and Matlab staff participated in a 90-day joint regimen of work that included a complete team jointly conducting all aspects of work—household visitation, management information compilation, staff meetings, clinical backup, and supervision.

Problems and difficulties that arose in the course of this counterpart program were reviewed by joint ICDDR,B-MOHFP implementation committees and were then documented and communicated to senior officials for discussion and review. This process aimed to diagnose problems in the government system, with the transfer experiment providing a convenient framework for a review of how the system functioned, or failed to function, when confronted with the challenge of undertaking change.

An early outcome of this process of review was to institute domiciliary DMPA services in Extension Project areas based on the Matlab model. In the early stages of the Extension Project, FWA were to be trained to give injections, provide counseling, and advise women on the use of DMPA. Although not explicitly designed as a study of contraceptive introduction, the Matlab system for domiciliary DMPA services represented a departure from usual procedures and a significant component of the Extension Project intervention system. In project comparison areas, only clinic-based paramedical staff members were allowed to provide injectables, a policy requiring clients to travel an average of 4 miles for such services. In both training and counterpart areas, paramedical backup services were provided. Thus, the only difference between the two treatment cells of Extension Project areas concerns the extent of joint work with ICDDR,B staff on practical field problems associated with changes in the work regimen.

TABLE 2 First-Method DMPA Life Table Continuation Rates for Domiciliary Services in Matlab and Two Government of Bangladesh Extension Project Subdistricts

Ordinal Month Following Adoption	Matlab[a]	Cumulative Probability of Continuing in Extension Project Areas[b]	
		Sirajganj	Abhoynagar
6	85.8	75.8	81.9
9	75.9	50.7	65.0
12	68.7	35.2	45.7
15	61.9	25.9	28.5
18	57.5	16.1	25.6
21	53.0		
24	48.7		

[a]SOURCE: Akbar, Koenig, and Phillips (1988)
[b]SOURCE: Smith et al. (1986).

The Impact of DMPA Introduction in Extension Project Areas

Initial findings from the Extension Project experience with DMPA were encouraging. As in Matlab, DMPA was popular among users and service providers alike. It is viewed as a medicinal modality, owing to the injection procedure, and workers initially welcomed the additional option of providing the method along with their usual options of oral contraceptive pills or condoms. Information was disseminated, in Matlab fashion, by female workers who visited households to discuss the available methods, including the new DMPA option. Workers were not encouraged to emphasize DMPA. Although the introduction procedure went smoothly, it was soon obvious that domiciliary DMPA services in the government program would not replicate the Matlab experience. Both adoption and continuation rates were considerably lower in Extension Project areas than had been the case in Matlab. This is shown by the analysis presented in Tables 2 and 3.

Table 2 presents cumulative first-method continuation rates for the Matlab Project and two Extension Project subdistricts, Abhoynagar, located near the western border of Bangladesh with India, and Sirajganj, located in central Bangladesh on the Jamuna River. In Matlab, 68.7 percent of all DMPA adopters continued to use DMPA for 12 months or more, and nearly half are still using DMPA after 24 months. In Sirajganj, only one-third continued for 1 year,

TABLE 3 Generalized Logit Regression Coefficients for the Effect of
Treatment, Worker Contact, and Client Characteristics on the Probability
of DMPA Use

	Regression Model		
Independent Variables	Treatment Only	Treatment with FWA Contact	Treatment with Covariates
Treatment[a]			
Training only	+1.12 (+4.14)**	+0.46 (+2.40)	+0.71 (+3.45)**
Counterpart support	+1.82 (+6.90)**	+0.89 (+4.69)**	+1.13 (+5.58)**
Worker-client contact			
FWA household visit		+2.86 (+17.36)**	+2.54 (+14.52)**
Client characteristics:			
Age			-0.08 (-5.07)**
Children ever born			+0.17 (+4.57)**
Education			+0.01 (+0.19)
Index of landholding			+0.10 (+1.34)
Index of wealth			-0.02 (-0.31)
Desire additional child			-0.40 (-1.77)
Intend to use contraceptives			+0.15 (+1.00)
Constant	-5.65 (-23.24)**	-6.94 (-23.45)**	-5.06 (-11.12)**

NOTE: Number of individuals, 5,556; number of observations, 18, 352;
number of time points, 5.

[a]The omitted class is the comparison area.

*p < .05.
**p < .01.

and very few continued for 2 years. In Abhoynagar, continuation
rates are somewhat higher than in Sirajganj, but nonetheless, are
substantially lower than corresponding rates in Matlab. As a consequence, the early success in recruiting acceptors was offset by high
rates of discontinuation. In Extension Project areas, DMPA never
contributed more than 5 percentage points to the overall prevalence
rate.

While this finding falls short of the achievement in the Matlab Project, evidence suggests that the introduction of domiciliary
DMPA had a modest impact on the overall prevalence of use. This

is demonstrated by the regression models presented in Table 3.[6] The dependent variable for the regressions is the 90-day probability that a married woman aged 15 to 44 will be using DMPA, adjusting for past use patterns and future use dynamics. As a mean point prevalence, it represents the average proportion of women who use DMPA at any point over a 15-month period. The treatment-only model examines the effect of training and training counterparts on the prevalence of DMPA use. The constant term (−5.65) represents the logit of the mean comparison area prevalence (0.35 percent) for the 15-month introductory period. The low prevalence of DMPA use in comparison areas suggests that clinic-based DMPA services produce little discernible impact. The effect of domiciliary DMPA was statistically significant in training only areas, accounting for a net 90-day effect of +1.12, corresponding to an average increase of only 1.1 percent to the prevalence rate. The corresponding logit coefficient for areas where counterparts were used was 1.82, representing a 2.1 percent prevalence rate increase. When such effects are compounded over time, they gradually accumulate, but the effect of DMPA introduction was obviously substantially less than the effect of domiciliary DMPA services in Matlab.

The analysis in column 2 of Table 3 shows that the column 1 effect is, in part, attributable to the independent role of household services. A visit by an FWA in a 90-day period has a considerably greater effect than intervention by the entire Extension Project. That the net effects of treatment in column 2 are substantially less than the gross effects in column 1 suggests that treatments have had an impact by accelerating the frequency of FWA contacts with clientele.[7] This

---

[6]The data for the present analysis are described in Appendix A. The regression method employed in Table 3 represents an extension of maximum likelihood logit regression to the problem of analyzing discrete outcome information that is time dependent. The Extension Project demographic research system permits observation of a sample of households in 90-day intervals and linkage of information over time. In the analysis, a period of 15 months is observed, corresponding to a maximum of five observations per individual, but often less owing to sample loss on a given round of interviewing. A two-step procedure is employed that first estimates rounded logit coefficients by maximum likelihood, and subsequently adjusts for time dependency with a weighted least-squares correction of coefficients and standard errors. (See Zeger, Liang, and Self, 1985; Moulton, Zeger, and Liang, 1989). The regression procedure is reviewed in Appendix B.

[7]Phillips et al. (1988) have shown that the impact of the Extension Project is explained, nearly entirely, by the effect of treatments on the frequency of client exchanges.

important effect of outreach is robust to the introduction of multiple statistical controls. This is illustrated by the regression results shown in column 3 of Table 3. Demographic characteristics, indices of economic status, and baseline reproductive preferences—all potentially important influences on the adoption of DMPA—introduce little change in the effect of FWA-client exchanges, estimated in column 2 of Table 3. Outreach has thus had a net incremental effect on the use of DMPA that cannot be explained by the client characteristics specified in column 3 of Table 3.

The introduction of DMPA domiciliary services in government areas thus had substantial effects under the most optimal treatment conditions—about 2 percent per quarter, or 8 percent in a year when counterparts were deployed to demonstrate the method and other elements of the Matlab Project system in the initial stage of use. In the absence of counterparts, effects on prevalence were half as great, ranging around 4 percent. Although this represents a significant contribution of DMPA in the first year of introduction, high discontinuation rates imply that the long-term impact of DMPA introduction will be no greater than first-year effects, and they may even diminish with time.

Reasons for the failure of the Extension Project to replicate the success of the Matlab Project with DMPA have been the subject of considerable investigation and review. Most important among these explanations concern the quality of care in the government program and determinants of the frequency of worker-client exchanges. We consider each problem in turn, with reference to the operational contrasts presented in Table 1.

1. *The staffing pattern.* For an FWA to effectively administer domiciliary DMPA services requires injections at 90-day intervals, with initial injections provided within the first 5 to 7 days of the menstrual cycle. An early observation of the Extension Project concerned the fundamental constraints on the domiciliary program that arise from this requirement. Even if visit cycles were reduced substantially through more efficient field routines, the current MOHFP worker density cannot sustain a major domiciliary DMPA program. As caseloads increase, clients due for follow-up injections are increasingly dispersed, and the capacity of workers to respond to complex client needs diminishes. The critical worker density required for effective administration of domiciliary DMPA services varies by locality, but should permit routine visitation every month or more often. Only

then can special provision be made for interrupting work routines to provide DMPA services.

Early identification of this problem led to a decision by the government of Bangladesh to expand the FWA staff by one-third by hiring 10,000 additional workers. Extension Project experimentation with this strategy suggests that the visit cycle may be reduced by as much as one-half, but that the mean duration between client visits is still too long to permit effective replication of the Matlab model.

If work routines could be specified so that each worker has responsibility for a delineated area, the existing staff density would be sufficient to offer a very broad package of MCH and family planning outreach services to rural households. Under current staffing and structural arrangements, however, this reorganization of work routines is not possible. The separation of health and family planning cadre into separate organizational structures and the prominent role of male workers perpetuate the pattern of infrequent visit cycles from any single type of field worker, so that any MCH or family planning services requiring domiciliary services will languish. DMPA, as a modality that requires methodical revisits, will be particularly difficult to introduce in the public sector, given current structural constraints.

The problem of staffing pattern and worker roles extends to clinical services. To be credible as referral centers, clinics should be open daily, stocked with supplies, and linked to the field routine with reliable management information. Considerable effort has been addressed to the problems of developing clinical backup for FWA in Extension Project areas, but the legacy of problems with clinical services may have detracted from the efficacy of the domiciliary DMPA program.

2. *The work cycle.* An early finding of the Extension Project was that lax task planning impeded DMPA work. In the absence of simple-to-use records for guiding household visitation, and methodical planning of service cycles, work routines were unpredictable to clients. Much has been achieved in Extension Project areas in introducing basic concepts of task planning, but rules imposing targets for copper T and sterilization are intrinsically disruptive. Targets should be set in terms of operational aims—households to be visited, tasks to be performed, and so on. Workers confronted with the task of meeting method-specific targets often viewed DMPA as somehow undermining their performance and increasing their task load. The target system clearly weakened provider commitment to DMPA in

government areas. In Matlab, where there are no contraceptive targets, but rather strict rules regarding work cycles, such problems never arose.

3. *Service content.* As stated earlier, structural and staffing problems weakened the climate of health care in the MOHFP program in ways that may have diminished the credibility of FWA. Seemingly minor differences between the Matlab and MOHFP systems exacerbated such problems. In the MOHFP system, for example, two injectable modalities are available, each with different syringe requirements, needle bore requirements, and visit cycles. In the Extension Project an early decision was taken to standardize injectable modalities so that only DMPA was available. Considerable confusion prevails elsewhere in Bangladesh, however, detracting from the overall efficacy of injectables in Bangladesh (Jonas et al., 1986).

Problems of system support greatly complicate the provision of ancillary supplies in the MOHFP system. Each component of the DMPA program—needles, syringes, autoclaves, kerosene, cotton, etc.—became an independent bottleneck compounding the provision of supplies. Considerable incremental demand for DMPA could be met if the method were dispensed in single-dose, nonreusable, presterilized packets with needles attached. Matlab Project logistics, while seemingly expensive, are relatively simple to manage and probably more cost-effective than are the logistics of the complex MOHFP operation.

Further compounding problems of system support is the inadequate system of medical rounds for field stations. Although progress on this issue was achieved in the Extension Project, there is a general lack of attention to medical backup and in service training in the MOHFP. As technical problems emerge, as has often been the case in the Matlab Project, it is important to review operations and continuously orient paramedical staff. The high discontinuation rates for DMPA, for example, have not been the subject of a routine clinical review of what is going wrong. In the absence of adequate mechanisms to ensure that the climate of care and service quality are generally sound, contraceptive introduction languishes.

4. *System support.* Although very little distinguishes the formal training system in Matlab from the training rendered in Extension Project areas, basic service support systems do not provide the continuous orientation to technical issues that workers require. Much attention in the Extension Project has focused on developing

appropriate management information and mechanisms of meetings and supervision that put the system to work. Nonetheless, lapses in recordkeeping, logistics, and communication were sufficiently frequent as to undermine the FWA's confidence that the system would support the DMPA program if caseloads increased. FWA were thus understandably reluctant to offer DMPA, since they could not be assured that requisite supplies would sustain the program. Targets, in any case, conveyed the message that other methods were more important than DMPA and that lapses in this program were not a matter of critical concern.

CONCLUSION

The litany of operational problems associated with the field trial of domiciliary DMPA services in the MOHFP system could continue. The intention, however, was to note that introductory studies, if focused solely on the use-effectiveness of a method, client satisfaction, and acceptability, can lead to spurious conclusions about the acceptability of a new modality in the system at large. Trials should study cohorts of women rather than cohorts of adopters of some method, and research designs should examine the role of contraceptive innovation when clientele are exposed to several contraceptive options and service providers must confront the practical problems of contraceptive introduction under realistic operational circumstances. The use of comparison areas, where new methods are not introduced but services are otherwise similar, permits analysis of the role of new methods as determinants of overall use dynamics.

An important conclusion to be reached from this research, however, relates less to the problems encountered in the Extension Project than to the considerable potential that exists to improve the impact of the Bangladesh program if the barriers to its effective operation can be systematically redressed. No single element of the Matlab Project explains its success—including the role of DMPA. No single element of the Matlab Project, in turn, can replicate that success in the public sector. Systemic changes are needed that address critical structural and operational barriers to improving the quality of care. If instituted, such changes could generate the organizational context in which new contraceptive technologies can have major demographic effects.

ACKNOWLEDGMENTS

Data for this analysis were provided by the MCH-FP Extension Project of the International Centre for Diarrhoeal Disease Research, Bangladesh (ICDDR,B), a project directed by Michael A. Koenig, Associate Population Council, ICDDR,B in Dhaka. DMPA introduction and collaborative work with the Government of Bangladesh is coordinated by A. A. Zahidul Huque.

Analytical software for generalized logit regression was developed by David Leon of the Population Council's Regional Office for South and East Asia in Bangkok, Thailand. Lawrence Moulton of the Department of Biostatistics, School of Public Health, University of Michigan, provided useful suggestions for software design.

This study was funded by grants to the International Centre for Diarrhoeal Disease Research, Bangladesh, and the Population Council by the U.S. Agency for International Development.

REFERENCES

Akbar, J., M.A. Koenig, and J.F. Phillips
    1988   The use-effectiveness of depot-medroxy progesterone acetate in Matlab, Bangladesh. Unpublished manuscript.
Bhatia, S., W.H. Mosley, A.S.G. Faruque, and J. Chakraborty
    1980   The Matlab Family Planning Health Services Project. *Studies in Family Planning* 11(6):202–212.
Hossain, M.B., and J. Phillips
    1984   A Factor Analysis of Economic Status Indicators from Four Rural Thanas of Bangladesh. Paper presented at the Annual Meeting of the Bangladesh Population Association, Dhaka, Bangladesh. August.
Jonas, E., M.A. Koblinsky, Z. Huque, and D. Balk
    1986   An overview of injectable contraceptives with special application to Bangladesh. Working Paper no. 6. MCH-FP Extension Project, Dhaka, Bangladesh. Unpublished manuscript.
Moulton, L.H., S.L. Zeger, and K.-Y. Liang
    1989   Some generalized regression models for longitudinal data. In J.H. Dwyer and F. Fienlieb, eds., *Statistical Models for Longitudinal Models for Health*. Oxford: Oxford University Press. Forthcoming.
Mozumder, A.B.M. K. Alam, J.F. Phillips, D. Leon, and M.B. Hossain
    1986   The Sample Registration System: A Microcomputer System for Monitoring Demographic Dynamics and Health and Family Planning Service Operations in Rural Bangladesh. Paper presented at the Annual Meeting of the Population Association of America, San Francisco, April 3–5.
Phillips, J.F.
    1988   Translating pilot project success into national policy development: Two projects in Bangladesh. *Asia-Pacific Population Journal* 2(4):3–28.

Phillips, J.F., W. Stinson, S. Bhatia, M. Rahman, and J. Chakraborty
  1982   The demographic impact of the Family Planning Health Services
         Project in Matlab, Bangladesh. *Studies in Family Planning* 13(5):
         131–140.
Phillips, J.F., R. Simmons, G. Simmons, and M.D. Yunus
  1984   Transferring health and family planning service innovations to the
         public sector: An experiment in organization development in Bangla-
         desh. *Studies in Family Planning* 15(2):62–73.
Phillips, J.F., R. Simmons, M.A. Koenig, and J. Chakraborty
  1988   The determinants of reproductive change in a traditional society:
         Evidence from Matlab, Bangladesh. *Studies in Family Planning.*
         Forthcoming.
Simmons, R., M.A. Koblinsky, and J.F. Phillips
  1986   Client relations in South Asia: Programmatic and societal determi-
         nants. *Studies in Family Planning* 17(6):257–268.
Simmons, R., L. Baqee, M. A. Koenig, and J.F. Phillips
  1988   Beyond supply: The importance of female family planning workers in
         rural Bangladesh. *Studies in Family Planning* 19(1):29–38.
Smith, C., A.A. Zahidul Huque, M.A. Koblinsky, F. Rahman, A.A. Molla, M.
Alam, M. Rahman, W. Kamal, and K.M. Rahman
  1986   Domiciliary Injectable Contraceptive Programme in Abhoynagar and
         Sirajganj Upazilas. Operations Research Paper no. 54. International
         Centre for Diarrhoeal Disease Research, Dhaka, Bangladesh. Unpub-
         lished manuscript.
Zeger, S.L., K.Y. Liang, and S.G. Self
  1985   The analysis of binary longitudinal data with time independent co-
         variates. *Biometrika* 72:31–38.

APPENDIX A

The Data

The demographic monitoring system for the Extension Project, the sample registration system (SRS), is a longitudinal data base that was implemented in October 1982 for evaluating project impact.[8] Each round of the SRS consists of visits of teams of ICDDR,B male and female interviewers to approximately 19 percent of the house-holds in 13 service areas, termed *unions*. A round of interviewing is completed in 90 days, during which approximately 6,800 households are visited. Data collection and processing are designed to ensure the linkage of current records with previously collected information providing an integrated data base, a procedure that generates linked and edited longitudinal data on demographic dynamics, indicators of contact between workers and clientele, and intermediate variables

---

[8]The SRS design is described in Mozumder et al. (1986).

on contraceptive use dynamics. Linked records also document characteristics of the social and economic status of households and the baseline reproductive preferences of members.[9]

Table A-1 presents baseline characteristics for the SRS respondents who make up the study population for the present analysis. All were currently married women of reproductive age and are distributed according to contraceptive use status in the period immediately prior to intervention.[10] Sample characteristics of the study population do not differ appreciably from those of populations in studies performed elsewhere in Bangladesh. The sample is made up of young, high-parity women who have an average of 1.2 years of schooling. Illiteracy is high and the economy is dominated by farming, handicrafts, and trading. The proportion of Hindus in the population is similar to the national average. Surprisingly, over 70 percent of the baseline respondents wanted no more children, although only 17 percent were using contraception. Of the women not using contraceptives, 55 percent stated that they intended to use a method in the future. Knowledge of methods is nearly universal, and most respondents are aware of sources of supplies and services (86 percent). Of the respondents half were contacted by a male worker and nearly two-fifths were contacted by a female worker in the 90 days prior to the baseline survey. Baseline data thus suggest that significant household services were being provided prior to the onset of Extension Project activities.[11]

In addition to the data presented in Table A-1, data are available on economic status. A survey of economic status was conducted in the baseline period in which information on landholding, possession of modern objects, and other indicators of wealth was gathered. To simplify analyses, these data have been scaled into two indices, one

---

[9]Baseline SRS interviews elected responses on reproductive preferences, current contraceptive use intentions and practice, and other issues.

[10]In the present analysis, the interviewing of clients regarding servcies and contraceptive behavior corresponds to the first interview round prior to introduction of project interventions, a period that was approximately 6 months after completion of the baseline survey, which commenced April 1, 1983. Table A-1 records the use status of respondents at that time, according to characteristics recorded in the earlier survey.

[11]Subsequent work on developing research techniques suggests that baseline data may seriously overestimate contact rates owing to reference period errors in the recall of dates of visits, whereby any recent visit is included in the 90-day reference period. Longitudinal data are less subject to such biases because respondents can be referred to the most recent visit.

TABLE A-1 Baseline Characteristics of Users and Nonusers in the SRS Sample

Variable	Users Mean	Standard Deviation	Nonusers Mean	Standard Deviation	All Women Mean	Standard Deviation
Continuous variables						
Age	30.5	7.5	28.8	9.6	29.1	9.3
Education	2.1	3.0	1.0	2.1	1.2	2.3
Children ever born	4.6	2.6	4.0	3.2	4.1	3.1
Categorical variables						
Religion						
Muslim	76.7		89.1		87.0	
Others	23.3		10.9		13.0	
Want more children?						
Yes	16.2		29.1		27.0	
No	83.8		70.9		73.0	
Intend to contracept?						
Yes	100.0		45.1		54.4	
No	0		54.9		45.6	
Know source of supply or services?						
Yes	95.8		83.3		85.5	
No	4.2		16.7		14.5	
Contacted by male worker in the past 90 days?						
Yes	56.5		48.4		49.7	
No	43.5		51.6		50.3	
Contacted by female worker in the past 90 days?						
Yes	48.5		37.0		38.9	
No	51.5		63.0		61.1	
Total number in sample	1,153		5,669		6,822	

SOURCE: Phillips et al. (1988).

correlating with land ownership and wealth typically derived from agricultural income and the other an index of wealth from sources other than land. The two scales are uncorrelated, with means of 0 and standard deviations of 1. In the absence of accurate information on household income, such indices are useful for characterizing economic status in rural Bangladesh in 1984 (Hossain and Phillips, 1984).

APPENDIX B

Presented here is the generalized logit regression estimation procedure of Moulton et al. (1989). A test of the hypothesis that services outreach affects contraceptive behavior is provided by estimation of unknown parameters in the following model.

$$\text{logit } p_{it} = \alpha + \sum_{j=1}^{J} \beta_j + \sum_{k=1}^{K} \gamma_k Z_k \qquad (B-1)$$

Where p_{it} is the 90-day probability that individual i is contracepting at time t among a sample of N observations of women who were nonusers at t, and Z_k is the kth attribute of women and their households defining reproductive motives in the baseline, assumed to be fixed with time.

The unknown parameters, to be estimated by maximum likelihood, are α, a constant, β_j the effect of treatment or FWA exchanges, and γ_k the effect of the kth characteristic client i.

A potential limitation of Equation B-1 is that conventional logistic regression procedures assume that successive observations of individual i are independent. Since contraceptive status at one observation interval covaries with the status of individual i at other points of time, estimates of β_I are biased. To adjust for time dependency we estimate β_t separately for each time point and combine estimates of β_t through a weighted least-squares calculation proposed by Moulton, Zeger, and Liang (1989) and Zeger, Liang, and Self (1985).

Part V
Consequences for Resources

Introducing New Contraceptive Technologies in Developing Countries

JACQUELINE SHERRIS AND GORDON W. PERKIN

The successful development and then introduction of a new contraceptive technology onto the market involves a number of interrelated activities. These activities are designed to ensure that the new technology is safe and acceptable to intended users and can be adequately and promptly supplied to users, and that the continuing effectiveness and safety of the technology in a given population can be appropriately monitored. Once a safe and appropriate method has been developed, the major activities involved in contraceptive introduction can be divided into three overall categories: supply, promotion, and surveillance.

THE CONTEXT

The process of developing new methods has changed dramatically in recent years. Whereas a few decades ago public and private sector roles in the development of new contraceptives were quite distinct, more recently the public sector has been forced to take responsibility for a wider array of activities. This is primarily because private sector manufacturers have reduced their investment in contraceptive development due, in part, to the uncertainties of the public sector market in developing countries and the private sector market in developed countries and to the product liability issues associated with many contraceptive methods, especially in the United States (Lincoln and Kaeser, 1988).

Previously, the role of the public sector was limited primarily to generating an idea for a new method and then in carrying out clinical trials and acceptability studies. These studies, which include survey research, small-scale qualitative research, and evaluation of anthropological data, have been crucial to ensuring that the technology fits the needs and preferences of the intended users (Sherris and Perkin, 1987). After collaborating with public sector agencies during the early stages of method development and testing, private sector manufacturers assumed the burden of manufacturing the product and of liability risks, and completed the business of bringing the method to the market. This included carrying out market research, obtaining regulatory approval, arranging distribution, and assessing and allocating royalties and fees.

Now, public sector agencies frequently must take on many of the marketing and licensing activities previously carried out by private sector manufacturers. In some cases, the pharmaceutical manufacturer has become primarily a supplier to a public sector agency, providing the product but leaving the public sector agency to carry out most other activities and to assume all liability risks. This is especially likely with methods aimed at a large audience in a developing country since some of the important criteria for a method in a developing country—limited need, highly trained personnel, low cost, and extended use—are not compatible with maximum profits.

In this new product development environment, it may be necessary for a number of different national and international agencies to work together to develop and successfully introduce a new contraceptive method. For instance, the Population Council has collaborated with public and private sector organizations in the development and introduction of NORPLANT®, the subdermal implant system for long-term delivery of levonorgestrel. NORPLANT® was developed by the council's International Committee for Contraception Research (ICCR) over a 15-year period and is now manufactured and sold by a commercial company. Following successful clinical testing by ICCR and Family Health International (FHI), NORPLANT® was registered and approved for use in a number of family planning programs throughout the world. The Population Council also initiated the development of several copper T intrauterine devices (IUDs), the most recent of which, the copper T-380A, is now widely available throughout the world.

SUPPLY

Supplying new methods to programs in developing countries demands different strategies, depending on the method. Currently, international donor agencies, especially the U.S. Agency for International Development, play a major role in supplying contraceptive commodities, especially oral contraceptives (OCs), IUDs, and condoms. A few developing countries purchase commodities on the international market. For most, however, limited national health budgets combined with the shortage of foreign exchange preclude this option. A few countries have begun producing their own contraceptives.

Because of the increasing demand for contraceptive supplies in many developing areas combined with the tightening of available funding, donor agencies are finding it more and more difficult to meet the recurring need for various methods of contraception. The countries in greatest need often are those with the most limited health care funds and the weakest foreign exchange situation and most cannot purchase contraceptives on the international market. Therefore, in some countries, the feasibility of local production of specific methods is being investigated.

In deciding whether local production of contraceptives is a feasible option in a given country, a number of factors must be assessed. While the issues surrounding local production have been extensively addressed elsewhere (Free, Mahoney, and Perkin, 1984), it is useful to review briefly some of the arguments that have been proposed for and against local production.

Arguments for local production include the following:

- Contraceptives may be viewed as strategic commodities essential for national survival.
- Local production ensures continuity of supply and facilitates long-term planning for a national population strategy.
- Significant manufacturing inputs are available in many developing countries.
- Excess pharmaceutical production capacity exists in some developing countries.
- Local production allows for effective donor assistance while reducing donor dependency.
- Local production develops skills and infrastructure.
- Local packaging of contraceptives facilitates development of culturally appropriate packaging and instructional materials.

- By remaining constant over a long period of time, locally produced goods and packages can build and retain brand familiarity.
- Local production can engender national pride.

Arguments against local production include the following:

- Local production could increase the cost of contraceptive commodities to the remainder of the public sector.
- Donor supply of contraceptives to qualified host countries can be expected to continue as long as needed.
- Technological and quality requirements of contraceptive production are not readily achieved in developing country settings.
- The cost of locally produced products must be compared with that for centrally procured goods.
- Publicly operated contraceptive or drug industries do not have a good track record.
- Local contraceptive production is not the most effective use of development capital.
- Alternative supply options may be more acceptable to some international organizations.

As these arguments suggest, a decision to undertake production of contraceptives must be preceded by careful analysis of the pros and cons to local production in a given situation. The long-term demand for a new method must be assessed, the technological capability in the country must be surveyed, the cost of locally manufactured products must be estimated, the degree of success of similar projects in the country must be reviewed, and the capability to continually monitor product quality must be evaluated. The feasibility of manufacturing sophisticated methods that demand a high degree of quality control and technical expertise (for instance, OCs, injectables, and implants) must be assessed especially carefully.

Perhaps the most appropriate way to view local production for most countries is as a continuum of activities, ranging from packaging of imported, bulk products on the one hand to complete processing, testing, and packaging on the other. For example, IUD production operations can range from assembly and packaging of purchased components to full-scale molding operations. Large-scale IUD production operations commonly have contractors perform some or all of the following procedures: blend the plastic material for the IUD frame, manufacture the copper components, make molds, perform injection molding and extrusion, and sterilize the finished product.

The development of local industries for testing and/or packaging of bulk products may be one way in which the interests of donors, manufacturers, and developing country governments can be aligned in favor of local participation in the production of needed commodities. Because the costs involved are inherently more dependent on labor and material costs, packaging and testing may lend themselves particularly well to local enterprise in some developing countries. With this approach, the developing country becomes a partner rather than a passive recipient in the supply of its own family planning commodities. Furthermore, product packages and package inserts can be effectively adapted to local cultural conditions.

Local production is by no means the best option for all countries. Where local production has been deemed feasible, however, locally produced contraceptives play an important role in meeting the overall family planning needs of a country (see Table 1 for a list of the developing countries where local production is contributing to contraceptive supply). In the People's Republic of China, for instance, local production of condoms, IUDs, injectables, spermicides, and OCs will provide about 55 million couples with contraceptive protection annually by 1989. The U.N. Fund for Population Activities projects to produce those contraceptives were begun in 1979, with technical assistance obtained from the Program for the Introduction and Adaptation of Contraceptive Technology. The donor cost of providing the technical assistance necessary to establish local manufacturing projects has been dramatically lower than the cost of providing commodities. In the early 1980s, the one-time donor cost of assisting in the establishment of a factory to manufacture condoms locally was just over $2 million; the annual cost of providing the number of condoms produced by the factory would have been almost $4.9 million. The one-time cost of establishing an OC factory was about $2.25 million; the annual cost of providing the OCs would have been about $16.7 million.

A reliable source of supply for a new contraceptive product must be supported by an appropriate and efficient logistics system to store and distribute the product. The logistics system is involved from the moment the product is ready to be transported in the country until it is in the hands of the user. When assessing the impact of a new product on a logistics system, the following kinds of questions must be addressed:

- Are special storage conditions required?
- Does the product have a shelf-life limitation?

TABLE 1 Current Status of Contraceptive Production in Selected
Countries, by Method Produced

Country	Injectable	OC	IUD	Condom
Argentina		P(M)		P(M)
Bangladesh		P(M), G(uc)		G(ud)
Bolivia		P(M)		
Brazil		P(M)	P(L)	P(L), P(M)
Chile		P(M)		
China (People's Republic of)	G	G	G	G
Colombia		P(M)		
Cuba		G	G(uc)	
Egypt		G	G(uc)	G(uc)
Ecuador		P(M)		P(L), P(M)
India		G, P(M)	P(L, uc), G(ud)	G,P(M)
Indonesia	P(M)	G, P(M)	G	G
Kenya				(uc)
Korea (Republic of)				P(L)
Malaysia				P(L), P(M)
Mexico	P(L), P(M)	P(M)	P(L)	P(L)
Nigeria				(uc)
Pakistan		P(M)	P(L) ?	G(uc)
Philippines		P(L) ?		
Taiwan				P(M)
Thailand	P(L)	P(M)		P(ud)
Turkey		P(M)		G(ud)
Venezuela		P(M)		
Vietnam			G(uc)	G

NOTE: G = Government-controlled; P = private owner; (L) = local,
primarily owned by business people in the country; (M) = multinational,
ranging from local packaging of imported products to complete
manufacture in the country; (uc) = under consideration; (ud) = under
development.

SOURCE: Adapted from Free, Mahoney, and Perkin (1984:Table 2).

- How much warehouse space is required?
- Is product or package integrity compromised by suboptimal storage or transit conditions?
- What, if any, are the visual signs of product deterioration?
- What sort of quality assurance tests should be completed on stored products to ensure product safety and efficacy?

Ensuring that these questions have been fully addressed in adapting a logistics system to accommodate a new method can greatly enhance the method's widespread acceptance and availability.

PROMOTION

Promotion of a new contraceptive method involves making the method widely available to potential users in the most acceptable manner possible. Promotion encompasses providing accurate and understandable information, a convenient source of local supply and resupply, and access to health care services for insertion and removal (if necessary) and management of side effects. A number of carefully planned and orchestrated promotional activities are crucial to the successful introduction of a new method. These activities generally take four major directions.

- Developing the most appropriate image for the method (including packaging, display materials, product name, etc.).
- Selecting the most appropriate and efficient channels for product distribution.
- Providing training and informational materials about the method to decision makers and health care providers.
- Developing print and other materials explaining the correct use of the method to users and prospective users.

To ensure the success of these promotional activities, studies must be carried out to assess what kinds of materials and strategies will be the most appealing and useful to various target groups (users, health care workers, clinicians, retailers, and decision makers). In many cases, data obtained from premarket studies can provide valuable information on user and provider concerns about a new method. Supplementary surveys can provide additional information on how much prospective providers and users know about the method and what characteristics of the method are most and least appealing. Qualitative research (for instance, focus group discussions) generally can be used to develop and pretest prototype materials, such as package inserts and informational booklets, to ensure that they are culturally appropriate (Zimmerman and Perkin, 1982; Zimmerman et al., 1988). Figure 1 shows how Nepalese booklets describing OCs have been adapted for two different ethnic groups in Nepal.

An important part of promotional activities associated with the introduction of any new method is developing an appropriate image for the method. Culturally appropriate names, packaging, and

FIGURE 1 Booklets describing OCs adapted for two different ethnic groups in Nepal. Source: From an oral contraceptive booklet prepared for Nepali villages, Family Planning and Maternal and Child Health Project, Nepal (PIACT).

promotional messages can all contribute to whether a method is perceived as acceptable by potential users. Much has been learned about developing appropriate images for contraceptive products from contraceptive social marketing programs (programs that use established commercial distribution networks and strategies to make contraceptives more widely available). For instance, many social marketing programs have found that the most acceptable names for condoms suggest strength, masculinity, and protection, for instance *Dhaal*, meaning "shield," in Nepal; *Raja*, meaning "king," in Bangladesh; and *Panther* in Jamaica. Packaging design, especially the choice of pictures and logos, can be very important. In Bangladesh, for instance, research revealed that potential customers thought that the woman pictured on the original Maya OC package looked sickly. A new package design, with a stylized drawing of an attractive, prosperous-looking woman, was viewed much more favorably. Broad-based promotional campaigns have been used to define a product's image. In Honduras, for example, women's fears about Perla OCs were addressed through radio advertising featuring physicians explaining how most minor side effects of OCs stop after a few months (Sherris, Ravenholt, and Blackburn, 1985).

Also important in any product introduction plan is the delivery system through which a product reaches users. Some delivery systems are more appropriate for some contraceptive methods than others. For example, condoms will be more likely to reach one major potential user population—younger males—if they are distributed through small shops and pharmacies rather than through the health care system. The attributes of some methods limit the type of distribution system that can be used to provide the method. IUDs or NORPLANT® implants, for instance, require trained health care personnel for insertion and removal; thus, they generally must be provided through a clinic-based system. Methods that require frequent resupply, such as OCs, are best suited to delivery systems that take the service close to the user, such as community-based programs or contraceptive social marketing programs (Hutchings and Saunders, 1985). Table 2 summarizes the appropriateness of different delivery systems for specific contraceptive methods.

Training decision makers and health care providers about the new methods—both about method characteristics and how best to provide the method—is essential to successful product introduction. If providers are uncertain about a new method, their attitudes can have a serious adverse effect on the acceptability of the method. In some countries, health care workers have been reluctant to provide OCs, claiming that they are not safe and that many nonliterate women are unlikely to take pills properly and consistently. Providing health care workers with complete, culturally appropriate information on a method, as well as on how to explain the method to their clients, is especially important in this type of situation.

Appropriate training of health care workers has been very important in the introduction of NORPLANT®. Of course, training in the correct insertion and removal is crucial. There have been a number of reports of NORPLANT® users experiencing difficulty in having implants removed because few health care workers in their village or region have been trained in the proper removal technique. In some cases, removal has been difficult to obtain because qualified clinicians have refused to remove the devices on request (Zimmerman

TABLE 2 Appropriateness of Different Delivery Systems for Specific
Contraceptive Methods

Methods	Clinic- Based Delivery	Community- Based Distribution	Subsidized Commercial Distribution
Hormonal[a]			
OC	LA[b]	A	A
Injectable	A	A	A/LA[c]
Implant	A	I	I
IUD			
Inert	A	I	I
Copper	A	I	I
Barrier			
Condom	LA	A	A
Vaginal spermicide	LA	A	A
Diaphragm/cap	A	I	I
Periodic abstinence	A	LA	I
Permanent sterilization	A	I	I
Noncontraceptive (menstrual regulation/ abortion)	A	I	I

NOTE: A = Appropriate; LA = less appropriate; I = inappropriate.

[a]Hormonal methods are provided through community-based distribution and
subsidized commercial systems on a resupply basis. An initial visit with
medical or paramedical staff is preferable for these methods.
[b]A designation of less appropriate does not suggest that a delivery system
should not offer that method but, rather, that the methods may be more
effectively provided through another system.
[c]The appropriateness of delivering injectable contraceptives through
subsidized commercial distribution systems is highly variable by country.

SOURCE: Adapted from Hutchings and Saunders (1985:Table 4).

et al., 1988). It also has been very important for health care workers
to be well-trained in counseling techniques to use when explaining
NORPLANT® and how it compares to other methods, what to expect during insertion, how to deal with common side effects, and so
on. Ensuring that providers clearly explain new methods to their
clients and take the time to listen to clients' concerns will improve
the quality of care provided in family planning clinics.

The Program for Appropriate Technology in Health (PATH) has collaborated with the Population Council and FHI in the introduction of NORPLANT®, particularly in developing print materials explaining NORPLANT® to nonliterate users. Results of focus group discussions made it clear that in introducing NORPLANT®, its primary benefits had to be stressed and apprehensions about side effects (especially changes in bleeding patterns) and insertion and removal had to be addressed. Informational materials have been developed that describe implants as safe, effective, long-lasting contraceptives that are easily reversible. In addition, the insertion and removal procedures are described so that women know what to expect and are not frightened by rumors suggesting, for example, that the use of NORPLANT® involves major surgery. PATH also has developed print materials for nonliterate users to assist in the introduction of the copper T-380A IUD in a number of countries. Special emphasis has been given to explaining the insertion and removal procedures, the common side effects of IUD use, and the importance of appropriate follow-up, especially if any signs of serious complications occur. Figure 2 shows how a Bangladeshi booklet on the copper T-380A explains to nonliterate women the importance of returning to a clinic for follow-up if abnormal bleeding persists for 6 months after insertion.

SURVEILLANCE

Once a new method is introduced, it is important that procedures are put into place so that the safety of the method in actual, wide-scale use can be monitored. This system of monitoring is called postmarketing surveillance. Developed countries frequently have established procedures for postmarketing surveillance, primarily voluntary adverse drug reaction (ADR) systems through which health care providers report on unexpected events associated with the use of a new drug or medical device. Developing countries often do not have well-developed procedures for postmarketing surveillance (Gardner, 1987).

Surveillance of a new method is important for the following reasons.

• Since only limited numbers of people use a new contraceptive before it is marketed, rare events associated with widespread use of the method may not be detected.

FIGURE 2   Explanation in a Bangladeshi booklet on the copper T-380A IUD for nonliterate women and the importance of returning to a clinic for follow-up if abnormal bleeding persists for 6 months after insertion. Source: From an oral contraceptive booklet prepared for Nepali villages, Family Planning and Maternal and Child Health Project, Nepal (PIACT).

- Postmarketing conditions are much less controlled than pre-market conditions and usually encompass a broader and more diverse population. Therefore, different kinds of method-related effects, both beneficial and harmful, may be observed.

Postmarketing surveillance is especially important in developing countries since country-specific data often are not available about the effects of new drugs or medical devices.

There are three primary reasons for carrying out postmarketing surveillance in a given developing country. First is the issue of safety and effectiveness in the local population. There may be prevalent endemic diseases, nutritional conditions, or local medical practices that were not encountered in the area where clinical testing of the product took place. Some indigenous characteristics may affect not only the way in which the product should be prescribed and used but also how it affects various physiological functions. For instance, there has been concern that OCs may not be appropriate for women with sickle cell anemia, a common genetic disease in many African countries. Few data are available on this issue, however.

Second is the possibility that a new product may provide a unique benefit to the local population. For instance, postmarketing surveillance of OCs in some Asian countries has shown that OC use benefits Asian women not only by reducing pregnancy-associated morbidity and mortality but also by reducing iron deficiency anemia (Fortney and Potts, 1984).

Third, postmarketing surveillance may be important for resolving the controversy about some methods. For instance, injectable contraceptives have been the center of widely publicized opposition by various groups. Although injectables may be considered safe, effective, and particularly suitable by the health care officials of a given country, postmarketing surveillance frequently has been necessary to validate their safety under local conditions.

Public sector agencies involved in introducing a new contraceptive method into a developing country family planning program frequently must take the lead in developing a plan for surveillance of the method. Such plans would likely include promoting an appropriate ADR reporting system. They also may include designing and carrying out appropriate epidemiological studies.

CONCLUSION

In the changing environment of contraceptive development and introduction, international public sector agencies and developing country family planning programs often must work together to appropriately introduce and promote contraceptive technologies. The success of a new method involves careful attention to a broad range of issues, most important, how the method will be supplied and distributed, how providers and users will be informed and educated about the method, and how the safety of the method will be monitored once it is widely available. Experience has shown that in addressing these issues, local conditions and needs must be taken into account at all stages of planning and implementation.

ACKNOWLEDGMENT

The authors gratefully acknowledge the assistance of Jane Hutchings and Richard Mahoney of PATH in the preparation of this paper.

REFERENCES

Free, M.J., R.T. Mahoney, and G.W. Perkin
   1984   *Transfer of Contraceptive Production Technology to Developing Countries*. PIACT paper 9. Seattle, Wash.: Program for the Introduction and Adaptation of Contraceptive Technology.
Fortney, J., and M. Potts
   1984   The pill and Asian women. *Outlook* 2(3):2–4.
Gardner, J.S.
   1987   Postmarketing surveillance of pharmaceuticals. *Outlook* 5(1):2–5.
Hutchings, J., and L. Saunders
   1985   *Assessing the Characteristics and Cost-effectiveness of Contraceptive Methods*. PIACT paper 10. Seattle, Wash.: Program for the Introduction and Adaptation of Contraceptive Technology.
Lincoln, R., and L. Kaeser
   1988   Whatever happened to the contraceptive revolution? *Family Planning Perspectives* 20(1):20–24.
Sherris, J.D., and G.W. Perkin
   1987   Cultural perspectives on contraceptive technology. *Technology in Society* 9(3/4):323–337.
Sherris, J.D., B.B. Ravenholt, and R. Blackburn
   1985   Contraceptive social marketing: Lessons from experience. *Population Reports* J(3):J-773–J-812.
Zimmerman, M.L., and G.W. Perkin
   1982   *Print Materials for Nonreaders: Experiences in Family Planning and Health*. PIACT paper 8. Seattle, Wash.: Program for the Introduction and Adaptation of Contraceptive Technology.
Zimmerman, M.L., E. Crane, J. Haffrey, and D. Szumowksi
   1988   The use of focus group research in assessing the acceptability of NORPLANT® implants in four countries. Unpublished internal document, PATH. Seattle, Wash.: Program for Applied Technology in Health.

Financing the Delivery of Contraceptives: The Challenge of the Next Twenty Years

DUFF G. GILLESPIE, HARRY E. CROSS,
JOHN G. CROWLEY, AND SCOTT R. RADLOFF

INTRODUCTION

The developing world has dramatically changed its attitudes and behavior toward fertility in the past 20 years. When the U.S. Agency for International Development (AID) started its program in the mid-1960s, there were perhaps 15 million family planning users in the Third World, excluding the People's Republic of China.[1] Today, there are more than 200 million. Prevalence for all methods has increased during the same period, from 15 percent of married women of reproductive age in the late 1960s to about 40 percent in 1988. These dramatic shifts in behavior have accompanied changes in governmental and donor policies. The perception of governments and donors has been transformed from one of near indifference and inaction 25 years ago to one of intense concern and activity today. In the mid-1960s, donor support for family planning amounted to a few million dollars. Today, that figure exceeds one-half billion dollars. The changing political environment is highlighted by the fact that most developing country governments currently have population policies favoring lower fertility.

The revolutionary shift in contraceptive behavior will likely continue and has very serious financial implications. Concurrent with an increased use of family planning has been an equally impressive expansion of organized family planning programs and a wider range of fertility regulation technologies. This paper examines the costs

---

[1] Because of its large population, the People's Republic of China is excluded throughout this paper since its inclusion would skew the analysis.

of buying and providing contraceptives over the past 20 years and estimates what these costs will be over the next 20 years.

The estimates are based on a number of assumptions concerning demand and supply for family planning. Undoubtedly, one could alter some of the assumptions underlying this analysis and arrive at different cost figures—perhaps higher, perhaps lower. However, there can be little doubt that relative and absolute increases in costs above current levels would remain staggering. Governments and private organizations need to address now the future funding needs suggested by these cost estimates. Indeed, if they do not, the moderate increase in contraceptive use rates (far lower than what countries such as Brazil have already achieved) assumed in this paper will not occur.

Recent survey data have confirmed a substantial demand for limiting and spacing births in developing countries. While use of family planning services has been growing in most countries, there is evidence of a considerable unmet demand for services (Boulier, 1984). A primary goal among donors and governments of developing countries is to expand access to information and services in a way that closes the gap between demand and use. By focusing attention on projected costs, it is hoped that this paper will help to stimulate the resources and commitments needed to ensure that supply increases sufficiently to meet future demand. Before presenting the results, the assumptions about demand and supply underlying the analysis will be reviewed.

CONTRACEPTIVE DEMAND

How is demand for family planning going to change between now and the year 2010? Demand can be considered in *quantitative* as well as *qualitative* terms.

How Much Demand?

A rough indicator of potential demand is the absolute number of married women of reproductive age. In the 30-year period from 1980 to 2010, this figure will more than double and exceed 800 million women, representing an increase of 425 million women in just over one generation. (A high degree of confidence is placed on this estimate since most of these women have already been born.)

An indicator of satisfied demand is the contraceptive prevalence rate (CPR) for all methods among married women aged 15 to 49.

A calculation based on United Nations (U.N.) estimates places the 1970 CPR at under 20 percent. By 1980, prevalence had risen to 32 percent, and today it most likely exceeds 40 percent (United Nations, 1987). Using the methodology of Bongaarts and Stover (1986), contraceptive prevalence rates are estimated at 52 percent for the year 2000 and 58 percent for the year 2010. These estimates assume that total fertility rates in the developing world will follow the U.N. medium-variant projections.[2]

The U.N. medium-variant fertility decline may be achieved if recent improvements in contraceptive prevalence observed in a number of countries are sustained and repeated elsewhere. Recent surveys show that prevalence is rising in many developing countries. In Thailand, it climbed from 36 percent in 1975 to 67 percent in 1987. Colombia witnessed an increase from 45 to 63 percent in the decade between 1976 and 1986. Even African countries are beginning to show signs of rising contraceptive prevalence rates. In Kenya, prevalence more than doubled in the 6 years between 1978 and 1984, from 7 to 17 percent (Population Information Program, Johns Hopkins University, 1985).

The absolute numbers of women of reproductive age and the prevalence rates can be used to estimate future levels of contraceptive use. Figure 1 presents these estimates graphically. (See Appendix Table A-1 for underlying numeric rules and explanatory note.) In 1980, there were about 130 million couples using family planning methods. By the year 2000, just 11 years from now, there will be 350 million users in the Third World. The number will reach nearly half a billion (475 million) by the year 2010 if current trends continue. These numbers signal a dramatically expanding market for family planning services.

How Will Demand Change?

Not only are large increases in the quantity of demand anticipated, but the character of demand is expected to change almost as significantly. The principal assumptions are that socioeconomic

---

[2]While demographers generally rely on the U.N. medium-variant projection series, the course of fertility decline hinges on the pace of socioeconomic improvements and program efforts to stimulate demand and supply. The actual path of fertility decline will likely fall within the U.N. high- and low-variant estimates (see Table A-2 in Appendix A). Recent evidence indicates that developing country fertility rates may be closer to the high-variant path (Haub and Kent, 1988).

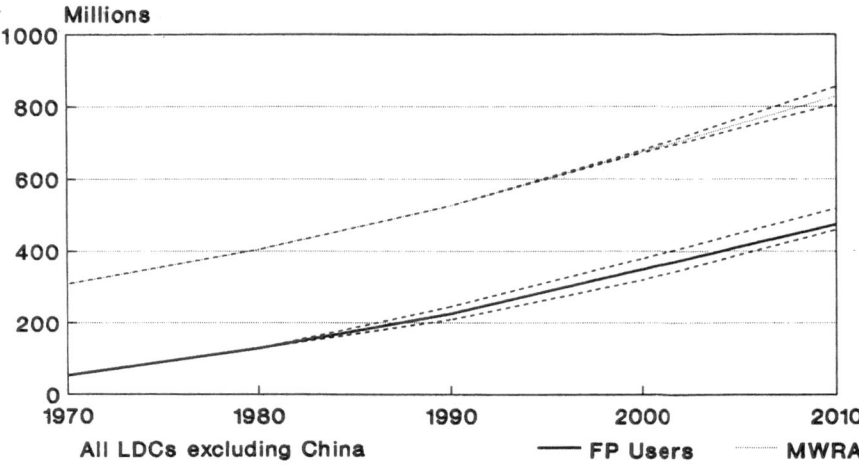

FIGURE 1   Projection of married women of reproductive age (MWRA) and
family planning (FP) users for all developing countries excluding the People's
Republic of China.

conditions in developing countries will improve and that high rates
of urbanization will continue. Family planning programs are also
assumed to continue to stimulate demand through information and
education efforts and by expanding access to services.

Life expectancy has been shown to be a good proxy for socioeconomic conditions (Lapham and Mauldin, 1985). This indicator has
risen steadily since World War II. In 1970, life expectancy in developing countries was 50 years; today, it is 57 years. By 2010, the United
Nations estimates that it will reach 64 years (United Nations, 1986).
This trend portends continued improvements in socioeconomic conditions, despite the periodic setbacks that can be expected in some
countries. Similarly, the shift of populations from rural to urban
areas will continue. In 1970, about one-quarter of the developing
world's population lived in urban areas; by the year 2010 more than
half are estimated to be urban dwellers (United Nations, 1986).

Improvements in social and economic status (measured by higher
incomes, more education, and improved health) and urbanization are
generally associated with better access to family planning information and services. These conditions also result in the desire for fewer
children and the increased use of family planning for limiting as well
as spacing births (National Academy of Sciences, 1982).

TABLE 1 Aggregate Demographic, Socioeconomic, and Family Planning Program Indicators in Developing Countries, 1970-2010

Characteristic	1970	1980	1990	2000	2010
Demographic Indicators					
Population (million)	1,815.2	2,316.8	2,912.6	3,589.3	4,303.0
WRA (15-49 millions)	410.6	538.7	703.2	899.8	1,104.4
MWRA (15-49 millions)	307.9	404.0	527.4	674.8	828.3
TFR	5.7	4.8	4.1	3.4	3.0
CPR	17.3	32.0	43.0	51.7	58.0
FP users	53.3	129.3	226.7	349.1	475.5
Socioeconomic Indicators					
Life expectancy	49.9	53.7	57.0	60.9	64.2
Percent urban	27.9	32.9	38.3	44.3	50.7
Family Planning Program Indicator					
Program effort	22.7	33.0	43.3	53.6	63.9

NOTE: See Table A-1 in Appendix A for explanatory notes.

To summarize, improved socioeconomic conditions and urbanization are associated with (1) rising general demand for family planning services, (2) more motivated demand for family planning, and (3) greater proportions of users relying on family planning for limiting rather than spacing births. These trends are modifying the profile of contraceptive users, resulting in discernible shifts to more effective and long-term methods.

Table 1 presents key trends in demographic, socioeconomic, and family planning program indicators underlying this analysis.

CONTRACEPTIVE SUPPLY

Unlike projecting demand, it is not easy to forecast future levels and patterns of supply. Whether the supply of family planning will increase to meet expected increases in demand over the coming 20 years is a major, and in large measure unanswerable, question for this analysis. The factors underlying future supply of family planning information and services are more varied and more complex than for demand (where 90 percent of the women who are potential family planning consumers 20 years from now are already living).

First, new contraceptive technologies could conceivably revolutionize contraceptive use and costs 20 or 30 years from now. Contraceptive technology has improved considerably since the 1960s. Compared with 20 years ago, family planning users have the choice of safer and more effective contraceptives. While this trend might generally be expected to continue into the next century, the development of a technology that would revolutionize contraceptive use is difficult to predict.

Clinical trials for two new methods, NORPLANT® and Net-90, portend an increased availability of contraceptives that can meet the demand for longer-lasting methods. These new methods have the added advantage that they are potentially more attractive to users. NORPLANT®, for example, may require only a few hours of clinic time over a 5-year period. Not only is NORPLANT® less intrusive and less time-consuming than the alternative (oral contraceptives), but there are fewer side effects with this new method, further increasing its attractiveness. Technology has played and, it is hoped, will continue to play a key role in helping family planning users shift to methods that more closely match their fertility intentions and preferences.

Second, family planning programs of the future may or may not reflect past trends. The family planning program effort has been defined as the combination of policy, financial, and program indicators which describe the total environment for family planning use (Mauldin and Berelson, 1978; Lapham and Mauldin, 1985). The program effort in developing countries improved substantially between 1970 and 1980 (see Table 1). The challenge of continuing such improvements in the future is formidable. This is especially so as more low-income countries, particularly those in sub-Saharan Africa, initiate family planning activities.

Third, the resources allocated to family planning by donors and developing country governments are difficult to predict with confidence. Donor resources for family planning have more than doubled over the period from 1971 and 1987 (Speidel, 1988). When considered in constant dollar terms, however, donor resources have increased only slightly. The future of funding for family planning among donors depends on allocations for foreign assistance and on the priority given to population assistance. As more developing country governments have adopted population policies, many are allocating increased resources to support family planning services. The future levels of funding for family planning by governments will obviously be constrained by overall government resources as well as the priority each places on population programs.

Fourth, levels of education and income of the populations in developing countries can be expected to increase, in general, over the next 20 years. The magnitude and distribution of these increases, which are difficult to predict, will determine the ability of the higher-income segments of these populations to pay for services. Because the elasticity of demand for private health and family planning services with respect to income is high, a larger future role can be anticipated for the for-profit private sector as people have more discretionary income (Lewis and Kenney, 1988). The extent to which the for-profit private sector responds to this demand is also difficult to predict and depends, in part, on regulations that affect local production, import, and distribution of family planning commodities.

THE PROJECTION ANALYSIS

Based on the foregoing assumptions about future demand for contraception, a projection analysis was undertaken that was made up of three elements:

• Estimates of current method mix and future changes in this mix.

• Estimates of the future number of contraceptive users and commodity requirements.

• Future commodity costs estimates.

Projecting future demand for family planning has been conducted by other analysts (e.g., Bulatao, 1985, and Bongaarts, 1986). What distinguishes the analysis presented in this paper is the attention given to method mix. A methodology is presented for estimating future changes in method mix based on observed cross-sectional differences in mix among countries having differing levels of socioeconomic and family planning development.

Alternative shifts in method mix associated with the introduction of new family planning methods are evaluated in terms of their commodity cost implications. Cost comparisons are made between a mix made up of currently available contraceptive methods (baseline A) and two alternative scenarios that assume small shifts (scenario B) and moderate shifts (scenario C) to two new contraceptive methods—NORPLANT® and the Net-90 injectable. These two new methods are chosen for this analysis because they are expected to become commercially viable in the 1990s. While other methods like the vaginal ring and the monthly injectable might also become available, NORPLANT® and Net-90 are used as examples in order to keep the analysis manageable. For analytical purposes, it is assumed that these new methods will achieve significant combined market shares of 3 and 6 percent under scenarios B and C, respectively, by the year 2000.

Briefly, the methodology used to estimate future demand, method mix, and costs consists of the following computations.

Estimating Current and Future Method Mix

Current Method Mix

Method mix data from 50 less developed countries (LDCs) surveyed between 1976 and 1986 were used to construct averages for each of three geographic regions—Africa, Asia and the Near East, and Latin America (United Nations, 1987; supplemented by Demographic and Health Surveys). These 50 LDCs represent over 75 percent of the population of all LDCs. Regional averages are weighted by married women of reproductive age (MWRA) to produce a 1980 method mix estimate for all LDCs.

Future Method Mix

To estimate future (and 1970) method mix, contraceptive use is assumed to change as countries undergo socioeconomic and family planning program development. Using method mix data as described above, the percentage of contraceptors currently using a given method is regressed on two commonly accepted indicators of socioeconomic development (life expectancy and urbanization) and a composite measure of program performance (Lapham and Mauldin, 1985).

The resulting set of six method-specific regression equations is used to estimate future method mix, based on U.N. estimates for future levels of life expectancy and urbanization and assuming that the 1972-1982 trend in program effort will continue (see Tables A-3a and A-3b in Appendix A).

Estimating Current and Future Users and Commodity Requirements

Current CPR

An estimate of current (1980) contraceptive prevalence is derived in the same way as method mix described in above, using CPR estimates from 50 surveyed LDCs.

Future Contraceptive Use and Commodity Requirements

As a basis for estimating future contraceptive prevalence, it is assumed that fertility in LDCs will follow the U.N.'s medium-variant projection series. The projection analysis employs Bongaarts's family planning demand methodology (Bongaarts and Stover, 1986).

Comparative Estimates of Use and Commodity Requirements

The methodology of Bongaarts (1986) is used to generate three scenarios of future contraceptive use and commodity requirements. These illustrate how the introduction of new contraceptive methods might affect total costs of family planning commodities. These three scenarios include the following: (1) baseline A projection which assumes that no new contraceptive methods are introduced over the next 20 years; (2) scenario B projection, which assumes that there is a small shift toward two new methods (NORPLANT® and the Net-90 injectable); and (3) scenario C projection, which assumes that there is a moderate shift toward these two methods over time.

In scenario B, 6 percent of all users are assumed to shift to these methods by the year 2010. In scenario C, a 12 percent shift to these methods is assumed. Recognizing that new methods may attract new users, for the purpose of this analysis, NORPLANT® is assumed to displace some sterilization and, to a lesser degree, intrauterine device (IUD) use. The Net-90 injectable is assumed to displace pills and, to a lesser degree, IUD use.

Estimating Future Commodity and Service Delivery Costs

Commodities

To determine commodity costs associated with meeting the projected method-specific demand for family planning in each scenario,

1988 unit prices paid by AID are applied as multipliers. Cost estimates are based on constant 1988 dollars (see Table C-1 in Appendix C).

Services

The total cost of providing family planning services in LDCs is the sum of the commodity costs plus service delivery costs. A value of $19.82 is assumed to be the average cost of delivering contraceptive services for 1 couple-year of protection. This estimate is derived from international averages (Bulatao, 1985).

FINDINGS

The analytic framework described above produces estimates of method mix, contraceptive commodity costs, and service delivery costs for the period from 1970 to 2010.

Method Mix

The regression analysis suggests that as socioeconomic conditions improve, family planning users will shift away from temporary and nonsupply methods to longer-term methods.[3] Figure 2 depicts this shift over the period from 1970 to 2010. Estimates for currently available methods (baseline A) are presented in Table 2.

The most dramatic shift occurring in the baseline A projection is the steep decline in the use of nonsupply methods. In 1970, nonsupply methods accounted for half of all contraceptive use. By the year 2010, these methods will comprise only about 15 percent of the total. A second notable shift occurs with longer-term methods—sterilization and IUDs. As expected, projected use of these longer-term methods increases over time, with sterilization more than doubling between 1970 and 2010. According to this estimate, in the absence of new contraceptive methods, sterilization will account for one-third of all contraceptive use 20 years from now. Use of IUDs will nearly double over this period, while the combined use of more temporary methods (i.e., pill, condom, and other supply) will increase more modestly from 30 to 39 percent. Overall, by the year 2010 the proportion of

---

[3]Temporary methods include pills, condoms, and other supply methods. Non-supply methods include withdrawal, rhythm, and folk methods. Longer-term methods include sterilization and IUDs.

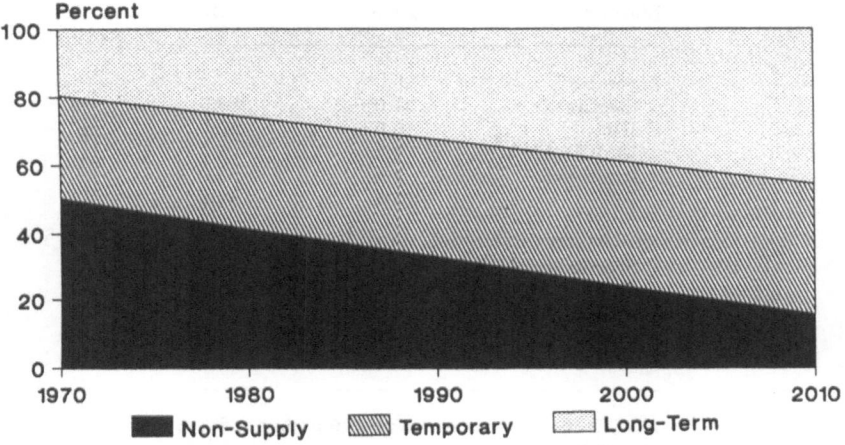

FIGURE 2   Changing method mix.

TABLE 2   Contraceptive Method Mix Estimates for LDCs, Baseline A, No New Methods, in Percent

Method	1970	1980	1990	2000	2010
Sterilization	12.9	18.0	23.0	28.0	33.0
IUD	6.6	8.0	9.3	10.9	12.4
Pill	22.1	22.7	23.2	24.1	24.6
Condom	3.0	4.0	4.9	5.9	6.7
Other supply	4.9	5.7	6.3	7.0	7.6
Nonsupply[a]	50.5	41.6	33.3	24.1	15.7
Total	100.0	100.0	100.0	100.0	100.0

[a]Nonsupply methods include withdrawal, rhythm, and folk methods.

NOTE: See Table A-4 in Appendix A for explanatory notes.

TABLE 3 Contraceptive Method Mix for LDCs, 2000-2010, Scenario B and C Projections, in Percent

Method	2000	2010
Scenario B		
Sterilization	27.0	30.9
IUD	10.0	10.6
NORPLANT^R	1.5	3.0
Injectable	1.5	3.0
Pill	23.1	22.5
Scenario C		
Sterilization	25.9	28.8
IUD	9.1	8.8
NORPLANT^R	3.0	6.0
Injectable	3.0	6.0
Pill	22.0	20.4

NOTE: See Tables A-5 and A-6 in Appendix A for explanatory notes.

demand for longer-term methods will more than double from 1970 levels.

The next step in the method mix analysis is to factor in market shares for NORPLANT® and Net-90. In scenario B, these methods increase their combined market share to account for 6 percent by 2010; in scenario C, they increase to 12 percent. Because they are longer-term methods, it is assumed that they will substitute for other longer-term methods. NORPLANT®, under these scenarios, will substitute for sterilization and, to a lesser extent, for the IUD. Net-90 will substitute for the pill and, to a lesser extent, for the IUD. The results of these market share shifts in the years 2000 and 2010 for the affected methods are presented in Table 3.

Contraceptive Users and Commodities

Future contraceptive use by method required to achieve the U.N. medium-variant fertility levels is presented in Table 4. The number of users grows about ninefold over this 40-year period. The number of supply method users grows by more than 15-fold over the same period. This dramatic increase results, in part, from a growth in numbers of MWRA, which increase by about 2.5 times over the period. It is also due to a rising rate of contraceptive prevalence,

TABLE 4 Contraceptive Users by Method for LDCs, 1970-2010, Baseline A, No New Methods, in Millions

Method	1970	1980	1990	2000	2010
Sterilization	6.9	23.3	52.1	97.8	183.6
IUD	3.5	10.3	21.4	38.1	69.0
Pill	11.8	29.5	52.6	84.1	136.8
Condom	1.6	5.2	11.1	20.6	37.3
Other supply	2.6	7.4	14.3	24.4	42.3
Nonsupply	26.9	53.7	75.5	84.1	87.3
Total users	53.3	129.4	227.0	349.1	556.3
Supply users	26.4	75.7	151.5	265.0	400.9

NOTE: See Table B-1 in Appendix B for explanatory notes.

which increases by more than threefold over the period. Supply method prevalence increases even more sharply over this period—by about fivefold.

Commodity and Service Delivery Costs

The foregoing projections, when coupled with unit costs, yield estimates of future commodity costs by method. Figure 3 provides a graphic comparison of total commodity costs under the three method mix scenarios (see Tables C-2 to C-4 in Appendix C for underlying numerical values and explanatory notes).

Costs escalate dramatically under each of these three scenarios. With the introduction of new contraceptive methods in scenarios B and C, commodity costs increase even more quickly. Under scenario B, which assumes a small shift toward new methods, total commodity costs increase by about 30 percent over the baseline by the year 2010. Under scenario C, which assumes a stronger shift toward these methods, there is an increase of about 60 percent over baseline costs. These cost increases are due largely to the introduction of Net-90, which is substantially more expensive than the methods for which it is substituted (see Table C-6 in Appendix C).

Considered alone, these increased costs seem inordinately large. Commodity costs are, however, only a fraction of total service costs. When combined with service delivery costs, the cost differentials associated with the introduction of new methods become greatly attenuated, as illustrated in Figure 4 (see Table C-7 in Appendix C

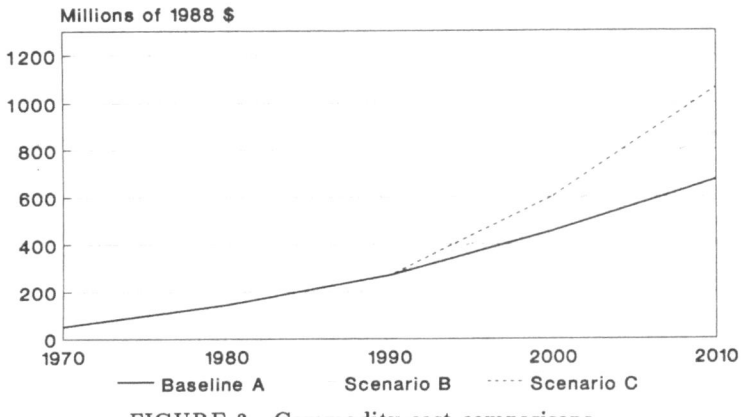

FIGURE 3   Commodity cost comparisons.

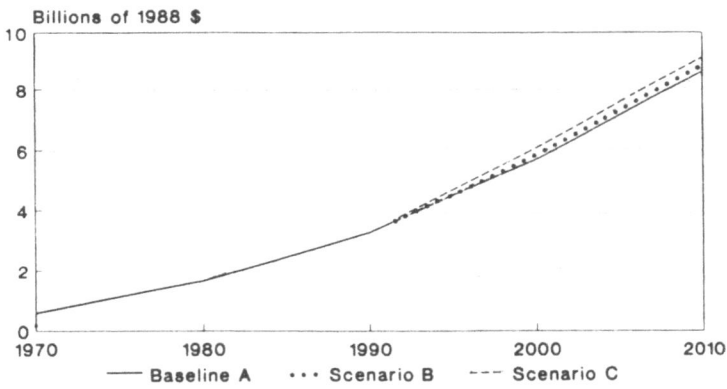

FIGURE 4   Total service delivery costs.

for underlying numerical values and explanatory notes). Costs under scenario B increase by about 2 percent over the baseline by the year 2010, and under scenario C they increase by about 4 percent. Seen in this light, supply costs are relatively unaffected by shifts to new contraceptive methods. However, service delivery costs are assumed here to be fixed over time and across methods. A more complete analysis would consider the service delivery costs associated with specific types of methods and the added costs of introducing new methods.

What is notable in this cost projection is the dramatic increase in service delivery costs over this 40-year period. Considered in constant dollars, there is about a 15-fold increase in costs. Resources required to meet projected family planning demand in the year 2010 are nearly triple those that are required today. This translates to cost increases averaging more than $250 million annually over the next 22 years.

DISCUSSION

A plethora of demographic and program data are used in this analysis. A number of straightforward assumptions are made about demand for family planning in order to project future method mix, the potential number of contraceptive users, and the associated commodity and delivery costs under different method mix scenarios. Throughout the analysis, a conservative approach has been taken to estimate the financial needs for family planning commodities and services. In particular, estimates of commodity costs are low since they are based on AID procurement prices, which are among the lowest anywhere in the world.

Similarly, the overhead cost of $19.82 per couple-year of protection (CYP) is an underestimate since it is largely based on successful countries in Asia and Latin America. Many of the additions to the pool of family planning users in the next 20 years will come from sub-Saharan Africa, where costs will probably be much higher than this estimate. The delivery cost is also assumed to be fixed, regardless of method. However, methods that provide multiple-year protection may have lower associated annual service costs when amortized over a multiple-year period. Methods that require clinic facilities, highly trained staff, and frequent follow-up (such as NORPLANT®) may have higher associated annual service costs. Lastly, new methods may have higher associated service costs during their introductory period, to the extent that they require service staff retraining, changes in delivery system structure, new equipment purchases, and introductory IEC efforts.

The analysis, therefore, may underestimate the cost of providing family planning services in the Third World over the next two decades. Nevertheless, the total cost is calculated at nearly $9 billion annually by the year 2010. This figure represents nearly three times the amount of money and effort currently being invested in family planning. The cumulative amount of money necessary to cover costs for the two decades (1990–2010) is estimated to approach $120 billion (in 1988 dollars).

The principal conclusions are twofold: (1) Most important, no matter what calculus one uses, the cost and effort to provide services over the next 20 years will be enormous. The annual estimate for the year 2010 is between $8 billion and $9 billion. Even if the estimate is low or high by a few billion dollars, the results are still staggering. Resources must increase by more than $250 million each year, on average, to enable projected declines in fertility to take place. (2) The cost of contraceptives will not have a major influence on the overall cost structure of family planning. By themselves, the cost of commodities varies considerably, depending on method mix, but when considered as part of overall service delivery, there is minimal effect on the total annual bill. Of course, new methods that have higher service delivery costs could affect total costs considerably.

Perhaps a more significant role of new contraceptive technology is its potential effect not on *supply* but on *demand* for family planning. The availability of methods that are longer term, effective, safe, and attractive to the user can stimulate future demand for contraceptives (Reboussin et al., 1987; Knodel, Chamratrithirong, and Debavalya, 1987). Contraceptive technology should continue to be innovative in order to produce methods that can satisfy consumer needs and preferences.

CHALLENGE FOR THE FUTURE

All of the above—generating demand, furnishing supply, and developing better contraceptive technologies—will require large amounts of resources over the next two decades.

The rising need for resources is occurring at a time when donor funding has actually declined in constant dollar terms. When considered against the rising demand for services in developing countries, donor resources went further 20 years ago than they do today. This places us in a resource bind. Donors may be unable or unwilling to carry the bulk of the responsibility for family planning in the future. Donors face formidable challenges in responding effectively to future resource requirements:

- available funds need to be used more effectively, and
- local governments and the private sector need to be stimulated to provide greater resources.

Where will the resources come from to meet future needs? In 1980, the costs of family planning were shared almost equally among donors, developing country governments, and the private sector. Even under the most optimistic assumptions about increases in contributions, the sheer numbers of new users will mean that the donors' share of the total will decline substantially over the next two decades (Gillespie, 1987). Local governments and the private sector, then, must make up the considerable difference.

Given these severe financial constraints, what can be done? At AID we realize that we have to be more imaginative and thoughtful in our approaches. To make the resources go farther we are:

1. stimulating new sources of investment in family planning;
2. concentrating on activities that are highly leveraged, that is, that can multiply our investments many times over;
3. improving the efficiency (management) of our family planning programs; and
4. improving contraceptive technology.

Stimulating New Sources of Investment

A relative decline of resources has caused us to look at potential new sources of support for family planning. A World Bank study estimates that 80 percent of the new funds needed to expand family planning services will have to come from developing country governments and the private sector (Bulatao, 1985). Stimulating governments, businesses, and consumers to assume the future costs of family planning is an appropriate and necessary role for donors.

Concentrating on Leveraged Activities

One key to coping successfully with resource constraints is to ensure that activities which are undertaken have a multiplier effect in the future. Therefore, AID supports a range of activities that affect resource allocations today and in the future. Among the most important are efforts to encourage policy reforms, operational improvements, and a greater availability of more effective and inexpensive contraceptives.

For example, countries can make the contraceptive marketplace more attractive for the private sector with relatively minor, but highly leveraged, changes such as eliminating import duties, allowing contraceptive advertising, and offering tax or other incentives to businesses.

Improving Efficiency of Programs

To stretch resources, existing systems must be made to work better. After all, the major cost of family planning is not the commodities but the systems used to deliver them. We can obtain more per dollar if available resources are used more efficiently. AID is placing more emphasis on good management. Additional money is being invested in training to improve the management skills of family planning program managers. Assistance in training for improved logistics management has also been expanded. More efficient contraceptive distribution systems can increase coverage without increasing costs. AID continues to support operations research as a way of testing the efficacy and efficiency of service delivery programs. Various research studies have shown that better-quality services can increase acceptance and promote the continued use of family planning methods (Lipton, Dixon-Mueller, and Lee, 1987).

Donors have other potential approaches to improved efficiencies that could have large payoffs. Donors and developing world governments should explore possibilities such as local production and consortium purchasing of contraceptives—keeping in mind the need to continue to provide a wide spectrum of high-quality products. Finally, and perhaps most immediately, there should be a much greater coordination between donors than presently exists—not only to avoid redundancies but also to build on each other's strengths.

Improving Contraceptive Technology

Contraceptive technology can have a major influence on the supply and demand for family planning services. New and improved products will increase the safety and effectiveness of contraceptive use in the future. Safer and more effective contraceptives will, in turn, stimulate the demand for family planning and at the same time reduce unmet demand. Perhaps more importantly, new contraceptive technology can affect service delivery costs. We have seen that the major cost component of family planning services is delivery. Contraceptives that have low initial fixed costs and low recurrent delivery costs will lower the average cost of family planning services and thus increase availability. Given the enormous financial needs outlined in this paper, the delivery costs of contraceptives should be an important factor in future research funding.

REFERENCES

Bongaarts, J.
1986   The transition in reproductive behavior in the Third World. *World Population and U.S. Policy.* New York: W.W. Norton and Co.

Bongaarts, J., and J. Stover
1986   *Target Setting Model, A User's Manual.* Population Council Working Paper no. 130. New York: The Population Council.

Boulier, B.
1984   Unmet Need for Contraception: Evaluation of Measures and Estimates for Thirty-Six Developing Countries. World Bank Working Paper. The World Bank, Washington, D.C.

Bulatao, R.
1985   Expenditures on Population Programs in Developing Regions. World Bank Staff Working Paper no. 679. The World Bank, Washington, D.C.

Gillespie, D.
1987   Mobilizing Resources to Meet Demand for Family Planning. Paper presented at the International Conference on Better Health for Women and Children through Family Planning, Nairobi, Kenya, October 5–9, 1987. The Population Council, New York.

Haub, C., and M. Kent
1988   Using population data. Population Reference Bureau. *Population Today* 16(5):6.

Knodel, J., A. Chamratrithirong, and N. Debavalya
1987   *Thailand's Reproductive Revolution.* Madison, Wis.: University of Wisconsin Press.

Lapham, R., and P. Mauldin
1985   Contraceptive prevalence: The influence of organized family planning programs. *Studies in Family Planning* 16(3):117–137.

Lewis, M.A., and G. Kenney
1988   *The Private Sector and Family Planning in Developing Countries: Its Role, Achievements and Potential.* Washington, D.C.: The Urban Institute.

Lipton, H., R. Dixon-Mueller, and P. Lee
1987   Client-provider transactions: An introduction and conceptual overview. *Organizing for Effective Family Planning Programs.* Washington, D.C.: National Academy Press.

Mauldin, P., and B. Berelson
1978   Conditions of fertility decline in developing countries. *Studies in Family Planning* 9(5):90–147.

National Academy of Sciences
1982   *Determinants of Fertility in Developing Countries: An Overview and A Research Agenda.* Committee on Population and Demography, Report No. 16. Washington, D.C.: National Academy Press.

Population Crisis Committee
1985   A guide to modern contraceptive methods. Wallchart. Population Crisis Committee, Washington, D.C.

Population Information Program, Johns Hopkins University
1985   Fertility and family planning surveys: An update. *Population Reports* Series M, no. 8.

Reboussin, D., J. DaVanzo, E. Starbird, T. Boon Ann, and S. Hadi Abdullah
   1987   *Contraceptive Method Switching over Women's Reproductive Careers.*
           Report R-3547-PC/RC. Santa Monica, Calif.: The Rand Corporation.
Speidel, J.
   1988   Resource needs for population and family planning activities in less
           developed countries. Unpublished paper.
Trias, M.
   1988   Looking at the costs of family planning. *Communique* 9(1):1–4.
United Nations
   1986   *World Population Prospects, Estimates and Projections as Assessed
           in 1984.* New York: United Nations.
   1987   World contraceptive use. Wallchart. United Nations, New York.

APPENDIX A

Projection of Contraceptive Method Mix

TABLE A-1 Aggregate Demographic, Socioeconomic, and Family Planning Program Indicators in Developing Countries, 1970-2010

Characteristic	1970	1980	1990	2000	2010
Demographic Indicators					
Population (million)	1,815.2	2,316.8	2,912.6	3,589.3	4,303.0
WRA (15-49 millions)	410.6	538.7	703.2	899.8	1,104.4
MWRA (15-49 millions)	307.9	404.0	527.4	674.8	828.3
TFR	5.7	4.8	4.1	3.4	3.0
CPR	17.3	32.0	43.0	51.7	58.0
FP users	53.3	129.3	226.7	349.1	475.5
Socioeconomic Indicators					
Life expectancy	49.9	53.7	57.0	60.9	64.2
Percent urban	27.9	32.9	38.3	44.3	50.7
Family Planning Program Indicator					
Program effort	22.7	33.0	43.3	53.6	63.9

NOTES: Throughout the analysis, LDC estimates exclude the People's Republic of China. Sources for indicators as follows: Population, women of reproductive age (WRA), total fertility rate (TFR), life expectancy, and urban estimates are drawn from United Nations population projections (medium variant) 1986. Married women of reproductive age (MWRA) is derived from WRA and assumes that 75 percent of the women aged 15-49 are married. Contraceptive prevalence rate (CPR) for 1980 is derived from U.N. data (1987) and augmented by recent Demographic and Health Surveys. Contraceptive prevalence rates for remaining years are derived by using the family planning use estimation methodology in Bongaarts and Stover (1986). This methodology estimates future numbers of contraceptive users and the associated commodity requirements given assumptions about fertility trends (in this case, the U.N. medium-variant TFR estimates), other proximate determinants of fertility (assumed to be fixed throughout the projection period based on 1980 regionally weighted averages), method mix (derived from the regression analysis presented in Tables A-3a and A-3b), and the effectiveness of each method (midrange estimates taken from Population Crisis Committee [1985]). Family planning (FP) users are derived by applying CPRs to MWRA. Program effort is adapted from Lapham and Mauldin (1985) estimates for 1972 and 1982. Point estimates were derived by using linear interpolation and extrapolation.

TABLE A-2 Aggregate LDC Demographic and Family Planning Program
Indicators, 1970-2010

Characteristic	1970	1980	1990	2000	2010
Married Women of Reproductive Age (millions)					
High variant				679.5	855.0
Medium variant	307.9	404.0	527.4	674.8	828.3
Low variant				670.9	807.2
Total Fertility Rate					
High variant			4.4	3.9	3.3
Medium variant	5.7	4.8	4.1	3.4	3.0
Low variant			3.7	3.0	2.4
Contraceptive Prevalence Rate					
High variant			39.7	43.6	53.8
Medium variant	17.3	32.0	43.0	51.7	57.4
Low variant			46.6	51.8	64.2
Family Planning Users (millions)					
High variant			209.4	319.4	460.0
Medium variant	53.3	129.3	226.7	349.1	475.5
Low variant			246.0	347.4	518.2

NOTES: Sources for indicators as follows: WRA and TFR estimates are
drawn from United Nations (1986) population projections (medium
variant). MWRA is derived from WRA and assumes that 75 percent of the
women aged 15-49 are married. CPR for 1980 is derived from U.N. data
(1987) and augmented by recent Demographic and Health Surveys. CPRs
for the remaining years are derived using the family planning use
estimation methodology of Bongaarts and Stover (1986). FP users are
derived by applying CPRs to MWRA.

TABLE A-3a Method Mix Determination Regression Equations

Variables in Equation	Regressor					
	(1) Sterilization		(2) IUD		(3) Pill	
	B	(t)	B	(t)	B	(t)
Life expectancy	0.216	(0.49)	0.136	(0.70)	0.617	(1.40)*
Percent urban	-0.034	(-0.18)	0.150	(1.85)**	0.077	(0.42)
Program effort	0.434	(3.62)***	0.010	(0.19)	-0.194	(-1.62)*
	Summary Statistics					
Intercept	-6.82		-4.64		-6.46	
R^2	0.340		0.164		0.091	
Total F	7.91**		3.01*		1.53	

NOTE: Method mix data are drawn from 50 national surveys conducted between 1976 and 1986. Life expectancy and percent urban data are drawn from U.N. (1986) estimates for 1980. Program effort data are drawn from Lapham and Mauldin (1985) analysis of family planning programs conducted in 1982.

* = significant at .20 level.
** = significant at .10 level.
*** = significant at .05 level.

TABLE A-3b Method Mix Determination Regression Equations

Variables in Equation	Regressor					
	(4) Condom		(5) Other Supply		(6) Nonsupply	
	B	(t)	B	(t)	B	(t)
Life expectancy	0.295	(2.32)***	0.129	(0.99)	-1.394	(-2.63)***
Percent urban	0.055	(-1.04)	-0.041	(-0.77)	-0.097	(-0.44)
Program effort	0.016	(0.47)	0.042	(1.18)	-0.308	(-2.14)***
	Summary Statistics					
Intercept	-10.55		-1.29		129.76	
R^2	0.188		0.107		0.438	
Total F	3.54*		1.84		11.96***	

NOTE: Method mix data are drawn from 50 national surveys conducted between 1976 and 1986. Life expectancy and percent urban data are drawn from U.N. (1986) estimates for 1980. Program effort data are drawn from Lapham and Mauldin (1985) analysis of family planning programs conducted in 1982.

* = significant at .20 level.
*** = significant at .05 level.

TABLE A-4 Contraceptive Method Mix Estimates for LDCs, Baseline A, No New Methods, in Percent

Method	1970	1980	1990	2000	2010
Sterilization	12.9	18.0	23.0	28.0	33.0
IUD	6.6	8.0	9.3	10.9	12.4
NORPLANT®	--	--	--	--	--
Injectable	--	--	--	--	--
Pill	22.1	22.8	23.2	24.1	24.6
Condom	3.0	4.0	4.9	5.9	6.7
Other supply	4.9	5.7	6.3	7.0	7.6
Nonsupply	50.5	41.6	33.3	24.1	15.7
Total	100.0	100.0	100.0	100.0	100.0

NOTES: Sterilization includes male and female methods; other supply methods include injectables, foam, tablets, and diaphragms; nonsupply methods include withdrawal, rhythm, and folk methods.

The 1980 method mix is derived by using prevalence data from 50 LDCs (representing over 75 percent of the population in all LDCs, except the People's Republic of China) surveyed between 1976 and 1986. A regionally weighted average method mix for all LDCs was then calculated.

To estimate future (and 1970) method mix, contraceptive use was hypothesized to change as countries undergo socioeconomic and family planning program development. Two indicators of socioeconomic development (life expectancy and urbanization) and a composite measure of program performance (Lapham and Mauldin, 1984) were regressed on the percentage of contraceptors using each method (regression results are presented in Tables A-3a and A-3b). Using U.N. estimates for future life expectancy and urbanization and assuming that the 1970-1980 trend in program performance will continue, future (and 1970) contraceptive method mix was estimated by applying the regression coefficients to estimated future levels of socioeconomic and family planning program development.

Totals may not equal 100 because of rounding.

TABLE A-5 Contraceptive Method Mix Estimates for LDCs, Scenario B, Small Shift to New Methods, in Percent

Method	1970	1980	1990	2000	2010
Sterilization	12.9	18.0	23.0	27.0	30.9
IUD	6.6	8.0	9.3	10.0	10.6
NORPLANT®	--	--	--	1.5	3.0
Injectable	--	--	--	1.5	3.0
Pill	22.1	22.8	23.2	23.1	22.5
Condom	3.0	4.0	4.9	5.9	6.7
Other supply	4.9	5.7	6.3	7.0	7.6
Nonsupply	50.5	41.5	33.3	24.1	15.7
Total	100.0	100.0	100.0	100.0	100.0

NOTE: Totals may not equal 100 because of rounding.

TABLE A-6 Contraceptive Method Mix Estimates for LDCs, Scenario C, Moderate Shift to New Methods, in Percent

Method	1970	1980	1990	2000	2010
Sterilization	12.9	18.0	23.0	25.9	28.8
IUD	6.6	8.0	9.3	9.1	8.8
NORPLANT®	--	--	--	3.0	6.0
Injectable	--	--	--	3.0	6.0
Pill	22.1	22.8	23.2	22.0	20.4
Condom	3.0	4.0	4.9	5.9	6.7
Other supply	4.9	5.7	6.3	7.0	7.6
Nonsupply	50.5	41.5	33.3	24.1	15.7
Total	100.0	100.0	100.0	100.0	100.0

NOTE: Totals may not equal 100 because of rounding.

APPENDIX B

Projection of Contraceptive Users

TABLE B-1 Contraceptive Users by Method for LDCs, 1970-2010,
Baseline A, No New Methods, in Millions

Method	1970	1980	1990	2000	2010
Sterilization	6.9	23.3	52.1	97.8	156.9
IUD	3.5	10.3	21.4	38.1	59.0
NORPLANT®	--	--	--	--	--
Injectable	--	--	--	--	--
Pill	11.8	29.5	52.6	84.1	116.9
Condom	1.6	5.2	11.1	20.6	31.9
Other supply	2.6	7.4	14.3	24.4	36.2
Nonsupply	26.9	53.7	75.5	84.1	74.6
Total users	53.3	129.4	227.0	349.1	475.5
Supply users	26.4	75.7	151.5	265.0	400.9

NOTE: Users by method generated through the family planning use
methodology of Bongaarts and Stover (1986) based on the baseline A
method mix shift presented in Table A-4.

TABLE B-2 Contraceptive Users by Method for LDCs, 1970-2010, Scenario B, Small Shift to New Methods, in Millions

Method	1970	1980	1990	2000	2010
Sterilization	6.9	23.3	52.1	93.9	146.7
IUD	3.5	10.3	21.4	34.9	50.3
NORPLANT®	--	--	--	5.3	14.3
Injectable	--	--	--	5.3	14.3
Pill	11.8	29.5	52.6	80.6	106.8
Condom	1.6	5.2	11.1	20.6	31.8
Other supply	2.6	7.4	14.3	24.4	36.1
Nonsupply	26.9	53.7	75.5	84.1	74.5
Total users	53.3	129.4	227.0	349.1	474.8

NOTE: Users by method generated through the family planning use methodology of Bongaarts and Stover (1986) based on the scenario B method mix shift presented in Table A-5.

TABLE B-3 Contraceptive Users by Method for LDCs, 1970-2010, Scenario C, Moderate Shift to New Methods, in Millions

Method	1970	1980	1990	2000	2010
Sterilization	6.9	23.3	52.1	90.3	136.6
IUD	3.5	10.3	21.4	31.7	41.7
NORPLANT®	--	--	--	10.5	28.5
Injectable	--	--	--	10.5	28.5
Pill	11.8	29.5	52.6	76.7	96.8
Condom	1.6	5.2	11.1	20.6	31.8
Other supply	2.6	7.4	14.3	24.4	36.1
Nonsupply	26.9	53.7	75.5	84.1	74.4
Total users	53.3	129.4	227.0	348.8	474.4

NOTE: Users by method generated through the family planning use methodology of Bongaarts and Stover (1986) based on Scenario C method mix shift presented in Table A-6.

APPENDIX C

Projection of Commodity and Service Delivery Costs

TABLE C-1 Unit Costs for Contraceptive Commodities

Method	Commodity Costs (dollars)
Sterilization	9.60 per procedure
IUD (copper T-380)	0.92 per unit
NORPLANT®	16.75 per unit
Net-90	2.75 per unit
Pill	0.12 per cycle
Condom	0.05 per piece
Other supply	6.15 per unit
Nonsupply	0.00

NOTE: The unit costs for IUD, the pill, and the condom are the prices paid by AID in 1988. The sterilization cost reflects only the price for the medical supplies associated with the procedure and is obtained from cost analysis by PROFAMILIA in Colombia (Trias, 1988). The unit cost for other supply methods is an average of the annual unit costs for injectables, foam, tablets, and diaphragms. To derive method-specific annual commodity costs, the unit costs are multiplied by the number of commodities needed to achieve 1 CYP.

TABLE C-2 Commodity Cost Estimates for LDCs, Baseline A, No New Methods, in Millions of 1988 Dollars

Method	1970	1980	1990	2000	2010
Sterilization	11	28	47	75	112
IUD	1	2	4	7	11
Pill	18	46	82	131	182
Condom	7	23	50	93	143
Other supply	16	46	88	150	223
Nonsupply	0	0	0	0	0
Total	53	145	271	456	671

NOTE: CYP costs presented in Table C-1 are applied to the estimated number of users by the method presented in Table B-1 to produce these cost estimates.

TABLE C-3 Commodity Cost Estimates for LDCs, Scenario B, Small Shift to New Methods, in Millions of 1988 Dollars

Method	1970	1980	1990	2000	2010
Sterilization	11	28	47	75	103
IUD	1	2	4	7	9
Pill	18	46	82	131	167
Condom	7	23	50	93	143
NORPLANT®	--	--	--	25	68
Injectable	--	--	--	58	157
Other supply	16	46	88	150	222
Nonsupply	0	0	0	0	0
Total	53	145	271	533	869

NOTE: CYP costs presented in Table C-1 are applied to users by the method presented in Table B-2 to produce these cost estimates.

TABLE C-4 Commodity Cost Estimates for LDCs, Scenario C, Moderate Shift to New Methods, in Millions of 1988 Dollars

Method	1970	1980	1990	2000	2010
Sterilization	11	28	47	69	92
IUD	1	2	4	6	7
Pill	18	46	82	120	151
Condom	7	23	50	93	143
NORPLANT®	--	--	--	50	136
Injectable	--	--	--	115	314
Other supply	16	46	88	150	222
Nonsupply	0	0	0	0	0
Total	53	145	271	603	1,065

NOTE: CYP costs presented in Table C-1 are applied to users by the method presented in Table B-3 to produce these cost estimates.

TABLE C-5 Contraceptive Commodity Cost Estimates for LDCs, in Million of Dollars

Scenario	1970	1980	1990	2000	2010
Baseline A	53	145	271	456	672
Scenario B	--	--	--	533	869
Scenario C	--	--	--	602	1,065

TABLE C-6 Annual Commodity Costs, New Versus Substitute Methods, Scenario C Market Shares, in Millions

Method	2000		2010	
	Change in Market Share (%)	Change in Commodity Costs ($)	Change in Market Share (%)	Change in Commodity Costs ($)
New methods	+6.0	165.0	+12.0	449.9
NORPLANT®	+3.0	50.0	+ 6.0	136.4
Net-90	+3.0	115.0	+ 6.0	313.5
Substitutes	-6.0	18.9	-12.0	55.6
Sterilization	-2.1	5.8	- 4.2	20.5
IUD	-1.8	1.5	- 3.6	3.7
Pill	-2.1	11.6	- 4.2	31.4
Annual costs				
Baseline A		456.3		672.0
Scenario C		602.3		1,065.4
Total increase		146.0		393.4
Percent increase				
Total		(32.0)		(58.5)
Due to NORPLANT®		(9.5)		(16.9)
Due to Net-90		(22.5)		(41.6)

TABLE C-7 Total Service Delivery Cost Estimates for LDCs, Millions of 1988 Dollars

Method	1970	1980	1990	2000	2010
Baseline A	576	1,645	3,274	5,709	8,618
Scenario B	--	--	--	5,783	8,803
Scenario C	--	--	--	5,847	8,993

NOTE: Service delivery costs (exclusive of commodities) are assumed to average $19.82 per couple year of protection, regardless of method. This is based on a cross-national average of $21.73 per user (from Bulatao, 1986) less a per user average cost for commodities of $1.91, as estimated for 1980 (see Table C-2). Total costs presented here include commodity costs.

Appendix

METHODS OF FERTILITY REGULATION LIKELY TO BE AVAILABLE WITHIN 10-15 YEARS[1]

METHOD	BASIC DRUG	MODE OF ADMINISTRATION	PROBABLE EFFECTIVENESS	PROBABLE SIDE EFFECTS AND SAFETY	FACTORS AFFECTING ACCEPTABILITY	DELIVERY REQUIREMENTS
Implants or Injectables						
Single silastic implants [2]	Various progestins	Inserted under skin of upper arm	High; less than 1 pregnancy per 100 women per year	Irregular menstrual bleeding	Effective for 1-3 years; removable at any time	Requires clinic staff to insert and remove; regulations governing steroid contraceptives
12-18 month biodegradable implant or pellets	Levonorgestrel (Capronor), norethindrone, desorgestrel	Implant or pellets inserted under skin	Under investigation; probably high	Irregular menstrual bleeding	Convenience because of infrequent administration; would not require removal	Requires clinic staff to insert; regulations governing steroid contraceptives
Once a month injectable	Norethindrone enanthate or depot-medroxy-progesterone acetate + estrogen	Injection given once a month	High; less than 1 pregnancy per 100 women per year	Irregular menstrual bleeding	Acceptance of injectables	Requires clinic staff or anyone who administers injections; regulations governing steroid contraceptives
3-month injectable	Norethindrone (microspheres), levonorgestrel butanoate or other progestin	Injection given once every 3 months	High; less than 1 pregnancy per 100 women per year	Irregular menstrual bleeding; absence of menses	Convenience, preference for injectables; offers an alternative to Depo Provera	Requires clinic staff or anyone who administers injections; regulations governing steroid contraceptives

Vaginal Use of Steroids

Vaginal pill	Levonorgestrel + estrogen	Inserted into vagina daily	High; less than 1 pregnancy per 100 women per year	Reduces steroid side effects	Avoids gastro-intestinal effects; some women may dislike touching genitals	Regulations governing steroid contraceptives
Levonorgestrel-releasing vaginal ring	Levonorgestrel	Self-inserted and worn continuously for 3 months	About 3.5 pregnancies per 100 women per year	Irregular menstrual bleeding	Some women may dislike touching genitals; can be removed regularly for washing	Regulations governing steroid contraceptives
Progesterone-releasing vaginal ring	Progesterone	Self-inserted and worn continuously for 3 months	Unknown — probably extends lactational amenorrhea for up to 1 year	Safety improved by use of natural hormone	Acceptable for use by lactating women; some women may dislike touching genitals; can be removed regularly for washing	Regulations governing steroid contraceptives

Intra-Uterine Devices

Levonorgestrel-releasing IUD	Levonorgestrel	Same as other IUDs	High	Less menstrual blood loss than with other IUDs	Convenience; 4-year effective duration of action	Requires clinic staff to insert and remove; regulations governing steroid contraceptives and IUDs

1 Methods listed are selected because they show promise after having reached the stage of clinical tests. Omission from this list does not imply that a method is not promising. It may only be an indication that the method is early in the research process or that no clinical data are available to evaluate.

2 *Italicized* entry indicates new method.

METHOD	BASIC DRUG	MODE OF ADMINISTRATION	PROBABLE EFFECTIVENESS	PROBABLE SIDE EFFECTS AND SAFETY	FACTORS AFFECTING ACCEPTABILITY	DELIVERY REQUIREMENTS
Flexible copper IUD	Copper	Same as other IUDs	Under investigation; probably high	Lower expulsion rate	Convenience; possibly 5 years duration	Requires clinic staff to insert and remove; regulations governing IUDs
Menses-Inducing Methods						
Contragestational steroid and prostaglandin (PG)	Mifepristone (RU-486) + a PG analogue	RU-486 orally for 1-3 days + a prostaglandin vaginal suppository, injection or tablets	95% effective during first 8 weeks of pregnancy	Incomplete cases need immediate medical attention; otherwise risk of hemorrhage and/or infection	Religious and personal views regarding pregnancy	Requires medical supervision and back-up to treat complications
Vaccine against hCG	hCG beta subunit or terminal peptide	Initial injection + booster shot(s) followed by booster every 1-2 years	High, but not yet tested	No apparent side effects within first year of phase I studies	Infrequent administration; probably reversible, requires boosters	Requires clinical staff to administer
Male Methods						
Gossypol pill	Gossypol	Daily pill for 3 months followed by a pill 2-3 times a week	High; less than 1 pregnancy per 100 couples per year	Still under investigation; possible renal effects and irreversibility	Male method that does not lower libido; low cost; could be used as a component of "couple" method alternating years of pill use	Could be sold over the counter if safety issues resolved satisfactorily

Method	Agent	Administration	Effectiveness	Side effects	Characteristics	Delivery
LHRH + androgen	LHRH analogue + steroid	Probably will require monthly injection of peptide + periodic injectable or implant supplementation with steroid	Unknown as yet	Possible androgen metabolic effects; long-term LHRH effects unknown	Will require complex mode of administration; cost may be high	Requires clinical supervision
Percutaneous vas occlusion	Chemical sclerosing agent or polymers	Injected into vas deferens	High	Unknown	Permanent male method for chemicals; reversible for polymers; no incision	Requires trained clinic staff
Barrier Methods						
Anti-viral medicated condom	Several being studied	Worn over penis	Similar to current condoms (low user effectiveness)	None apparent	Protects against STDs; HIV; coital related method	Could be sold over the counter
Female condom	None necessary; could be medicated	Self-inserted within vagina	Unknown	None apparent; effect on sexual pleasure under study	Protects against STDs, HIV; some women may dislike touching genitals; coital related method	Could be sold over the counter
Disposable diaphragm	None; could be medicated	Inserted vaginally; discarded after use	Unknown	None apparent	No storage or cleaning required; some women may dislike touching genitals	Clinic staff for proper fitting and instruction

Inventory prepared for the Conference on Demographic and Programmatic Consequences of Contraceptive Innovations, sponsored by the Committee on Population, National Academy of Sciences.

Index

World Fertility Survey (WFS), 68, 107, 128,
    159, 164, 166
World Health Organization (WHO), 107, 111,
    132, 161, 162, 163, 166
  antipregnancy vaccine and, 15
  CVRs and, 160

World Health Organization (WHO) (*cont.*)
  definition of health, 153

Yaounde, 118
Yugoslavia, 177, 179

Zimbabwe, 42